JYL STEINBACK

AMERICA'S HEALTHIEST MOM

P9-DZP-040

THE BUSY MOM'S
SLOW
COOKER
COOKBOOK

Meredith® Books
Des Moines, Iowa

The Busy Mom's Slow Cooker Cookbook
by Jyl Steinback
Editor: Stephanie Karpinske, R.D.
Contributing Editor: Janet Figg
Contributing Designer: Mary Pat Crowley
Copy Chief: Terri Fredrickson
Publishing Operations Manager: Karen Schirm
Edit and Design Production Coordinator: Mary Lee Gavin
Editorial Assistants: Cheryl Eckert, Kairee Windsor
Marketing Product Managers: Aparna Pande, Isaac Petersen,
    Gina Rickert, Stephen Rogers, Brent Wiersma, Tyler Woods
Book Production Managers: Pam Kvitne, Marjorie J. Schenkelberg,
    Rick von Holdt, Mark Weaver
Contributing Copy Editor: Kim Catanzarite
Contributing Proofreaders: Gretchen Kauffman, Susan J. Kling,
    Elise Marton
Photographers: Marty Baldwin, Blaine Moats
Food Stylists: Paige Boyle, Dianna Nolin, Charles Worthington
Prop Stylist: Sue Mitchell
Indexer: Spectrum Communication Services, Inc.

Meredith₀ Books
Executive Director, Editorial: Gregory H. Kayko
Executive Director, Design: Matt Strelecki
Senior Editor/Group Manager: Jan Miller
Senior Associate Design Director: Ken Carlson

Publisher and Editor in Chief: James D. Blume
Editorial Director: Linda Raglan Cunningham
Executive Director, Marketing: Jeffrey B. Myers
Executive Director, New Business Development: Todd M. Davis
Executive Director, Sales: Ken Zagor
Director, Operations: George A. Susral
Director, Production: Douglas M. Johnston
Business Director: Jim Leonard

Vice President and General Manager: Douglas J. Guendel

Meredith Publishing Group
President: Jack Griffin
Senior Vice President: Bob Mate

Meredith Corporation
Chairman and Chief Executive Officer: William T. Kerr
President and Chief Operating Officer: Stephen M. Lacy

In Memoriam: E.T. Meredith III (1933-2003)

All of us at Meredith₀ Books are
dedicated to providing you with
the information and ideas you
need to create delicious foods.
We welcome your comments
and suggestions. Write to us at:
Meredith Books, Cookbook
Editorial Department, 1716
Locust St., Des Moines, IA
50309-3023.

If you would like to
purchase any of our cooking,
crafts, gardening, home
improvement, or home
decorating and design books,
check wherever quality books
are sold. Or visit us at:
meredithbooks.com

About the Author

Jyl Steinback, dubbed America's Healthiest Mom, is an author, personal trainer, lifestyle consultant, fitness instructor, spokesperson, and nutrition expert. "Life is full of choices," she says, "and you can make a change."

A St. Louis native, Jyl earned a degree in elementary education with a minor in physical education from Arizona State University. She began providing personal training more than 25 years ago, targeting those who needed to improve their health because of medical problems. Jyl soon expanded her focus to families because she recognized that many health challenges were associated with eating and lifestyle choices made in the home.

She also realized early in her career that by teaching children the importance of proper nutrition and exercise and how to incorporate them into their lifestyles, she could help reduce childhood obesity and other health problems. Her enthusiastic, energetic, open but structured approach has been a success with individuals and schools that have utilized her programs. Over the years as Jyl has practiced what she recommends to others, her family has become known as America's Healthiest Family.

Jyl also has worked with cities, communities, and private companies to develop programs that help participants make changes in their lives, lose weight, and become healthier. An advocate for choice, change, and life-long commitment, Jyl says, "I am passionate about helping people live a lifestyle that improves the quality of their life and also that of future generations. I love to watch people change their lives for the better and feel extraordinary about themselves."

A nutrition expert, Jyl has developed thousands of healthy recipes, focusing on making family meals easy, quick, and delicious. Her cookbooks have sold more than 2 million copies. She also has provided corporations with customized cookbooks featuring recipes using their products, provided the products are consistent with a healthy lifestyle.

Jyl started and directed the exercise program for Elizabeth Arden in Beverly Hills. She has written for *Healthy Living, First for Women, eDiet, Let's Live, Women's Own,* and others. She has been featured in *People, Women's World, Better Homes and Gardens,* and *Family Circle* and has been a guest on CNN, Food Network, HGTV, *Good Day New York, The Morning Show,* and *Good Morning Arizona.*

"I am passionate about helping people live a lifestyle that improves the quality of their lives. I love to see people change their lives for the better and feel extraordinary about themselves."

Jyl is the founder of Family Fit Lifestyle, Inc., which provides information to consumers about diet, nutrition, recipes, exercise, equipment, and lifestyle balance.

Jyl and her family live in Scottsdale, Arizona, where she provides consulting and personal training and serves as healthy lifestyles advisor to local and national media. In addition, she is a spokesperson for the Arizona Heart Institute, the National Heart Institute, and selected companies that focus on long-term consumer health. Some of her favorite hobbies are being with her kids, hiking, in-line skating, and volunteering in local schools teaching health and wellness.

Acknowledgements

Thank you all from the bottom of my heart. I couldn't do it without any of you, and I am eternally grateful to each and every one of you.

Jamie, you did it, sweetie—first year down and lots more excitement on its way. This is just the beginning of an incredible journey, and I am so grateful you are allowing me to go along for the ride. You are an amazing and beautiful woman. I am blessed and lucky that you are my daughter and friend. I love you, Jams, more than life itself.

Scott, your smile is electrifying, and I am so proud of the young man you have become. You are going into sixth grade, and you still have a heart of gold. Keep up your dreams—you deserve them all—and you will make them happen. I love you, Scott!

Mom and Dad (Betty and Bill Levy), I love you— thank you for life and making it absolutely beautiful. How lucky I am to have both of you as my parents—and I count my blessings every day. You gave me my sunny disposition, my heart on my sleeve, and my passion to help the world be a better place. Thank you.

Grandma, I love you.

Jacie, thank you for always going the extra 10 miles to make my life great. And everybody's life you touch. It is because of you I got my honor in the "Hall of Fame," and it was truly an amazing experience. Thank you! You belong in the Hall of Fame yourself for the never-ending love you give back to everyone you touch. You have an incredible, beautiful heart, and I am so lucky you are my sister. I love you.

Jeff, Diane, Alex, and Casey, I love you all very much! Your support and values in life are inspirational along with your drive and passion to help other people become the best that they can be in this life. Thank you for always being there! Please go to journeyhome.org. Journey Home is a nonprofit, charitable organization whose mission is to nurture human potential and foster personal and organizational growth.

Mikki Eveloff, without a doubt you are one of the most astonishingly talented and creative women I have ever had the pleasure to work with. Mikki, you are a gift in my life and a joy to work with day after day, project after project. Thank you for "you" and your special friendship.

Debbie Kohl, my phenomenal friend and nutritionist. Thank you for your hard work, patience, persistence, and for always being there. I appreciate everything that you do—thank you.

Jeff Wardford, I admire your creativity and patience to make things run smoothly and to be at the right place at the right time. I am grateful for your sound advice and beautiful friendship. You are a gift in my life, and I am extremely grateful for all that you are and all that you do. We are a great team, Jeff. Thank you!

Pam Nelson, my personal earth angel. Thank you for always being there and being a very special friend and wonderful person.

Coleen O'Shea, my talented literary agent. Thank you for your persistence and always following through on your commitments. We have been together for more than five years, and I am eternally grateful for all the wonderful things that you do. Thank you, Coleen.

Stephanie Karpinske, you are an extraordinary editor, and I appreciate all of your hard work and dedication. Thank you, Stephanie.

Amy Nichols, you are on fire, girl—creative, outgoing, and full of life. Thank you for being an excellent PR agent and friend. I appreciate all that you do and all that you are. Thank you!

Linda Cunningham and everyone at Meredith Books, it is a pleasure and a gift to work with you on this wonderful book. Thank you for your time and extraordinary energy to make everything the best that it can be. Thank you.

Table of Contents

Table of
Contents

Spanish Rice Pork Casserole

5

Slow Cooking Today

The slow cooker made a grand entrance onto the cooking scene during the '70s, and since that time, millions of people have been creating, cooking, and crocking their way to slow-cooked delicacies. Convenient, cost-efficient, timesaving, and easy to use, slow cookers may be the answer to fast food with a twist.

The traditional roast beef-mashed potato meal has gone by the wayside to be replaced by ready-made, fast-food, or take-out meals. As food options shift from the home to outside sources, American waistlines continue to expand. This is not a healthy repercussion. While not everyone wants to don miniskirts and platform shoes, the cooking habits of the '70s may bring Americans back to happier days. Reverting to the health craze that marked that decade, slow cooking may provide an excellent opportunity to return to a time of family cooking. Toss all ingredients in one pot; walk away for several hours, all day, or overnight; and return to a delicious prepared meal. Stews, soups, casseroles, beef, pork, chicken, vegetables, and more are prepared with ease.

Slow-cooked meals are the perfect solution for busy people who dread dinner planning and preparation. They're put together effortlessly and economically with food items that are readily available in the supermarket.

What Crockery Cooking Brings to Everyone's Table

- **Cost efficiency:** Slow cooking transforms budget cuts of meat into tender, appetizing meals and eliminates the need for expensive prepared or take-out meals.
- **Time efficiency:** Cut cleanup time because you're using only one pot!
- **Energy efficiency:** When you cook on low heat, you use less energy than you would with a 100-watt lightbulb! A slow cooker doesn't heat up the kitchen on hot summer days.
- **Versatility:** Not only can a variety of recipes from appetizers to desserts be successfully prepared in the slow cooker, but you can also use your slow cooker to melt cheese for fondue or candy coatings for desserts.
- **Warming tool:** A slow cooker is great for beverages, rolls, and other food items you want to serve moist and warm.
- **Serving tool:** You can serve directly from the pot or use the slow cooker as a chafing dish to keep the food warm.
- **Healthy cooking method:**
  - The moist heat of slow cooking requires no butter or oil, saving on calories and fat.
  - Foods retain nutrients because vitamins are not boiled away.
  - Lower-fat meats cook best; remove skin from poultry before cooking.

- **Safe cooking method:** Even the low-heat setting raises the internal temperature of the food well beyond 140°F, the minimum temperature at which bacteria are killed.
- **Family time:** The ease of crockery cooking allows for family meals that encourage communication and does wonders for family relationships.

Selecting Your Slow Cooker

With so many slow cookers on the market, how do you know which one to choose? What is the difference between a CROCKPOT and a SLOW COOKER? What size is best? Should you select one with a removable liner or one with a liner that stays in place? How many settings will you need on your appliance?

- A slow cooker has a crockery insert that warms up slowly and evenly to a temperature of 200°F–300°F. Do not confuse this with other appliances that provide slow heat but cannot thoroughly cook foods. CROCKPOT is actually a brand name The Rival Corporation dubbed its slow cooker. There are many brands on the market, and selecting one is a matter of personal preference. You can check *Consumer Reports* or reviews of products online, if desired, before selecting a particular product.
- Slow cookers range in size from 1 to 6 quarts. Small 1- to 1½-quart versions are perfect for singles or hot party dips but will not accommodate most main dishes. A 3½-quart cooker is perfect for a couple, while a family of three or four will need a 3½- to 4½-quart cooker. Families of four or five will need a 4½- or 5-quart cooker, and a 6-quart cooker is better for larger families, potluck meals, or

parties. If you opt for one pot, select a 3½- to 4-quart model with a removable ceramic or stoneware liner. Make sure the liner is microwave-, oven-, and dishwasher-safe. This will offer the greatest versatility and ease in preparation, cooking, and cleanup.
- If you select a slow cooker without a removable liner, you'll have to line your cooker with a cooking bag or spray the inside with cooking spray before filling to prevent sticking.
- There are generally two heat settings, low and high. Low is 200°F and high is 300°F.
- Extras such as automatic timers and warming settings usually are unnecessary, as most recipes cook for such extended periods of time. These features generally increase the price of the slow cooker without much added value. If you are looking for the most value, select an appliance with basic features. With it you will be able to prepare most of the recipes in this book.
- Always check your crockery insert for cracks or deep scratches before using. Stoneware is extremely porous, and cracks and scratches can harbor dangerous bacteria.

Slow Cooking

In the Beginning
- **Read the entire recipe** so you understand the whole procedure before you begin.
- **Review the ingredient list** and make any necessary adjustments.
- **Line up ingredients,** appliances, and tools.
- **Prepare ingredients:** chop, mince, shred, cut, grate, etc.

- **Follow the recipe exactly** to ensure best results. You can make substitutions as long as they do not affect the basic chemistry of the recipe. See the substitution list on page 15.
- **Super timesaver**—clean up as you go!
- **Be cautious about doubling or tripling** slow cooker recipes. While this may be a simple process with standard cooking procedures, slow cooking is a whole different ball game. Doubling liquids and spices can throw a recipe out of whack, and it usually takes some experimentation to get it just right. Even then, the recipe might not work the same every time. If you want to double a recipe, start by increasing spices or liquid by one and a half times; add more spices or liquid at the end if the result seems too bland or too thick. You can always spice it up or thin it out, but the reverse is much more difficult!

Slow Cooking Basics

The general principles and recommendations for slow cooking are relatively standard, but you should ALWAYS read through your manufacturer's manual before using any new appliance.

1. Generally 1 hour on HIGH heat is equivalent to 2 to 2½ hours on LOW heat.

2. It is not necessary or recommended to preheat the slow cooker.

3. Spray the inside of the slow cooker with cooking spray before adding ingredients to prevent food from sticking.

4. Follow the layering instructions the recipe calls for. Generally vegetables do not cook as quickly as meat, so they are placed in the bottom of the appliance. Layer heavy vegetables such as potatoes, turnips, and carrots on the bottom, lighter vegetables such as corn and peas next, and meat above the vegetables. Add liquids and sauces last and mix the ingredients well before closing the lid.

5. Use only the amount of liquid specified in the recipe. It may not seem like enough until you consider the condensation-cover principle: As moisture accumulates and rises, condensation forms on the lid and the moisture returns to the food in the pot.

6. You can vary the type of liquid a recipe calls for as long as you substitute an equal amount (for example, ½ cup broth for ½ cup wine).

7. DO NOT lift the lid during cooking. Every time you lift the lid, heat escapes and cooking is set back by 20 to 30 minutes. If you want to check the progress of your recipe, spin the cooker lid until the condensation falls off and you can see inside. There is no need to stir unless specifically stated in the recipe.

8. The cooking time required depends on the type of food, the temperature setting, the temperature of the food when assembled and placed in the slow cooker, the size of the food pieces (chunks, shreds, minced, etc.), and the level to which the pot is filled. A 3-pound roast that took 8 hours to cook one week may take 9 hours to cook the next week, depending on fat content and other added ingredients. Newer slow cookers may cook at a hotter

temperature. To check the temperature of your slow cooker, fill it with 2 quarts of water, cover with the lid, and heat for 8 hours. Lift the lid and immediately check the water temperature with a thermometer; the temperature should read 185°F. If the temperature is higher, slightly reduce your cooking time to prevent foods from overcooking. If the temperature is lower, foods will not reach a safe temperature quickly enough and you should not use that particular slow cooker. Exchange or discard it.

9. Never fill the slow cooker less than one-half or more than three-quarters full, as foods will not cook properly. On the other hand, a slow cooker that's not full enough may cook too quickly. Foods on the bottom of the slow cooker cook faster because they are immersed in hot liquid.

10. Preparing Foods

- Cut or chop vegetables to the same size and place in the bottom of the slow cooker; they cook more slowly than meats in the moist heat. Most vegetables cook better when cut into small pieces or quartered.
- Thaw frozen vegetables in the refrigerator overnight or place them in a colander, run hot water over them for a couple of minutes, and drain well.
- Prevent potato discoloration by adding them to the slow cooker right before turning it on.
- Always remove skin from poultry and trim fat from meat before cooking. All of the recipes in this book call for boneless, skinless poultry and lean cuts of meat. Fats melt with

extended cooking times, adding an unpleasant texture to the food.

- Instead of soaking dry beans overnight, cook them on the low-heat setting overnight. If desired, add onion, garlic, and pepper.
- Soften beans completely before combining with sugar and/or acid foods. Boil dried beans, especially red kidney beans, before adding to a recipe. Cover the beans with three times their volume of unsalted water and bring to a boil. Boil 10 minutes, reduce heat, cover, and allow to simmer for 1½ hours or until beans are tender.
- Cut fruit right before adding it to the slow cooker. Fruit discolors quickly when exposed to air. Combine with sugar to draw out natural juices.
- Resist the natural urge to add salt. Salt draws flavors and juices out of meat and vegetables.
- You can prepare cakes and desserts in the slow cooker, but you'll need a small round

Slow Cooking

rack or vegetable steamer to place on the bottom, allowing heat to circulate around the cake pan. Smaller slow cookers cannot accommodate 8- or 9-inch cake pans; it is necessary to have at least a 5-quart slow cooker when preparing these desserts.

11. When preparing soup, add only enough water to cover the ingredients. If a thinner soup is desired, you can add more water during the last 20 to 30 minutes of cooking.

12. What to do during the last 30 to 60 minutes of cooking time:
   - If you want to thicken liquids, remove the lid and cook on high during the last half hour of cooking time.
   - Add tender vegetables, such as mushrooms, zucchini, or tomatoes, and quick-cooking vegetables during the last 45 minutes of cooking time so they do not overcook.
   - Add dairy products (milk, cream, sour cream, yogurt) during the last 30 minutes of cooking time unless otherwise indicated in recipe. To prevent curdling, mix the dairy product with an equal amount of cooking liquid from the dish being prepared.
   - Add spices during the last hour of cooking to prevent them from losing flavor. Try whole-leaf herbs and spices instead of ground for stronger flavor.
     - Some spices (e.g., cinnamon) tend to remain on the top of soups or stews. Add them at the end of cooking time so they can be stirred frequently.

   - Freshly ground black peppercorns retain their flavor better than pre-ground pepper, and you'll need less to get the same flavor.
   - Add pasta and rice during the last hour of cooking time; always make sure there is enough liquid. These foods require more liquid than other foods to cook properly.
   - Alternative method for pasta: Cook pasta in a pot of boiling water just until tender. Add the pasta to the slow cooker during the last half hour of cooking.
   - Long grain converted rice slow cooks better than other rice types. If it doesn't cook completely after the suggested time, add an extra 1 to 1⅔ cups of liquid per cup of rice.
   - The amount of water required for cooking rice depends on the type of rice. For example, processed white rice usually needs less water than long grain brown or wild rice, which can take up to 6 cups of water per cup of dry rice. Read the recipe carefully and follow directions.

13. If you want to double or triple a recipe, make sure you have a slow cooker large enough to handle it. Add enough water for a single recipe; add more as needed later.

14. Never put frozen foods in the slow cooker. Never thaw foods in the slow cooker. Defrost all foods before assembling and cooking so they'll reach the safe temperature of 140°F as quickly as possible.

15. Meats:
   - Most meat requires about 8 hours of cooking time on low heat.

- The longer meat cooks in the slow cooker, the more tender it becomes. At the minimum cooking time, meat is generally easier to cut; at the maximum cooking time, it is perfect for shredding.
- Cheaper cuts of meat actually work better in the slow cooker because they have less fat.
- In recipes that call for ground beef or ground poultry, brown ground beef or poultry in a skillet and drain fat before adding to the slow cooker.
- If desired, brown large pieces of meat before adding to the slow cooker to provide color and enhance flavor.
- If you don't want to brown meat, make a gravy to serve with it; this will hide any lack of color.
- When preparing a large pot roast, you can cut the meat into four to six smaller pieces to speed cooking. Layer sliced onions between the pieces for added flavor.
- Roasts can be cooked with a very small amount of water when set on low heat. The more fat or "marbling" the meat has, the less liquid is required for cooking.
- The best cuts of meat for stew are chuck, flank, or brisket. While these are tough and well-marbled meats, the slow cooking process is excellent for tenderizing them.
- The smaller the cut of meat, the less time it takes to cook.

16. If you prepare ingredients the night before and want to assemble them, add the dry ingredients to the slow cooker but wait to add liquid ingredients until ready to cook.

17. Do not leave prepared meals at room temperature for more than 2 hours before you refrigerate them. Do not reheat foods in the slow cooker because foods do not reach a safe temperature quickly enough to prevent bacteria growth. Instead, reheat foods in the microwave oven and serve immediately.

18. Do not store cooked food in the slow cooker's crockery liner; remove and place in sealed containers. Left in the liner, the food will not cool down quickly enough to prevent the growth of harmful bacteria.

19. DO NOT put your crockery insert into the microwave oven unless your instruction manual says the insert is microwave-safe.

Slow Cooking

20. High-Altitude Slow Cooking: Altitudes above 3,500 feet may require longer cooking times (about 1 to 2 hours longer), but recipes will react differently. Test your slow cooker to determine the cooking-water temperature. Cooking on the high setting rather than low will increase cooking temperatures and may produce better results. Have patience and experiment to determine what works best.

21. Cleanup:

- NEVER immerse the slow cooker in water.
- NEVER add cold water to a hot crockery insert. If you want to soak the insert after cooked food has been removed, pour hot water into the hot insert. This method will prevent cracking or breakage.
- Fill the slow cooker with hot, soapy water when it is cooled and allow it to soak for 15 to 20 minutes. Do not use harsh, abrasive cleaners or metal pads. Scrub with plastic sponges, nylon net pads, or cloths; rinse with hot water and dry with towels.
- To remove stains, fill the slow cooker three-quarters full with hot water and 1 cup white vinegar. Cover and cook on high heat setting for 2 hours. Let the slow cooker cool, soak, and clean as usual.
- Read the instruction manual to determine if it's safe to wash your crockery container in the dishwasher. This is a real timesaver!

Foods to Avoid

Not all foods are suited for the slow cooker. Foods that should not be used include

- Large, tender roasts such as prime rib, standing rib, or leg of lamb
- Tender steaks
- Chicken or turkey pieces with the skin on
- Pies, cakes, or cookies
- Most seafood
- Recipes with a large amount of natural cheese or other dairy product

Suggested Cooking Times

Cooking Time for Recipes Prepared in Oven or on Cooktop	Time on Low-Heat Setting (about 200°F)	Time on High-Heat Setting (about 300°F)
15–30 minutes	4–6 hours	1½–2½ hours
35–45 minutes	6–8 hours	3–4 hours
50 minutes–3 hours	8–18 hours	4–6 hours
Pot Roast	8–12 hours	4–5 hours
Stew	10–12 hours	4–5 hours
Ribs	6–8 hours	
Stuffed Peppers	6–8 hours	3–4 hours
Brisket	10–12 hours	
Corned Beef and Cabbage	6–10 hours	4–5 hours
Casserole	4–9 hours	2–4 hours
Rice	5–9 hours	2–3 hours
Meat Loaf	8–9 hours	
Soup	6–12 hours	2–6 hours
Chicken	7–10 hours	3–4 hours
Vegetables	2–4 hours	
Baked Potato	8–10 hours	
Artichoke	6–8 hours	2½–4 hours

Slow Cooker

Converting Recipes

While it's possible to convert many recipes to slow-cooker cooking, it's important to make the proper adjustments for successful results. It's impossible to give an exact conversion formula, but general guidelines allow you to experiment with some of your favorite recipes. You can plan about 8 hours on the low setting or 4 hours on the high setting for every hour in the oven. The most popular and easiest conversions are soup or stew recipes, casseroles, and less expensive cuts of meat that cook well at low, even temperatures. Generally the amount of liquid called for in a regular recipe is reduced because liquids do not evaporate in the slow cooker. The exception is cooking rice, beans, or pasta, which require almost twice as much liquid.

- Do not try to translate quick recipes. Select recipes that take 1 hour or more in the oven or on the stove top.
- Most uncooked meat and vegetable combinations require at least 8 hours on low heat setting.
- Reduce the liquid by half, unless rice or pasta is in the dish.
- Add liquids for sauces about an hour before dish is done.
- Add ground spices during the last hour of cooking.
- Reduce herbs by about half; add during last hour of cooking.
- Many ingredients do not hold up well for extended periods of time in the slow cooker. Rice, pasta, seafood, and milk will fare better if added during the last 1 to 2 hours of cooking. Add these ingredients 2 hours before serving if cooking on low-heat setting or 1 hour before serving if cooking on high-heat setting.
- Although it is not necessary to brown meats (except ground beef) before slow cooking, doing so adds color and enhances flavor.
- It is not necessary to cook vegetables before adding to slow cooker.
- If a recipe calls for soaking dry beans, you can cook them on low heat in the slow cooker overnight. Cover the beans with water, add 1 teaspoon of baking soda, and cook on low setting. Drain well and combine with ingredients as the recipe directs.

Quick Fixes

Thin, runny soup: Start with half the recommended amount of water. If soup is still too thin, remove the cover from the slow cooker an hour or two before serving.

Too salty: Add a teaspoon each of cider vinegar and sugar to the recipe. The combination of ingredients will neutralize the salt without altering the flavor.

Mushy vegetables: Do not use canned vegetables. These vegetables are precooked and tend to get mushy, lose their color, and even disintegrate over the long cooking process. Stick with fresh or frozen vegetables. When using frozen vegetables, always let them thaw before adding to the slow cooker.

Too runny (too much liquid): Take the cover off and cook on high for 30 to 45 minutes.

Swapping This for That in Your Favorite Crockery Recipes

Original Ingredient	Substitute	Adjustments
Fresh corn	Canned or frozen corn	
Oil for sauteing	Flavored vinegar, wine, or broth	
Any type of beans	Any type of beans	
Meat marinade	Dry seasoning mixes	Rub on meat
Ground turkey or chicken	Ground beef	
Ground beef	Ground turkey or ground chicken	
Chicken	Turkey	
Beef	Pork	Remove any fat from pork
Whole milk, half and half, cream	Fat-free milk	
3 fresh tomatoes	28-oz. can peeled whole tomatoes with juice	
Fresh mushrooms	Dried mushrooms (wood ear, porcini, enoki)	
2 cups sliced fresh mushrooms	4.5-oz. jar sliced mushrooms, drained	
Dry beans	Canned beans	Decrease water by 4 cups per cup of beans Reduce cooking time by half
Onions	Leeks, rutabagas, turnips	
1 cup wine	1 cup water or nonfat chicken broth + 1 tbsp. red or cider vinegar	
1 cup tomato juice	1 cup V-8 juice	
14½-oz. can diced tomatoes with green chiles	14½-oz. can diced tomatoes + 4-oz. can chopped green chiles, undrained	
14½-oz. can diced tomatoes with roasted garlic	14½-oz. can diced tomatoes + ½ tsp. garlic powder	
Cream of mushroom soup	Cream of chicken or cream of celery soup	
14½-oz. can Italian-style stewed tomatoes	14½-oz. can stewed tomatoes + 1 tsp. dried Italian seasoning	
Zucchini	Yellow summer squash	
4 chicken breast halves (1–1½ lbs.)	3- to 3½-lb. cut-up broiler-fryer chicken, skin removed	
¼ cup soy sauce	3 tbsp. Worcestershire sauce + 1 tbsp. water	

Slow Cooking

Healthy Eating Guide

As "America's Healthiest Mom," I'm always reading food labels and nutrition articles. But sometimes nutrition terms can be confusing. That's why I developed this little cheat sheet on nutrition terminology. I hope you find it helpful as you read and learn more about nutrition and healthy living.

Amino Acids: The building blocks of protein.

Antioxidant: A chemical or other agent that prevents free radicals from overreacting with body tissue and causing premature aging, cancer, heart disease, arthritis, and other diseases. Vitamins C and E, beta-carotene, alpha-lipoic acid, selenium, and zinc are common antioxidants.

Beta-carotene: One of the major carotenoids found in all orange and yellow fruits and vegetables; it is used by the body to make vitamin A and is a strong antioxidant.

Calcium: An important mineral for the development of strong bones and teeth and the prevention of osteoporosis. You must absorb calcium every day from the foods you eat because your body does not make it. When you do not have enough calcium, your body breaks down bone to obtain the mineral. You can get the amount of calcium required daily through a variety of foods. Milk and dairy products offer the best source of calcium. Green leafy vegetables are another.

Calorie: A unit by which energy is measured.

Carbohydrate: A nutrient that supplies calories to the body. One gram of carbohydrate yields about 4 calories.

Carnitine: An amino acid essential for the breakdown of fat into energy; it may also have properties that help fight heart disease and protect against toxins.

Cholesterol: A soft, waxy substance found in the fats in the bloodstream and in all of the body's cells. Used to build cell membranes, produce hormones, and manufacture bile acids. High levels of cholesterol in the blood are a major risk for coronary heart disease, which can lead to heart attack. There are two types of cholesterol: LDL ("bad") and HDL ("good"). If too much LDL (low-density lipoprotein) cholesterol circulates in the blood, it can eventually clog the arteries that lead to the

heart and brain. HDL (high-density lipoprotein) is known as the "good" cholesterol because a high level seems to protect against heart attack. A healthy diet includes a daily total cholesterol intake that does not exceed 300 milligrams, regardless of calorie intake.

Daily Reference Values: A set of dietary measurements. Includes daily amounts for total fat, saturated fat, cholesterol, carbohydrates, protein, fiber, sodium, and potassium that can be used as general guidelines for a healthy diet. They are not specific recommendations, because each person's nutritional requirements may be influenced by other factors.

Dietary Fiber: The part of plant materials that the body cannot digest. It passes out of the body as waste, moving food along through the stomach and intestines, and helps prevent constipation, other intestinal problems, and hemorrhoids. Fiber has been associated with a reduced incidence of colon cancer.

Dietary Reference Intakes (DRI): The DRIs are revised recommendations for vitamins and minerals that are developed from the Institute of Medicine. DRIs will gradually replace the Recommended Dietary Allowances, or RDAs. In addition, experts are developing DRIs for vitamins and minerals that currently have no RDAs.

Healthy Eating

DV (Daily Value): Used in the labeling of supplement and vitamin products in the United States, DV is used as a recommendation.

Enzyme: A catalyst for a biological reaction. For example, digestive enzymes break down food in the digestive process.

Essential Fatty Acids (EFA): Polyunsaturated fatty acids from seeds, oils (safflower, sunflower, corn), and deep-sea fish that play an important role in fat transport and metabolism, as well as the maintenance and functioning of cellular membranes.

Fat: A macronutrient in food that insulates the body, supplies fatty acids, and carries fat-soluble vitamins A, D, E, and K. One gram of fat yields about 9 calories. While fat is essential for good health, high levels of saturated fat and cholesterol in the diet are linked to increased blood cholesterol levels and greater risk of heart disease. The daily recommended intake of total fat is less than 30 percent of total calories. It is important to remember that 30 percent is a maxiumum.

Fat-Soluble Vitamins: Vitamins A, D, E, and K; they dissolve in liquid fat or fatty oils, not in water alone.

Folic Acid: Also referred to as vitamin B_4, folic acid helps with cell division, strengthens arterial walls, maintains healthy blood, and promotes the growth of the fetal nervous system. Good food sources include yeast, liver, nuts, eggs, and whole wheat.

Food Additive: Anything added to food to enhance aroma, color, flavor, texture, shelf life, or nutritional value.

Free Radical: An unstable group of atoms with unpaired electrons that react with anything within the body, causing cellular and genetic damage. Causes of free radicals include excess ultraviolet radiation, smoke, and environmental pollutants. Can be countered with antioxidants.

Functional Foods: Foods formulated to provide certain health benefits.

Health Claim: A supplement manufacturer's or retailer's claim that a certain product prevents, treats, or cures a given condition or disease.

High-Density Lipoprotein (HDL): The "good" cholesterol, HDL is responsible for returning triglycerides from the cells and blood vessels to the liver. A high HDL blood level is associated with a lowered risk of heart attack.

IU (International Unit): The international standard measure for determining the biological action of vitamins A, D, and E. One IU stands for different quantities, depending on the vitamin in question.

Low-Density Lipoprotein (LDL): The "bad" cholesterol, LDL transports triglycerides in the blood from the liver to the body's cells. A high level of LDL is associated with a higher risk of heart attack, indicating raised levels of artery-clogging cholesterol in the blood.

Lutein: An antioxidant found throughout the body but concentrated in the *macula lutea,* lutein is believed to help protect the eyes from free radical damage caused by the sun's harmful rays. Good food sources include spinach, peaches, squash, kale, and broccoli.

Lycopene: A carotenoid that helps convert beta-carotene into vitamin A and gives fruits and vegetables their bright colors. Good food sources include tomatoes, carrots, sweet potatoes, leafy greens, apricots, papayas, and watermelon.

Mcg (Micrograms): 1 microgram is one millionth of a gram.

Metabolism: The process of cells burning food to produce energy. It involves all the chemical and physical changes that take place within the body and facilitate the body's continued growth and functioning.

Mg (Milligrams): 1 milligram is one thousandth of a gram.

Micronutrients: Nutrients, such as vitamins and minerals, that the body needs only in very small amounts.

Minerals: Inorganic substances essential for health. Include calcium, phosphorous, potassium, sodium, sulfur, copper, zinc, iron, iodine, selenium, magnesium, and nitrogen.

Natural Foods: Organically grown foods that are produced without pesticides and/or are unprocessed.

Nutrient: A substance or food that provides the body with nourishing factors and promotes growth.

Nutrient Density: The nutrients a food provides relative to the calories it provides. The more nutrients and fewer calories, the higher the nutrient density.

Nutrition: The entire process of metabolizing nutrients including ingestion, digestion, absorption, and utilization.

Pantothenic Acid: Commonly found in almost all foods, pantothenic acid is a B vitamin that helps maintain an active metabolism and a healthy nervous system.

Phytochemical: The naturally occurring substances in plants or a term referring to the chemistry of plants and plant processes.

Phytomedicinals: Medicinal products that are derived from plants.

Potassium: Potassium is needed for the healthy, steady functioning of the nervous system. Potassium also supports the normal functioning of the heart, muscles, kidneys, and blood. Studies suggest that eating foods high in potassium helps to counter some of the effects of high sodium consumption on blood pressure. The recommended daily intake of potassium is 3,500 mg, regardless of calorie intake. Good food sources include fruits and vegetables such as bananas, apricots, dried plums, cantaloupe, potatoes, tomatoes, sweet potatoes, and green leafy vegetables, as well as milk, fish, and meats.

Healthy Eating

Protein: One of the three macronutrients that provide calories, protein is needed for the growth and repair of all human tissues. Protein provides the body with energy and heat, maintains the body's acid/alkali balance, and helps manufacture hormones, antibodies, and enzymes.

Pyridoxine: Also known as vitamin B_6, pyridoxine is important for releasing energy from proteins. Good food sources include poultry, fish, potatoes, liver, and bananas.

RDA (Recommended Dietary Allowance): The Institute of Medicine recommends safe levels of intake for essential nutrients, based on current scientific knowledge. RDAs are set to meet the known nutrient needs of most healthy people and are updated regularly; they are gradually being replaced by revised guidelines called Dietary Reference Intakes, or DRIs.

RDI (Reference Daily Intake): The RDI represents the upper tolerable limit of vitamin and mineral intakes that the U.S. Food and Drug Administration recommends for persons 4 or more years of age. Food label percentages (called Percent Daily Values, or %DV) are based upon the RDI. For example, if the RDI for calcium is 1,000 mg and a food label lists calcium as 100%, that product contains the RDI of calcium, 1,000 mg.

Refined Carbohydrates: Plant foods that have undergone a process that removed their coarse parts, such as wheat refined into flour.

Retinol: The chemical name for vitamin A, this fat-soluble vitamin is especially important for eye health but also aids skin and mucous membranes. Good food sources include egg yolks, butter, and all yellow and orange fruits and vegetables.

Riboflavin: The chemical name for vitamin B_2, riboflavin plays a part in the body's metabolic function. Good food sources include dark leafy greens, milk, red meat, and mushrooms.

Saturated Fat: Saturated fat has been shown to increase total blood cholesterol level. Eating too much fat or cholesterol has been linked to an increased risk of heart disease. A healthy diet provides less than 10 percent of total calories from saturated fat. As with total fat, the 10 percent reference value represents an upper limit.

Selenium: A trace mineral, selenium protects the immune system; maintains heart, liver, and pancreatic function; keeps tissues elastic; and works with vitamin E as an antioxidant. Good food sources include lobster, clams, crabs, whole grains, Brazil nuts, and oysters.

Serum Cholesterol: A soft, waxy substance present in all parts of the body, serum cholesterol is made by the body and obtained from fatty substances in the diet. Cholesterol is manufactured in the liver for normal body functions including the production of hormones, bile, and vitamin D.

Sodium: Sodium plays an essential role in regulating fluids and blood pressure. Many studies have shown that high sodium intake is associated with high blood pressure. The daily reference value for sodium represents an upper limit. Daily intake should not exceed 2,400 milligrams, regardless of calorie intake.

Thiamine: The chemical name for vitamin B_1, thiamine contributes to growth, digestion, and nerve health. Good food sources include whole wheat and pork.

Tocopherol: The chemical name for vitamin E, tocopherol keeps cells and blood healthy and assists vitamin A; it also reduces the damaging oxidation of compounds. Good food sources include soybeans, peanut butter, avocado, oats, eggs, hazelnuts, shrimp, wheat germ, and leafy greens.

Tolerable Upper Intake Level (UI): Maximum amount of intake advisable for a given nutrient before a risk could develop.

Toxins: Substances poisonous to the body.

Triglycerides: The chief form of fat in the diet and the major form of stored fat in the body. Serum levels of triglycerides indicate how much fat is moving through or clogging arteries.

Tryptophan: An amino acid that helps make up proteins and can be converted into niacin (vitamin B_7).

USRDA (United States Recommended Daily Allowances): Widely used recommendations on supplements, developed by the Food and Drug Administration (FDA).

Vitamin A: Fat-soluble vitamin that helps maintain healthy skin, eyes, bones, hair, and teeth and is essential to proper immune function.

Vitamin B_6: Important to formation of proteins, red blood cells, messengers in nervous system, structural compounds, and prostaglandins, as well as functioning of enzymes and maintenance of immune system.

Vitamin C: Important antioxidant; helps maintain health of bones, teeth, blood vessels, and connective tissues; enhances immune system; reduces the risk of death from heart attacks, strokes, and cancer.

Vitamin E: Fat-soluble antioxidant that protects cell membranes, fats, the immune system, and vitamin A from free radicals.

Vitamin K: Aids in the thickening of blood to prevent hemorrhaging when a wound has occurred. Commonly found in all green vegetables; helpful bacteria in the intestine also make it.

Vitamins: Essential nutrients needed for good health. Most are not produced by the body so must be obtained through the diet.

Water-Soluble Vitamins: Vitamin C and all B vitamins. Easily dissolve in water; therefore, overcooked or boiled foods risk losing these nutrients.

Healthy Eating

Understanding Food Labels

Serving Size: Average amount or portion size that the nutrition information on the label represents. If you eat more or less than the amount indicated, make adjustments for calories and all other nutrient values.

Servings Per Container: The number of servings in the container of food. If the package says three servings per package and you eat the entire package, multiply the nutrient values times three to determine your total intake.

Amounts Per Serving: The number of nutrients and calories for each serving of food. One of the most common mistakes is to ignore the number of servings per package. Always check the number of servings per package before you start eating.

Calories: The number of calories for each serving of food.

% Daily Value: The percents of daily values for fat, cholesterol, carbohydrate, sodium, potassium, and protein are based on a 2,000-calorie diet. These values may be higher or lower, depending on the number of calories in your diet. Aim for 100 percent for total carbohydrate, dietary fiber, vitamins, and minerals each day.

Total Fat: Fat supplies energy and promotes the absorption of fat-soluble vitamins A, D, and E, but high levels of saturated fat and cholesterol are linked to increased blood cholesterol levels and greater risk of heart disease. The daily recommended intake of total fat is less than 30 percent of total calories. With 9 calories per gram of fat, a person who consumes 2,000 calories a day should eat less than 66 grams of total fat. Total fat values include saturated and unsaturated fats. Saturated and trans fats raise LDL cholesterol levels in the blood, thereby increasing the risk of heart disease. Dietary cholesterol also contributes to heart disease. Unsaturated fats, such as monounsaturated and polyunsaturated, do not raise LDL cholesterol and are beneficial when consumed in moderation. Therefore, it is advisable to choose foods low in saturated fat, trans fat, and cholesterol as part of a healthful diet.

Cholesterol: The recommended daily intake of cholesterol is 300 milligrams or less, regardless of calorie intake.

Sodium: High sodium intake has been associated with an increase in cases of high blood pressure. The daily reference value for sodium represents an upper limit. The recommended daily intake is 2,400 milligrams or less, regardless of calorie intake.

Total Carbohydrate: The daily recommended intake of total carbohydrates is approximately 60 percent of total calories. Dietary carbohydrates also include the complex carbohydrates, starch, and fiber.

Protein: Protein provides the body with energy and also helps manufacture hormones, antibodies, enzymes, and muscle tissues. It also maintains a proper acid/alkali balance. Reference values established for protein are based on age and sex.

Beef Entrées 1

Gingered Beef and Vegetables

BBQ Beef

Easy | Do Ahead | Freeze | Serves: 12

3 lbs. beef round steak

¾ cup frozen chopped onions, *thawed and drained*

⅓ cup brown sugar

2 tsp. chili powder

⅓ cup ketchup

¼ cup cider vinegar

1 cup beer

½ cup tomato paste

whole wheat buns, tortillas, or pita breads

Spray inside of slow cooker with cooking spray. Trim any excess fat from round steak and cut steak into 1-inch pieces. Combine with remaining ingredients in slow cooker and mix well. Cover and cook on low heat for 10–12 hours or high heat for 6–7 hours. Remove beef from slow cooker; shred using 2 forks and place in large saucepan. Add 2 cups of sauce from slow cooker and stir to mix. Keep warm over low heat; serve on whole wheat buns, tortillas, or pita breads.

Nutrition Facts per serving: 216 cal., 5.4 g total fat, 72 mg chol., 137 mg sodium, 12 g carbo., 1 g fiber, 28 g pro.
Exchanges: 1 Other Carbo., 3 Lean Meat
Carb Choices: 1

Shopping List

Meat	Baking Goods
3 lbs. beef round steak	brown sugar

Frozen	Condiments
12-oz. pkg. frozen chopped onions	ketchup cider vinegar

Canned	Seasonings
6-oz. can tomato paste	chili powder

Packaged	Other
whole wheat buns, tortillas, or pita breads	12 oz. beer

Barbecue Beef and Beans

2½ lbs. beef stew meat, *cut into 1-inch cubes*

1 tsp. garlic powder

¼ tsp. pepper

1 cup barbecue sauce

1 cup nonfat beef broth

1 15-oz. can red kidney beans, *drained*

Spray large nonstick skillet with cooking spray. Add stew meat to skillet; sprinkle with garlic powder and pepper. Cook over medium heat, stirring frequently, until browned on all sides. Spray inside of slow cooker with cooking spray. Combine stew meat, barbecue sauce, and beef broth in slow cooker. Cover and cook on low heat for 4–6 hours. Add beans; increase heat to high and cook 20–30 minutes until heated through.

Nutrition Facts per serving: 459 cal., 12.8 g total fat, 159 mg chol., 816 mg sodium, 17 g carbo., 4 g fiber, 65 g pro.
Exchanges: ½ Starch, ½ Other Carbo., 7 Lean Meat
Carb Choices: 1

Beef
Entrées

Shopping List

Meat
2½ lbs. beef stew meat

Canned
14-oz. can nonfat beef broth
15-oz. can red kidney beans

Condiments
8 oz. barbecue sauce

Seasonings
garlic powder
pepper

Storage Tip: Immediately freeze any beef you do not plan to use within a few days. Store at 0°F or colder and label each package with content information and date. Prevent freezer burn by rewrapping beef in freezer paper, plastic freezer bags, or heavy-duty foil. Press out as much air as possible before sealing.

Two-Ingredient Barbecue Beef

1 lb. beef stew meat

8 oz. barbecue sauce

whole wheat buns, tortillas, or pita breads (optional)

Spray inside of slow cooker with cooking spray. Combine ingredients in slow cooker and toss to mix. Cook on low heat for 8–10 hours or high heat for 4–5 hours. Transfer meat and sauce to serving bowl; shred using 2 forks. Serve on whole wheat buns, tortillas, or pita breads, if desired.

Nutrition Facts per serving: 259 cal., 8 g total fat, 95 mg chol., 530 mg sodium, 7 g carbo., 1 g fiber, 37 g pro.
Exchanges: ½ Other Carbo., 4 Lean Meat
Carb Choices: 0

Shopping List

Meat
1 lb. beef stew meat

Condiments
8 oz. barbecue sauce

Optional
whole wheat buns, tortillas, or pita breads

Never allow cooked food to sit at room temperature for more than 2 hours; wrap and refrigerate as soon as possible to prevent contamination.

Saucy Barbecue Beef

Easy | Do Ahead | Serves: 6

1½ lbs. extra-lean ground beef
1 cup chopped onion
1 cup chopped green bell pepper
2 tbsp. brown sugar
⅛ tsp. ground allspice
2 tbsp. mustard
1 tbsp. white vinegar
1 cup ketchup
⅓ cup chopped celery
½ cup shredded carrot
whole wheat buns, whole wheat pita breads, or baked potatoes

Spray large nonstick skillet with cooking spray. Add ground beef to skillet and cook over medium heat, stirring frequently, until beef is browned and crumbled. Drain well. Combine ground beef with remaining ingredients in slow cooker and mix well; cover and cook on low heat for 6–8 hours. Serve over whole wheat buns, stuffed inside whole wheat pita breads, or as topping on baked potatoes.

Nutrition Facts per serving: 231 cal., 4.8 g total fat, 61 mg chol., 494 mg sodium, 22 g carbo., 1 g fiber, 22 g pro.
Exchanges: 2 Vegetable, ½ Other Carbo., 3 Lean Meat
Carb Choices: 1

Beef
Entrées

Shopping List

Produce	Baking Goods
large onion	brown sugar
large green bell pepper	
small bunch celery	**Condiments**
8-oz. pkg. shredded carrots	mustard
baking potatoes (optional)	white vinegar
	ketchup
Meat	
1½ lbs. extra-lean ground beef	**Seasonings**
	ground allspice
Packaged	
whole wheat buns or whole wheat pita breads (optional)	

Substitution Tip: If you need a substitution for allspice, combine equal amounts of ground cinnamon, cloves, nutmeg, and pepper.

Shredded Barbecue Beef

Easy | Do Ahead | Serves: 8

3½ lbs. boneless beef chuck,
  cut into 1-inch cubes
2½ cups ketchup
1 cup Diet Coke
½ cup dried minced onion
2 tbsp. beef bouillon granules
½ tsp. onion powder
  whole wheat buns,
  sourdough bread rolls, or
  pita breads

Spray inside of slow cooker with cooking spray. Combine all ingredients in slow cooker and mix well; cover and cook on low heat for 6–8 hours. Remove meat from slow cooker; shred using 2 forks. Return to slow cooker and heat through. Serve on whole wheat buns, sourdough bread rolls, or pita breads.

Nutrition Facts per serving: 365 cal., 12.3 g total fat, 112 mg chol., 1,091 mg sodium, 25 g carbo., 0 g fiber, 38 g pro.
Exchanges: 2 Other Carbo., 10 Lean Meat
Carb Choices: 0

Shopping List

Meat
3½ lbs. boneless beef chuck

Packaged
whole wheat buns, sourdough
  bread rolls, or pita breads

Condiments
20 oz. ketchup

Seasonings
dried minced onion
beef bouillon granules
onion powder

Other
12-oz. can Diet Coke

Packaged fresh beef has a "sell by" date printed on the food label, which represents the last day recommended for selling the product. Stores generally pull any products left on the shelf on the sell-by date. If the meat is properly refrigerated, it will remain fresh up to 3 days after the sell-by date. If you're not going to use it within that time, you should freeze it. Some labels may have a "use by" date rather than a sell-by date, which means the meat must be cooked or frozen by that date.

Barbecue Meatballs

Easy | Do Ahead | Freeze | Serves: 6

1½ lbs. extra-lean ground beef

¾ tsp. garlic powder

¼ tsp. pepper

1 tsp. chili powder

1 5-oz. can evaporated skim milk

1 cup quick-cooking oatmeal

¼ cup egg substitute

1¾ cups barbecue sauce

barbecue sauce (optional)

Spray inside of slow cooker with cooking spray. Combine ground beef, garlic powder, pepper, chili powder, evaporated milk, oatmeal, and egg substitute in medium bowl and mix well; shape into 1-inch meatballs. Place meatballs in slow cooker; pour barbecue sauce over top. Cover and cook on low heat for 7–8 hours. Serve with additional barbecue sauce for dipping, if desired.

Nutrition Facts per serving: 276 cal., 6.8 g total fat, 62 mg chol., 655 mg sodium, 22 g carbo., 1 g fiber, 28 g pro.
Exchanges: ½ Starch, 1 Other Carbo., 3 Lean Meat
Carb Choices: 1

Beef Entrées

Shopping List

Meat
1½ lbs. extra-lean ground beef

Dairy
egg substitute

Canned
5-oz. can evaporated skim milk

Packaged
quick-cooking oatmeal

Condiments
16-oz. bottle barbecue sauce

Seasonings
garlic powder
pepper
chili powder

Optional
barbecue sauce

Fabulous Meatballs

1½ cups ketchup

¼ cup + 2 tbsp. horseradish

¼ cup + 2 tbsp. lemon juice

1 cup grape jelly

1½ tsp. Dijon mustard

1 lb. extra-lean ground beef

¼ cup egg substitute

3 tbsp. soft dry bread crumbs

¼ tsp. pepper

Shopping List

Meat
1 lb. extra-lean ground beef

Dairy
egg substitute

Packaged
bread or bread crumbs

Condiments
12 oz. ketchup
6 oz. horseradish
6 oz. lemon juice
8 oz. grape jelly
Dijon mustard

Seasonings
pepper

Spray inside of slow cooker with cooking spray. Combine ketchup, horseradish, lemon juice, jelly, and mustard in slow cooker and mix well. Cover and cook on high heat while preparing meatballs. Combine ground beef, egg substitute, bread crumbs, and pepper in large bowl and mix well; shape into 1-inch balls. Preheat oven to 400°. Line baking sheet with foil and spray with cooking spray. Arrange meatballs on baking sheet; bake 15–20 minutes. Add meatballs to slow cooker; stir to coat with sauce. Reduce heat to low; cover and cook 6–8 hours.

Nutrition Facts per serving: 331 cal., 3.4 g total fat, 41 mg chol., 889 mg sodium, 59 g carbo., 1 g fiber, 16 g pro.
Exchanges: 4 Other Carbo., 2 Lean Meat
Carb Choices: 4

When purchasing beef, do not select meat that has begun to turn gray, has dried-out edges, does not smell fresh, has yellowed fat on the edges, has a slimy feel, or is packed with excess liquid. These are signs of possible contamination or spoilage.

Meat Loaf and Potato Supper

Easy | Do Ahead | Serves: 8

2 lbs. extra-lean ground beef

1 cup seasoned bread crumbs

½ cup nonfat half and half

½ cup barbecue sauce

½ cup egg substitute

¾ cup chopped onion

5½ cups roasted onion potato cubes

Spray inside of slow cooker with cooking spray. Combine ground beef, bread crumbs, half and half, barbecue sauce, egg substitute, and onion in medium bowl and mix well. Shape mixture into loaf. Place potatoes in bottom of cooker; place meat loaf on top of potatoes. Cover and cook on low heat for 8–10 hours.

Nutrition Facts per serving: 308 cal., 5.5 g total fat, 61 mg chol., 443 mg sodium, 33 g carbo., 3 g fiber, 27 g pro.
Exchanges: 1 Starch, 1 Other Carbo., 3 Lean Meat
Carb Choices: 2

Beef
Entrées

Shopping List

Produce
large onion
2 16-oz. pkgs. roasted onion potato cubes

Meat
2 lbs. extra-lean ground beef

Dairy
4 oz. nonfat half and half
egg substitute

Packaged
seasoned bread crumbs

Condiments
barbecue sauce

Seasoned Bread Crumbs: Combine 1 cup fine dry bread crumbs, 1 tbsp. onion powder, 1 tbsp. dried parsley, ½ tsp. garlic powder, ½ tsp. oregano, and 2 tablespoons + 2 teaspoons nonfat Parmesan cheese in a tightly covered container; shake until mixed. Store in a tightly covered container in the freezer for up to 6 months. Makes 1¼ cups.

Slow Cooker Beef and Potato Casserole

Easy | Do Ahead | Serves: 6

2 lbs. extra-lean ground beef

1 tsp. onion powder

¾ tsp. garlic powder

¼ cup frozen chopped onions, *thawed and drained*

1 10¾-oz. can low-fat tomato soup

½ tsp. pepper

5 medium potatoes, *peeled and sliced*

1 cup nonfat half and half

Spray large nonstick skillet with cooking spray. Add ground beef to skillet; sprinkle with onion powder and garlic powder. Cook over medium heat, stirring frequently, until beef is browned and crumbled. Drain well. Combine onions, soup, and pepper in medium bowl and mix well. Arrange potato slices in bottom of slow cooker; top with meat mixture. Pour soup mixture over top and mix. Cover and cook on low heat for 4–6 hours. Increase heat to high. Pour half and half into slow cooker. Cover and cook for 15–20 minutes.

Nutrition Facts per serving: 374 cal., 7 g total fat, 81 mg chol., 362 mg sodium, 41 g carbo., 3 g fiber, 32 g pro.
Exchanges: 2 Vegetable, 2 Starch, 3 Lean Meat
Carb Choices: 3

Shopping List

Produce
5 medium potatoes

Meat
2 lbs. extra-lean ground beef

Dairy
8 oz. nonfat half and half

Frozen
12-oz. pkg. frozen chopped onions

Canned
10¾-oz. can low-fat tomato soup

Seasonings
onion powder
garlic powder
pepper

More Than Just Mom's Meat Loaf

Easy | **Do Ahead** | **Freeze** | **Serves: 6**

1¼ lbs. extra-lean ground beef
1 tbsp. onion powder
1 cup frozen pepper stir-fry, *thawed, drained, and patted dry*
pepper to taste
1 tsp. poultry seasoning
1 tsp. garlic powder
1 tbsp. paprika
½ cup egg substitute
¼ cup nonfat half and half

Spray inside of slow cooker with cooking spray. Combine all ingredients in medium bowl and mix well. Shape mixture into loaf and place in cooker. Cover and cook on low heat for 4–5 hours.

Nutrition Facts per serving: 148 cal., 3.9 g total fat, 51 mg chol., 63 mg sodium, 4 g carbo., 1 g fiber, 20 g pro.
Exchanges: ½ Vegetable, 2½ Lean Meat
Carb Choices: 0

Beef Entrées

Shopping List

Meat
1¼ lbs. extra-lean ground beef

Dairy
egg substitute
nonfat half and half

Frozen
16-oz. pkg. frozen pepper stir-fry

Seasonings
onion powder
pepper
poultry seasoning
garlic powder
paprika

Get the best beef for your buck! The difference between ground beef, ground sirloin, and ground round is basically the difference in the amount of fat in the ground meat. Ground beef is 73% lean with 27% fat; ground chuck is 80% lean with 20% fat; ground sirloin is 85% lean with 15% fat; and ground round is 90% lean with 10% fat.

Easiest-Ever Meat Loaf

Easy | Do Ahead | Freeze | Serves: 8

½ cup egg substitute

¾ cup nonfat half and half

¾ cup seasoned dry bread crumbs

1 1-oz. packet dry onion soup mix

2 lbs. extra-lean ground beef

Line slow cooker with wide strip of aluminum foil, making sure foil comes up sides of cooker. Combine egg substitute, half and half, bread crumbs, and soup mix in large bowl and mix well. Add ground beef and mix; shape mixture into oval or rectangle and place in cooker without touching sides. Cover and cook on low heat for 6 hours or high heat for 3 hours.

Nutrition Facts per serving: 211 cal., 5.2 g total fat, 61 mg chol., 432 mg sodium, 12 g carbo., 1 g fiber, 24 g pro.
Exchanges: ½ Starch, 3 Lean Meat
Carb Choices: 1

Shopping List

Meat
2 lbs. extra-lean ground beef

Dairy
egg substitute
6 oz. nonfat half and half

Packaged
seasoned dry bread crumbs
1-oz. packet onion soup mix

Swedish Stuffed Cabbage

Easy | Do Ahead | Serves: 6

12 large cabbage leaves
1 lb. extra-lean ground beef
1 cup cooked rice
¼ cup egg substitute
¼ cup skim milk
1½ tsp. onion powder
¼ tsp. pepper
1 8-oz. can tomato sauce
  with roasted garlic
1 tbsp. brown sugar
1 tsp. lemon juice
1 tsp. steak sauce

Spray inside of slow cooker with cooking spray. Bring 4 cups water to a boil in saucepan. Add cabbage leaves; turn off heat and let leaves soak for 5 minutes. Remove leaves from water, drain, and let cool. Combine ground beef, cooked rice, egg substitute, milk, onion powder, and pepper in medium bowl and mix well. Place about ¼ cup meat mixture in center of each leaf, fold sides, and roll ends over meat. Arrange cabbage rolls in slow cooker, stacking if necessary. Combine tomato sauce, brown sugar, lemon juice, and steak sauce in small bowl and mix well. Pour tomato mixture over cabbage rolls. Cover and cook on low heat for 7–9 hours or high heat for 3½–4½ hours.

Beef Entrées

Nutrition Facts per serving: 175 cal., 3.2 g total fat, 41 mg chol., 285 mg sodium, 17 g carbo., 17 g pro.
Exchanges: 3 Vegetable, 2 Lean Meat
Carb Choices: 1

Shopping List

Produce	Canned	Condiments
large head cabbage	8-oz. can tomato sauce with roasted garlic	lemon juice steak sauce
Meat		**Seasonings**
1 lb. extra-lean ground beef	**Packaged** rice	onion powder pepper
Dairy	**Baking Goods**	
egg substitute skim milk	brown sugar	

Cabbage Rolls

12 large cabbage leaves
 1 lb. extra-lean ground beef
½ cup cooked rice
⅛ tsp. pepper
¼ tsp. dried thyme
¼ tsp. ground nutmeg
¼ tsp. ground cinnamon
 1 6-oz. can Italian tomato paste with roasted garlic
¾ cup water

Shopping List

Produce
large head cabbage

Meat
1 lb. extra-lean ground beef

Canned
6-oz. can Italian tomato paste
 with roasted garlic

Packaged
rice

Seasonings
pepper
dried thyme
ground nutmeg
ground cinnamon

Bring 4 cups water to a boil in saucepan. Add cabbage leaves; turn off heat and let leaves soak for 5 minutes. Remove leaves from water, drain, and let cool. Combine ground beef, rice, pepper, thyme, nutmeg, and cinnamon in medium bowl and mix well. Place 2 tablespoons of meat mixture in center of each cabbage leaf and roll firmly. Spray inside of slow cooker with cooking spray. Arrange cabbage rolls in slow cooker, stacking as necessary. Combine tomato paste and ¾ cup water in small bowl and mix well. Pour sauce over cabbage rolls. Cover and cook on low heat for 8–10 hours or high heat for 4–5 hours.

Nutrition Facts per serving: 152 cal., 3.1 g total fat, 41 mg chol., 263 mg sodium, 11 g carbo., 2 g fiber, 16 g pro.
Exchanges: 2 Vegetable, 2 Lean Meat
Carb Choices: 1

All beef sold in the United States must pass an inspection by the Food Safety and Inspection Service (FSIS) of the United States Department of Agriculture (USDA). The mandatory inspection concentrates on the safety and wholesomeness of the meat and not necessarily the quality. Tests determine if biological or chemical contamination is present in the meat.

Easy Beef and Vegetables

Easy | Do Ahead | Serves: 8

- ¼ cup flour
- ½ tsp. pepper
- 2 lbs. beef stew meat, *cut into 1-inch cubes*
- 4 carrots, *sliced on the diagonal*
- 3 potatoes, *diced*
- 2 medium onions, *chopped*
- ½ cup sliced celery
- 1½ cups nonfat beef broth
- 1 tsp. steak sauce
- ½ tsp. minced garlic
- 1 tsp. paprika

Spray large nonstick skillet with cooking spray. Combine flour and pepper in zip-top bag and shake to mix. Drop stew meat into bag and shake to coat with flour mixture. Add to skillet and cook over medium heat, stirring frequently, until browned on all sides. Spray inside of slow cooker with cooking spray. Place carrots, potatoes, onions, and celery in bottom of slow cooker; place meat on top of vegetables. Combine remaining ingredients and pour over meat and vegetables; stir to mix. Cover and cook on low heat for 10–12 hours or high heat for 5–6 hours.

Beef Entrées

Nutrition Facts per serving: 322 cal., 7.4 g total fat, 95 mg chol., 250 mg sodium, 23 g carbo., 3 g fiber, 39 g pro.
Exchanges: 3 Vegetable, ½ Starch, 4 Lean Meat
Carb Choices: 2

Shopping List

Produce	Baking Goods
4 carrots	flour
3 potatoes	
2 medium onions	**Condiments**
small bunch celery	steak sauce
Meat	**Seasonings**
2 lbs. beef stew meat	pepper
	minced garlic
Canned	paprika
14-oz. can nonfat beef broth	

Steak Stew

1½ lbs. beef round steak, *cut into 1-inch cubes*

1 14½-oz. can stewed tomatoes with bell pepper and onion, *do not drain*

1 8-oz. can tomato sauce with roasted garlic

1 medium onion, *sliced thin*

1 16-oz. pkg. frozen mixed vegetables, *thawed and drained*

1 tbsp. Worcestershire sauce

½ tsp. dried basil

¼ tsp. dried rosemary

¼ tsp. pepper

4 medium potatoes, *cut into ½-inch cubes*

Spray large nonstick skillet with cooking spray. Add steak cubes to skillet and cook over medium heat, stirring frequently, until browned on all sides. Spray inside of slow cooker with cooking spray. Combine all ingredients in slow cooker and mix well. Cover and cook on low heat for 8–10 hours or high heat for 4–5 hours.

Nutrition Facts per serving: 333 cal., 5.7 g total fat, 72 mg chol., 523 mg sodium, 37 g carbo., 8 g fiber, 32 g pro.
Exchanges: 4 Vegetable, 1 Starch, 3 Lean Meat
Carb Choices: 2

Shopping List

Produce
medium onion
4 medium potatoes

Meat
1½ lbs. beef round steak

Frozen
16-oz. pkg. frozen mixed vegetables

Canned
14½-oz. can stewed tomatoes with bell pepper and onion

8-oz. can tomato sauce with roasted garlic

Condiments
Worcestershire sauce

Seasonings
dried basil
dried rosemary
pepper

Beef Stew

1½ lbs. beef stew meat, *cut into 1-inch cubes*

¾ cup frozen chopped onions, *thawed and drained*

2 cups chopped celery

2 cups chopped carrots

½ lb. red potatoes, *cubed*

1 8-oz. can tomato sauce with roasted garlic

1 10¾-oz. can low-fat cream of mushroom soup

¼ tsp. pepper

Spray large nonstick skillet with cooking spray. Add stew meat to skillet and cook over medium heat, stirring frequently, until browned on all sides. Spray inside of slow cooker with cooking spray. Combine all ingredients in slow cooker and mix well. Cover and cook on low heat for 6–8 hours or high heat for 3–4 hours.

Nutrition Facts per serving: 342 cal., 10.9 g total fat, 102 mg chol., 575 mg sodium, 23 g carbo., 4 g fiber, 38 g pro.

Exchanges: 2 Vegetable, 1 Starch, 4 Lean Meat

Carb Choices: 2

Beef
Entrées

Substitution Tip: One cup of tomato sauce equals ¼ cup of tomato paste + ¾ cup water. For tomato sauce with roasted garlic, add about 1 tsp. garlic powder.

Shopping List

Produce	Canned
small bunch celery	8-oz. can tomato sauce with
¾ lb. carrots	roasted garlic
½ lb. red potatoes	10¾-oz. can low-fat cream
	of mushroom soup
Meat	
1½ lbs. beef stew meat	**Seasonings**
	pepper
Frozen	
12-oz. pkg. frozen chopped	
onions	

Beef in Red Wine Gravy

Easy | Do Ahead | Serves: 6

1½ lbs. beef stew meat, *cut into 1-inch cubes*

3 tbsp. dried minced onion

2 tsp. beef bouillon granules

3 tbsp. cornstarch

pepper to taste

1½ cups dry red wine

cooked no-yolk egg noodles (optional)

Spray inside of slow cooker with cooking spray. Place stew meat in slow cooker; sprinkle with onion, bouillon granules, cornstarch, and pepper. Pour red wine over beef; cover and cook on low heat for 10–12 hours or high heat for 5–6 hours. Serve over cooked no-yolk egg noodles, if desired.

Nutrition Facts per serving: 230 cal., 5.3 g total fat, 72 mg chol., 156 mg sodium, 7 g carbo., 1 g fiber, 27 g pro.
Exchanges: ½ Other Carbo., 3 Lean Meat
Carb Choices: 0

Shopping List

Meat
1½ lbs. beef stew meat

Baking Goods
cornstarch

Seasonings
dried minced onion
beef bouillon granules
pepper

Other
12 oz. dry red wine

Optional
no-yolk egg noodles

Freeze leftover wine to use in your favorite recipe. Simply pour wine into ice cube containers and freeze. Add to soups, stews, gravies, stir-fries, and more for fabulous flavor.

Vegetable Ground Beef Stew

Easy | **Do Ahead** | **Serves: 6**

- 1 lb. extra-lean ground beef
- 1 tsp. onion powder
- ¾ tsp. garlic powder
- 1½ cups nonfat beef broth
- ½ cup V-8 juice
- 1 tsp. sugar
- 1½ cups frozen chopped onions, *thawed and drained*
- 1½ cups chopped carrots
- 2 cups diced potato
- ¼ tsp. pepper

Spray large nonstick skillet with cooking spray. Add ground beef, onion powder, and garlic powder to skillet. Cook beef over medium heat, stirring frequently, until browned and crumbled. Drain well. Spray inside of slow cooker with cooking spray. Combine all ingredients in slow cooker and mix well; cover and cook on low heat for 8–10 hours or high heat for 4–5 hours.

Nutrition Facts per serving: 182 cal., 3.3 g total fat, 41 mg chol., 300 mg sodium, 19 g carbo., 3 g fiber, 17 g pro.
Exchanges: 1 Vegetable, ½ Starch, 2 Lean Meat
Carb Choices: 1

Beef
Entrées

Shopping List

Produce	Baking Goods
2 medium carrots	sugar
large potato	
	Seasonings
Meat	onion powder
1 lb. extra-lean ground beef	garlic powder
	pepper
Frozen	
12-oz. pkg. frozen chopped onions	
Canned	
14-oz. can nonfat beef broth	
6 oz. V-8 juice	

Savory Beef Roast

- ¼ cup Worcestershire sauce
- ¼ cup steak sauce
- 2 lbs. boneless beef bottom round
- ½ cup chopped onion

Combine Worcestershire sauce and steak sauce in small bowl and mix well. Pour sauce into slow cooker. Place meat on top and coat both sides with sauce. Sprinkle onion on meat; cover and cook on low heat for 10 hours or high heat for 5 hours.

Nutrition Facts per serving: 179 cal., 5.4 g total fat, 72 mg chol., 234 mg sodium, 3 g carbo., 0 g fiber, 27 g pro.
Exchanges: 3 Lean Meat
Carb Choices: 0

Shopping List

Produce
medium onion

Meat
2 lbs. boneless beef bottom round

Condiments
Worcestershire sauce
steak sauce

Always thaw meat in the refrigerator or microwave (at low-power setting). NEVER defrost meat at room temperature.

Eye of Round Roast with Mushroom Sauce

Easy | Do Ahead | Serves: 6

- 1½ lbs. boneless beef eye of round
- 1½ lbs. unpeeled potatoes, *quartered*
- 1 16-oz. pkg. frozen baby carrots
- 2 cups sliced fresh mushrooms
- ½ tsp. dried basil
- 1 10¾-oz. can low-fat cream of mushroom soup

Shopping List

Produce
1½ lbs. potatoes
½ lb. mushrooms

Meat
1½ lbs. boneless beef eye of round

Frozen
16-oz. pkg. frozen baby carrots

Canned
10¾-oz. can low-fat cream of mushroom soup

Seasonings
dried basil

Trim any visible fat from meat and cut meat to fit slow cooker. Combine potatoes, carrots, mushrooms, and basil in slow cooker; place meat on top of vegetables and cover with soup. Cover and cook on low heat for 10–12 hours or high heat for 5–6 hours.

Nutrition Facts per serving: 332 cal., 6.4 g total fat, 73 mg chol., 307 mg sodium, 36 g carbo., 6 g fiber, 32 g pro.
Exchanges: 2 Vegetable, 1 Starch, ½ Other Carbo., 3 Lean Meat
Carb Choices: 2

Beef Entrées

Read labels carefully. On some packaged beef a "lean" label simply refers to the fact that the excess fat has been trimmed from the beef; it may not indicate a lean cut. If you purchase cuts from the tenderloin or round, you can be sure they are lean.

Steak with Mushrooms and Gravy

Easy | Do Ahead | Serves: 6

1 12-oz. jar fat-free beef gravy

1 4-oz. can sliced mushrooms, *drained*

2 tbsp. Italian tomato paste with roasted garlic

¾ tsp. garlic powder

½ tsp. pepper

½ tsp. dried Italian seasoning

1½ lbs. boneless beef top round steak, *trimmed and cut into 6 equal pieces*

Shopping List

Meat
1½ lbs. boneless beef top round steak

Canned
4-oz. can sliced mushrooms
6-oz. can Italian tomato paste with roasted garlic

Condiments
12-oz. jar fat-free beef gravy

Seasonings
garlic powder
pepper
dried Italian seasoning

Spray inside of slow cooker with cooking spray. Combine gravy, mushrooms, tomato paste, garlic powder, pepper, and Italian seasoning in medium bowl and mix well. Spread half the gravy mixture in slow cooker; top with steak and remaining gravy mixture. Cover and cook on high heat for 1 hour. Reduce heat to low and cook for 6–7 hours.

Nutrition Facts per serving: 191 cal., 5 g total fat, 72 mg chol., 419 mg sodium, 5 g carbo., 1 g fiber, 28 g pro.
Exchanges: 1 Vegetable, 3 Lean Meat
Carb Choices: 0

Sirloin Tip Roast with Horseradish Sauce

- 1 tsp. salt
- 2 tsp. garlic powder
- ¾ tsp. dried oregano
- ¼ tsp. dried basil
- ½ tsp. pepper
- 1 4-lb. boneless beef sirloin tip roast, *trimmed and cut in half*
- ½ cup nonfat beef broth

Shopping List

Meat
4-lb. boneless beef sirloin
tip roast

Dairy
8 oz. nonfat sour cream

Canned
14-oz. can nonfat beef broth

Condiments
nonfat mayonnaise
prepared horseradish
lemon juice
Worcestershire sauce

Seasonings
salt
garlic powder
dried oregano
dried basil
pepper

Spray inside of slow cooker with cooking spray. Combine salt, garlic powder, oregano, basil, and pepper in a small bowl and mix well. Spread mixture over roast halves and spray with cooking spray. Spray large nonstick skillet with cooking spray and heat over medium-high heat. Add roast and cook until browned on all sides. Place roast halves in slow cooker. Add broth to skillet and cook, scraping to loosen browned bits. Pour broth over roast. Cover and cook on high heat for 1 hour. Reduce heat to low and cook 6–8 hours. Remove meat from slow cooker and let stand 15 minutes before slicing diagonally across the grain into thin slices. Scoop juices from slow cooker into gravy dish. Serve meat with juices and Horseradish Sauce.

Beef Entrées

Nutrition Facts per serving: 407 cal., 14 g total fat, 127 mg chol., 401 mg sodium, 21 g carbo., 2 g fiber, 46 g pro.
Exchanges: 1½ Starch, 5 Lean Meat
Carb Choices: 1

Horseradish Sauce: Combine ⅔ cup nonfat sour cream, ¼ cup nonfat mayonnaise, 2 tablespoons prepared horseradish, ¼ teaspoon lemon juice, and ½ teaspoon Worcestershire sauce in small bowl and mix well. Cover and refrigerate until ready to serve.

Shortcut Beef Stroganoff

Easy | Do Ahead | Serves: 6

1½ lbs. extra-lean ground beef

1½ tsp. onion powder

½ tsp. minced garlic

2 tbsp. flour

pepper to taste

¼ tsp. paprika

1 10¾-oz. can low-fat cream of mushroom soup

3 cups cooked no-yolk noodles

Shopping List

Meat
1½ lbs. extra-lean ground beef

Canned
10¾-oz. can low-fat cream of mushroom soup

Packaged
8-oz. pkg. no-yolk egg noodles

Baking Goods
flour

Seasonings
onion powder
minced garlic
pepper
paprika

Spray large nonstick skillet with cooking spray. Add ground beef to skillet and cook over medium heat, stirring frequently, until browned and crumbled. Drain well. Add onion powder, minced garlic, flour, pepper, paprika, and mushroom soup and mix well. Spray inside of slow cooker with cooking spray. Spoon beef mixture into slow cooker. Cover and cook on low heat for 6–7 hours. Serve over hot cooked noodles.

Nutrition Facts per serving: 292 cal., 5.7 g total fat, 62 mg chol., 220 mg sodium, 29 g carbo., 2 g fiber, 27 g pro.
Exchanges: 1½ Starch, 3 Lean Meat
Carb Choices: 2

Storage: The following recommended storage times will help you determine how long to keep raw or cooked beef.
   Steaks/roasts: Refrigerate 3–4 days; freeze 6–12 months.
   Ground beef: Refrigerate 1–2 days; freeze 3–4 months.
   Cooked beef (leftovers): Refrigerate 3–4 days; freeze 2–3 months.

Beef Stroganoff

Easy | Do Ahead | Serves: 6

¼ cup flour

½ tsp. Mrs. Dash seasoning

¼ tsp. pepper

2 lbs. beef stew meat, *cut into 1-inch cubes*

1 10¾-oz. can low-fat cream of mushroom soup

1 cup nonfat half and half

½ cup frozen chopped onions, *thawed and drained*

1 tbsp. Worcestershire sauce

2 tsp. beef bouillon granules

1 tsp. garlic powder

1 8-oz. pkg. nonfat cream cheese, *softened and cubed*

3 cups cooked noodles or rice

Spray large nonstick skillet with cooking spray. Combine flour, Mrs. Dash seasoning, and pepper in zip-top bag and shake until mixed. Drop stew meat into bag and shake to coat with flour mixture. Add meat to skillet and cook over medium heat, stirring frequently, until browned on all sides. Drain well. Spray inside of slow cooker with cooking spray. Place meat in slow cooker. Combine soup, half and half, onions, Worcestershire sauce, bouillon granules, and garlic powder in a medium bowl and mix well. Pour soup mixture over meat. Cover and cook on low heat for 5–6 hours. Increase heat to high; add cream cheese and cook, stirring occasionally, until cheese is melted. Serve over cooked noodles or rice.

Beef Entrées

Nutrition Facts per serving: 500 cal., 11.2 g total fat, 153 mg chol., 651 mg sodium, 36 g carbo., 2 g fiber, 58 g pro.
Exchanges: 2 Starch, 6½ Lean Meat
Carb Choices: 2

Shopping List

Meat	Canned	Condiments
2 lbs. beef stew meat	10¾-oz. can low-fat cream of mushroom soup	Worcestershire sauce
Dairy		**Seasonings**
8 oz. nonfat half and half		Mrs. Dash seasoning
8 oz. nonfat cream cheese	**Packaged**	pepper
	8-oz. pkg. noodles or rice	beef bouillon granules
		garlic powder
Frozen	**Baking Goods**	
12-oz. pkg. frozen chopped onions	flour	

Herbed Stroganoff with Mushrooms

Easy | **Do Ahead** | **Serves: 6**

1 tbsp. + 1½ cups nonfat beef broth, *divided*

1½ lbs. beef stew meat, *cut into 1-inch cubes*

2 cups sliced fresh mushrooms

1 tsp. minced garlic

½ tsp. dried oregano

¼ tsp. dried thyme

¼ tsp. pepper

1 bay leaf

⅓ cup dry sherry

1 cup nonfat sour cream

½ cup flour

⅓ cup water

4 cups cooked no-yolk egg noodles

Spray large nonstick skillet with cooking spray. Add 1 tablespoon beef broth and heat over medium-high heat. Add stew meat to skillet and brown on all sides. Drain well. Spray inside of slow cooker with cooking spray. Combine beef, mushrooms, minced garlic, oregano, thyme, pepper, and bay leaf in cooker. Pour sherry and remaining beef broth on top. Cover and cook on low heat for 8–10 hours or high heat for 4–5 hours. Remove bay leaf. If cooking on low, increase heat to high. Combine sour cream, flour, and water in small bowl and mix well. Add 1 cup hot liquid from slow cooker to flour mixture and blend well. Return mixture to slow cooker and stir to mix. Cover and cook on high heat for 30 minutes until mixture becomes thick and bubbly. Serve over hot cooked noodles.

Nutrition Facts per serving: 391 cal., 5.9 g total fat, 72 mg chol., 296 mg sodium, 40 g carbo., 3 g fiber, 38 g pro.
Exchanges: 2 Starch, ½ Other Carbo., 3 Lean Meat
Carb Choices: 3

Shopping List

Produce	Canned	Seasonings
8 oz. sliced fresh mushrooms	14-oz. can nonfat beef broth	minced garlic
		dried oregano
		dried thyme
Meat	**Packaged**	pepper
1½ lbs. beef stew meat	8-oz. pkg. no-yolk egg noodles	bay leaf
		Other
Dairy	**Baking Goods**	dry sherry
8 oz. nonfat sour cream	flour	

Stroganoff-Topped Potatoes

Easy | **Do Ahead** | **Serves: 6**

1½ lbs. extra-lean ground beef

2 medium onions, *sliced thin*

2 cups sliced fresh mushrooms

½ tsp. minced garlic

2 tbsp. flour

¼ tsp. paprika

1 10¾-oz. can low-fat cream of mushroom soup

1 cup nonfat sour cream

3 baking potatoes, *baked and sliced*

Spray large nonstick skillet with cooking spray. Add ground beef, onions, mushrooms, and garlic and cook over medium heat, stirring frequently, until beef is browned and crumbled. Drain well. Remove from heat. Add flour, paprika, and soup and mix well. Spray inside of slow cooker with cooking spray. Place beef mixture in slow cooker. Cover and cook on low heat for 6 hours or high heat for 3 hours. Just before serving, stir in sour cream and heat 10–15 minutes, stirring constantly. Serve beef mixture over sliced cooked potatoes.

Beef Entrées

Nutrition Facts per serving: 343 cal., 5.7 g total fat, 62 mg chol., 239 mg sodium, 40 g carbo., 4 g fiber, 28 g pro.
Exchanges: 1½ Vegetable, 2 Starch, 3 Lean Meat
Carb Choices: 3

Shopping List

Produce	**Canned**
2 medium onions	10¾-oz. can low-fat cream
8 oz. sliced mushrooms	of mushroom soup
3 baking potatoes	
	Baking Goods
Meat	flour
1½ lbs. extra-lean ground beef	
	Seasonings
	minced garlic
Dairy	paprika
8 oz. nonfat sour cream	

Beefy Macaroni

Easy | Do Ahead | Serves: 8

- 2 lbs. extra-lean ground beef
- 1 cup frozen chopped onions, *thawed and drained*
- ¼ cup frozen chopped green bell peppers, *thawed and drained*
- ½ tsp. minced garlic
- 2 14½-oz. cans ready-cut diced tomatoes with garlic, oregano, and basil, *do not drain*
- 1 cup V-8 juice
- ¼ tsp. pepper
- ½ tsp. dried Italian seasoning
- 2 cups uncooked macaroni

Spray large nonstick skillet with cooking spray. Add ground beef, onions, bell peppers, and garlic to skillet. Cook over medium heat, stirring frequently, until beef is browned and crumbled. Drain well. Spray inside of slow cooker with cooking spray. Combine meat mixture, undrained tomatoes, V-8 juice, pepper, and Italian seasoning in slow cooker and mix well. Cover and cook on low heat for 6–8 hours. Add macaroni, mix lightly, and cook 2–3 hours longer.

Nutrition Facts per serving: 227 cal., 4.8 g total fat, 61 mg chol., 276 mg sodium, 17 g carbo., 2 g fiber, 24 g pro.
Exchanges: 1 Vegetable, ½ Starch, 3 Lean Meat
Carb Choices: 1

Shopping List

Meat	Packaged
2 lbs. extra-lean ground beef	8-oz. pkg. macaroni

Frozen	Seasonings
12-oz. pkg. frozen chopped onions	minced garlic
10-oz. pkg. frozen chopped green bell peppers	pepper
	dried Italian seasoning

Canned
2 14½-oz. cans ready-cut diced tomatoes with garlic, oregano, and basil
8-oz. can V-8 juice

Mac and Cheese with Savory Tomato Sauce

Easy | Do Ahead | Serves: 4

- 1 lb. extra-lean ground beef
- 1½ tsp. onion powder
- ¾ tsp. garlic powder
- 1 15-oz. can spaghetti sauce
- ¼ cup water
- ¼ cup tomato sauce
- 2 tbsp. sugar
- 1½ tsp. vinegar
- ¼ tsp. dried Italian seasoning
- 6 oz. nonfat shredded mozzarella cheese
- 8 oz. macaroni, *cooked and drained*

Spray large nonstick skillet with cooking spray. Add ground beef to skillet; sprinkle with onion powder and garlic powder. Cook over medium heat, stirring frequently, until beef is browned and crumbled. Drain well. Spray inside of slow cooker with cooking spray. Place browned beef in cooker. Add spaghetti sauce, water, tomato sauce, sugar, vinegar, and Italian seasoning. Cover and cook on low heat for 4–6 hours. Add cheese and cooked macaroni. Cover and cook on low heat for 2 hours.

Nutrition Facts per serving: 491 cal., 5.4 g total fat, 61 mg chol., 644 mg sodium, 58 g carbo., 1 g fiber, 44 g pro.
Exchanges: 2 Vegetable, 3 Starch, 1 Very Lean Meat, 3 Lean Meat
Carb Choices: 4

Beef Entrées

Shopping List

Meat
1 lb. extra-lean ground beef

Dairy
6 oz. nonfat shredded mozzarella cheese

Canned
15-oz. can spaghetti sauce
6-oz. can tomato sauce

Packaged
8-oz. pkg. macaroni

Baking Goods
sugar

Condiments
vinegar

Seasonings
onion powder
garlic powder
dried Italian seasoning

Beef and Potato Hash

Easy | **Do Ahead** | **Serves: 4**

1 lb. extra-lean ground beef

¾ tsp. onion powder

½ tsp. garlic powder

3½ cups frozen potatoes O'Brien

2 8-oz. cans tomato sauce with roasted garlic

1 14½-oz. can ready-cut diced tomatoes with garlic, oregano, and basil, *do not drain*

½ cup nonfat shredded cheddar cheese

Spray large nonstick skillet with cooking spray. Add ground beef, onion powder, and garlic powder to skillet. Cook over medium heat, stirring frequently, until beef is browned and crumbled. Drain well. Combine cooked beef, potatoes, tomato sauce, and undrained tomatoes in slow cooker. Cover and cook on low heat for 6–8 hours or high heat for 3–4 hours. Just before serving, sprinkle with cheese.

Nutrition Facts per serving: 290 cal., 4.7 g total fat, 61 mg chol., 1,012 mg sodium, 28 g carbo., 5 g fiber, 29 g pro.
Exchanges: 2 Vegetable, 1 Starch, 3 Lean Meat
Carb Choices: 2

Shopping List

Meat
1 lb. extra-lean ground beef

Frozen
28-oz. pkg. potatoes O'Brien

Dairy
nonfat shredded cheddar cheese

Canned
2 8-oz. cans tomato sauce with roasted garlic
14½-oz. can ready-cut diced tomatoes with garlic, oregano, and basil

Seasonings
onion powder
garlic powder

Creamy Mushroom-Beef Casserole

Easy | Do Ahead | Serves: 4

1½ lbs. beef round steak, *cut into 1-inch cubes*

1 10¾-oz. can low-fat cream of mushroom soup

2 cups sliced fresh mushrooms

¼ cup instant minced onion

2 tbsp. beef bouillon granules

½ tsp. onion powder

½ cup skim milk

2 cups cooked rice or noodles

Spray large nonstick skillet with cooking spray. Add beef to skillet and cook over medium heat, stirring frequently, until browned on all sides. Spray inside of slow cooker with cooking spray. Combine all ingredients except rice or noodles in slow cooker. Cover and cook on low heat for 8–10 hours. Serve over cooked rice or noodles.

Nutrition Facts per serving: 497 cal., 13 g total fat, 170 mg chol., 878 mg sodium, 30 g carbo., 3 g fiber, 60 g pro.
Exchanges: 2 Starch, 6½ Lean Meat
Carb Choices: 2

Beef
Entrées

Shopping List

Produce
½ lb. fresh mushrooms

Meat
1½ lbs. beef round steak

Dairy
4 oz. skim milk

Canned
10¾-oz. can low-fat cream of mushroom soup

Packaged
8-oz. pkg. rice or noodles

Seasonings
instant minced onion
beef bouillon granules
onion powder

Substitution Tip:
You can substitute a 4- or 6-oz. can of sliced mushrooms (drained) for the fresh sliced mushrooms.

Italian Beef Spaghetti Sauce

Easy | **Do Ahead** | **Serves: 4**

- ¾ lb. extra-lean ground beef
- ½ tsp. onion powder
- 1 tsp. minced garlic
- 1 14½-oz. can ready-cut Italian diced tomatoes with garlic, oregano, and basil, *do not drain*
- 1 8-oz. can tomato sauce
- 2 cups sliced fresh mushrooms
- ½ cup chopped green bell pepper
- 2 tbsp. quick-cooking tapioca
- 1 tsp. dried Italian seasoning
- ⅛ tsp. crushed red pepper
- 2 cups hot cooked spaghetti

Spray large nonstick skillet with cooking spray. Add ground beef, onion powder, and minced garlic to skillet. Cook over medium heat, stirring frequently, until beef is browned and crumbled. Drain well. Spray inside of slow cooker with cooking spray. Combine undrained tomatoes, tomato sauce, mushrooms, bell pepper, tapioca, Italian seasoning, and red pepper in cooker; stir in meat mixture. Cover and cook on low heat for 8–10 hours or high heat for 4–5 hours. Serve over hot cooked spaghetti.

Nutrition Facts per serving: 254 cal., 4.2 g total fat, 46 mg chol., 508 mg sodium, 31 g carbo., 4 g fiber, 21 g pro.
Exchanges: 3 Vegetable, 1 Starch, 2 Lean Meat
Carb Choices: 2

Shopping List

Produce	Packaged
½ lb. mushrooms	quick-cooking tapioca
small green bell pepper	8-oz. pkg. spaghetti

Meat	Seasonings
¾ lb. extra-lean ground beef	onion powder
	minced garlic
	Italian seasoning
Canned	crushed red pepper
14½-oz. can ready-cut Italian diced tomatoes with garlic, oregano, and basil	
8-oz. can tomato sauce	

Beef and Pasta

Easy | Do Ahead | Freeze | Serves: 12

1½ lbs. extra-lean ground beef

1 tsp. garlic powder

1 tsp. onion powder

1 28-oz. can Italian-style petite-cut diced tomatoes, *do not drain*

1¼ cups nonfat beef broth

1½ cups uncooked tricolored rotini pasta

1 16-oz. can cannellini beans, *rinsed and drained*

1 15-oz. can garbanzo beans, *rinsed and drained*

¾ cup nonfat Parmesan cheese (optional)

Spray nonstick skillet with cooking spray. Add ground beef, garlic powder, and onion powder to skillet. Cook over medium heat, stirring frequently, until beef is browned and crumbled. Drain well. Combine beef, undrained tomatoes, and beef broth in slow cooker. Cover and cook on high heat for 1½–2 hours. Add pasta and cook 15–20 minutes. Add beans and cook until heated through. Garnish each serving with about 1 tablespoon cheese, if desired.

Nutrition Facts per serving: 237 cal., 3.1 g total fat, 30 mg chol., 400 mg sodium, 30 g carbo., 1 g fiber, 20 g pro.
Exchanges: 1 Vegetable, 1½ Starch, 1 Lean Meat
Carb Choices: 2

Beef Entrées

Shopping List

Meat
1½ lbs. extra-lean ground beef

Canned
28-oz. can Italian-style petite-cut diced tomatoes
14-oz. can nonfat beef broth
16-oz. can cannellini beans
15-oz. can garbanzo beans

Packaged
12-oz. pkg. tricolored rotini pasta

Seasonings
garlic powder
onion powder

Optional
nonfat Parmesan cheese

You can easily substitute extra-lean ground turkey, pork, or vegetable "beef" crumbles for ground beef in recipes that call for meat to be skillet-cooked prior to slow cooking.

Penne with Mushroom-Beef Sauce

Easy | Do Ahead | Serves: 8

1½ lbs. extra-lean ground beef

2 15-oz. cans tomato sauce

2 14½-oz. cans petite-cut diced tomatoes with roasted garlic and sweet onion, *do not drain*

2 6-oz. cans Italian tomato paste with roasted garlic

1 4-oz. can sliced mushrooms, *drained*

2½ cups frozen pepper stir-fry, *thawed and drained*

1 cup nonfat beef broth

2 tbsp. brown sugar

2 tsp. dried basil

1 tsp. dried oregano

¼ tsp. pepper

⅛ tsp. cayenne pepper

1 tsp. minced garlic

16 oz. penne pasta, *cooked and drained*

1 cup nonfat Parmesan chese

Spray large nonstick skillet with cooking spray. Add ground beef to skillet and cook over medium-high heat until browned and crumbled. Drain well. Spray inside of slow cooker with cooking spray. Combine ground beef and all ingredients except pasta and cheese in slow cooker and mix well. Cover and cook on high heat for 1 hour. Reduce heat to low and cook 6–7 hours. Add hot pasta to sauce and mix thoroughly. Sprinkle with cheese.

Nutrition Facts per serving: 471 cal., 4.6 g total fat, 46 mg chol., 1,447 mg sodium, 71 g carbo., 4 g fiber, 32 g pro.
Exchanges: 4 Starch, 2 Vegetable, 2 Lean Meat
Carb Choices: 5

Shopping List

Meat
1½ lbs. extra-lean ground beef

Dairy
4 oz. nonfat Parmesan cheese

Frozen
16-oz. pkg. frozen pepper stir-fry

Canned
2 15-oz. cans tomato sauce
2 14½-oz. cans petite-cut diced tomatoes with roasted garlic and sweet onion
2 6-oz. cans Italian tomato paste with roasted garlic

4-oz. can sliced mushrooms
14-oz. can nonfat beef broth

Packaged
16-oz. pkg. penne pasta

Baking Goods
brown sugar

Seasonings
dried basil
dried oregano
pepper
cayenne pepper
minced garlic

Lasagna

- 1½ lbs. extra-lean ground beef
- 1 tsp. onion powder
- 1¼ tsp. garlic powder, *divided*
- ¾ cup frozen chopped onions, *thawed and drained*
- 2 14½-oz. cans ready-cut Italian diced tomatoes with garlic, oregano, and basil, *do not drain*
- 2 12-oz. cans tomato sauce
- 1 cup nonfat ricotta cheese
- 2 cups nonfat shredded mozzarella cheese
- 2 tsp. sugar
- 1 tsp. dried parsley
- 1 tsp. dried Italian seasoning
- ½ tsp. pepper
- 8 lasagna noodles, *broken into bite-size pieces, cooked, and drained*

Spray large nonstick skillet with cooking spray. Add ground beef, onion powder, and 1 teaspoon garlic powder to skillet. Cook over medium heat, stirring frequently, until beef is browned and crumbled. Drain well. Spray inside of slow cooker with cooking spray. Place beef in slow cooker; add ¼ teaspoon garlic powder and remaining ingredients except noodles and mix well. Stir in noodles. Cover and cook on low heat for 7–9 hours or high heat for 3½–4½ hours.

Nutrition Facts per serving: 451 cal., 6.3 g total fat, 103 mg chol., 1,263 mg sodium, 45 g carbo., 2.7 g fiber, 47 g pro.
Exchanges: 2 Vegetable, 2 Starch, 5 Lean Meat
Carb Choices: 3

Beef
Entrées

Shopping List

Meat	Packaged
1½ lbs. extra-lean ground beef	8 oz. lasagna noodles
	Baking Goods
Dairy	sugar
8 oz. nonfat ricotta cheese	
8 oz. nonfat shredded mozzarella cheese	**Seasonings**
	onion powder
	garlic powder
Frozen	dried parsley
12 oz. frozen chopped onions	dried Italian seasoning
	pepper
Canned	
2 14½-oz. cans ready-cut Italian diced tomatoes with garlic, oregano, and basil	
2 12-oz. cans tomato sauce	

Goulash

½ lb. extra-lean ground beef

½ cup frozen chopped onions, *thawed and drained*

¼ cup frozen chopped green bell peppers, *thawed and drained*

3 cups V-8 juice

1½ cups macaroni, *cooked and drained*

¼ tsp. chili powder

¼ tsp. pepper

Shopping List

Meat
½ lb. extra-lean ground beef

Frozen
12-oz. pkg. frozen chopped onions
10-oz. pkg. frozen chopped green bell peppers

Canned
24 oz. V-8 juice

Packaged
8-oz. pkg. macaroni

Seasonings
chili powder
pepper

Spray large nonstick skillet with cooking spray. Add ground beef, onions, and bell peppers to skillet. Cook over medium heat, stirring frequently, until beef is browned and crumbled. Drain well. Add V-8 juice, macaroni, chili powder, and pepper to skillet; cook over low heat until most of the liquid is absorbed. Spray inside of slow cooker with cooking spray. Spoon mixture into slow cooker. Cover and cook on low heat for 2–3 hours.

Nutrition Facts per serving: 170 cal., 2.7 g total fat, 30 mg chol., 667 mg sodium, 21 g carbo., 3 g fiber, 14 g pro.
Exchanges: 1 Vegetable, 1 Starch, 1 Lean Meat
Carb Choices: 1

How much beef should you buy? The following recommendations are based on 3-ounce servings. Lean boneless cuts yield up to 4 servings per pound. Beef cuts with some bone yield up to 3 servings per pound. Bony cuts yield no more than 1½ servings per pound. One pound of ground beef produces about 4 cooked 3-ounce servings.

Slow Cooker Beef Meal

Easy | Do Ahead | Serves: 6

- 2 lbs. extra-lean ground beef
- 1¾ cups frozen chopped onions, *thawed and drained*
- 1 tsp. minced garlic
- 1 6-oz. can Italian tomato paste with roasted garlic
- 1 cup water
- 2 tbsp. steak sauce
- 2 tsp. red wine vinegar
- 1 tsp. dried oregano
- ¾ tsp. dried basil
- 1 tbsp. canned diced jalapeño pepper
- ¾ cup chopped green bell pepper

Spray large nonstick skillet with cooking spray. Add ground beef to skillet and cook over medium heat, stirring frequently, until beef is browned and crumbled. Drain well. Spray inside of slow cooker with cooking spray. Add beef and all ingredients except green bell pepper to slow cooker and mix well. Cover and cook on low heat for 7–8 hours or high heat for 3½–4 hours. If cooking on low heat, increase to high; add bell pepper and cook 15–20 minutes.

Nutrition Facts per serving: 246 cal., 6.2 g total fat, 81 mg chol., 376 mg sodium, 11 g carbo., 1 g fiber, 30 g pro.
Exchanges: 2 Vegetable, 4 Lean Meat
Carb Choices: 1

Beef
Entrées

Shopping List

Produce
medium green bell pepper

4-oz. can diced jalapeño peppers

Meat
2 lbs. extra-lean ground beef

Frozen
12-oz. pkg. frozen chopped onions

Canned
6-oz. can Italian tomato paste with roasted garlic

Condiments
steak sauce
red wine vinegar

Seasonings
minced garlic
dried oregano
dried basil

Peppered Beef

2 lbs. lean beef round steak, *sliced thin*

1 large green bell pepper, *sliced thin*

1 large red bell pepper, *sliced thin*

1 medium onion, *sliced*

1 cup nonfat beef broth

2 tbsp. low-sodium soy sauce

½ tsp. ground ginger

1½ tsp. minced garlic

1 tsp. Worcestershire sauce

Shopping List

Produce
large green bell pepper
large red bell pepper
medium onion

Meat
2 lbs. lean beef round steak

Canned
14-oz. can nonfat beef broth

Condiments
low-sodium soy sauce
Worcestershire sauce

Seasonings
ground ginger
minced garlic

Spray nonstick skillet with cooking spray and heat over medium-high heat. Add steak to skillet and cook, stirring constantly, just until browned. Spray inside of slow cooker with cooking spray. Place peppers and onion on bottom of cooker; top with meat (avoid stacking meat slices directly on top of one another). Combine remaining ingredients in small bowl and pour over meat. Cover and cook on low heat for 8–10 hours or high heat for 4–5 hours.

Nutrition Facts per serving: 184 cal., 5.4 g total fat, 72 mg chol., 307 mg sodium, 4 g carbo., 1 g fiber, 28 g pro.
Exchanges: 1 Vegetable, 3 Lean Meat
Carb Choices: 0

Fresh raw beef that has not been frozen is easily cut after it's left in the freezer for a few minutes to firm up.

Ginger-Soy Pepper Steak

2 lbs. lean round steak, *cut into strips*

1 large green bell pepper, *cut into strips*

1 large red bell pepper, *cut into strips*

1 medium onion, *sliced thin*

1 cup nonfat beef broth

2 tbsp. low-sodium soy sauce

½ tsp. ground ginger

½ tsp. minced garlic

1 tsp. Worcestershire sauce

Spray large nonstick skillet with cooking spray. Add steak to skillet and cook over medium heat until browned on both sides. Spray inside of slow cooker with cooking spray. Place pepper and onion slices in bottom of slow cooker; top with meat. Combine remaining ingredients and pour over meat and vegetables. Cover and cook on low heat for 8–10 hours or high heat for 4–5 hours.

Nutrition Facts per serving: 237 cal., 7.1 g total fat, 95 mg chol., 322 mg sodium, 4 g carbo., 1 g fiber, 37 g pro.
Exchanges: 1 Vegetable, 4 Lean Meat
Carb Choices: 0

Beef Entrées

Shopping List

Produce
large green bell pepper
large red bell pepper
medium onion

Meat
2 lbs. lean beef round steak

Canned
14-oz. can nonfat beef broth

Condiments
low-sodium soy sauce
Worcestershire sauce

Seasonings
ground ginger
minced garlic

Asian-Style Beef and Rice

1 lb. extra-lean ground beef

½ tsp. garlic powder

¾ cup chopped onion

1 6-oz. pkg. long grain and wild rice mix

1¾ cups water

¼ cup + 1 tbsp. low-sodium soy sauce, *divided*

1 8-oz. pkg. shredded cabbage

1 cup bean sprouts

1 cup shredded carrots

2 stalks celery, *sliced*

1 8-oz. pkg. sliced mushrooms

Spray large nonstick skillet with cooking spray. Add ground beef, garlic powder, and onion to skillet. Cook over medium heat, stirring frequently, until beef is browned and crumbled. Drain well. Spray inside of slow cooker with cooking spray. Spoon beef mixture into slow cooker. Add rice mix, water, and ¼ cup soy sauce to beef and mix. Cover and cook on high heat for 2 hours. Stir mixture. Add cabbage, bean sprouts, carrots, celery, and mushrooms. Cover and cook 30–45 minutes. Stir in remaining 1 tablespoon soy sauce and serve.

Nutrition Facts per serving: 359 cal., 5.4 g total fat, 61 mg chol., 1,446 mg sodium, 47 g carbo., 5 g fiber, 30 g pro.
Exchanges: 3 Vegetable, 2 Starch, 2½ Lean Meat
Carb Choices: 3

Shopping List

Produce
large onion
8-oz. pkg. shredded cabbage
bean sprouts
8-oz. pkg. shredded carrots
small bunch celery
8-oz. pkg. sliced mushrooms

Meat
1 lb. extra-lean ground beef

Packaged
6-oz. pkg. long grain and wild rice mix

Condiments
low-sodium soy sauce

Seasonings
garlic powder

Wild rice is not really rice at all. Popular for its nutty flavor and chewy texture, wild rice is actually a long-grained marsh grass that is combined with other rices or grains.

Beef and Broccoli

2 cups broccoli florets

1 medium onion, *thinly sliced*

1 14½-oz. can Italian-style diced tomatoes, *do not drain*

¾ cup nonfat beef broth

1½ tsp. dried Italian seasoning

¼ tsp. pepper

1 lb. extra-lean ground beef

1 tsp. minced garlic

2 tbsp. Italian tomato paste with roasted garlic

2 cups cooked rotini pasta

½ cup nonfat shredded cheddar cheese

Spray inside of slow cooker with cooking spray. Layer broccoli and onions in slow cooker. Combine undrained diced tomatoes, beef broth, Italian seasoning, and pepper in medium bowl; pour over vegetables. Cover and cook on low heat for 2½ hours. Spray large nonstick skillet with cooking spray. Add ground beef and minced garlic to skillet; cook over medium heat, stirring frequently, until beef is browned and crumbled. Drain well. Add beef mixture to slow cooker and mix well. Cover and cook 2 hours. Stir in tomato paste, rotini, and cheese. Cover and cook 30 minutes.

Nutrition Facts per serving: 323 cal., 5.6 g total fat, 61 mg chol., 543 mg sodium, 33 g carbo., 3 g fiber, 32 g pro.
Exchanges: 3 Vegetable, 1 Starch, 3 Lean Meat
Carb Choices: 2

Beef
Entrées

Shopping List

Produce
¾ lb. broccoli florets
medium onion

Meat
1 lb. extra-lean ground beef

Dairy
shredded nonfat cheddar
  cheese

Canned
14½-oz. can Italian-style
  diced tomatoes

14-oz. can nonfat beef broth
6-oz. can Italian tomato
  paste with roasted garlic

Packaged
8-oz. pkg. rotini pasta

Seasonings
dried Italian seasoning
pepper
minced garlic

Substitution Tip: Use a 10-oz. package of frozen broccoli florets or broccoli cuts, thawed and drained, in place of the fresh broccoli.

Gingered Beef and Vegetables

Easy | Do Ahead | Serves: 6

1½ lbs. beef eye of round steak, *cut into 1-inch cubes*

4 medium carrots, *sliced into ½-inch pieces*

½ cup sliced green onions

1 tsp. minced garlic

1½ cups nonfat beef broth

¼ cup low-sodium soy sauce

¾ tsp. ground ginger

¼ tsp. crushed red pepper

3 tbsp. cornstarch

3 tbsp. cold water

1 9-oz. pkg. frozen snap peas

½ cup frozen chopped bell peppers, *thawed and drained*

3 cups hot cooked brown rice

Spray inside of slow cooker with cooking spray. Combine steak, carrots, green onions, and minced garlic in slow cooker. Combine beef broth, soy sauce, ginger, and red pepper in small bowl and mix well; pour over steak and vegetables. Cover and cook on low heat for 10–12 hours or high heat for 5–6 hours. If cooking on low heat, increase to high. Combine cornstarch and water in small bowl and mix until smooth. Add to meat mixture and cook on high for 20–30 minutes until mixture thickens, stirring once while cooking. Stir in snap peas and bell peppers. Cover and cook 15–20 minutes. Serve over hot cooked brown rice.

Nutrition Facts per serving: 416 cal., 7.6 g total fat, 95 mg chol., 686 mg sodium, 42 g carbo., 3 g fiber, 42 g pro.
Exchanges: 2 Vegetable, 2 Starch, 4 Lean Meat
Carb Choices: 3

Shopping List

Produce
4 medium carrots
small bunch green onions

Meat
1½ lbs. beef eye of round steak

Frozen
9-oz. pkg. frozen snap peas
16-oz. pkg. frozen chopped bell peppers

Canned
14-oz. can nonfat beef broth

Baking Goods
cornstarch

Packaged
8-oz. pkg. brown rice

Condiments
low-sodium soy sauce

Seasonings
minced garlic
ground ginger
crushed red pepper

p. 24 BBQ Beef

Steak Stew p. 38

Beef and Pasta p. 55

Italian Beef Spaghetti Sauce p. 54

p. 76 Cincinnati-Style Chili

Chili Dogs p. 74

Chili Spice Sloppy Joes

Easy | Do Ahead | Serves: 4

- 1 lb. extra-lean ground beef
- 1 tsp. garlic powder
- ½ tsp. Mrs. Dash seasoning
- ¾ cup frozen chopped onions, *thawed and drained*
- ¾ cup chopped green bell pepper
- ½ tsp. soy sauce
- 3 tbsp. chili sauce
- 1 6-oz. can Italian tomato paste with roasted garlic
- 1 tsp. prepared mustard
- 1 tbsp. sugar
- 1 tbsp. vinegar
- whole wheat buns or baked potatoes
- pickle slices

Spray large nonstick skillet with cooking spray. Add ground beef, garlic powder, and Mrs. Dash seasoning to skillet. Cook over medium heat, stirring frequently, until beef is browned and crumbled. Drain well. Remove skillet from heat, add remaining ingredients, and mix well. Spray inside of slow cooker with cooking spray. Spoon meat mixture into slow cooker; cover and cook on low heat for 6–7 hours. Serve on whole wheat buns with pickle slices or use as topping for baked potatoes.

Nutrition Facts per serving: 228 cal., 4.6 g total fat, 61 mg chol., 603 mg sodium, 18 g carbo., 2 g fiber, 23 g pro.
Exchanges: 1 Other Carbo., 3 Lean Meat
Carb Choices: 1

Beef Entrées

Shopping List

Produce	Baking Goods
large bell pepper	sugar

Meat	Condiments
1 lb. extra-lean ground beef	soy sauce
	chili sauce
	mustard
Frozen	vinegar
12-oz. pkg. frozen chopped onions	
	Seasonings
	garlic powder
Canned	Mrs. Dash seasoning
6-oz. can Italian tomato paste with roasted garlic	
	Optional
	whole wheat buns or potatoes
	pickle slices

Chili Dogs

1 15-oz. can nonfat chili with beans

1 6-oz. can Italian tomato paste with roasted garlic

¼ cup minced green bell pepper

1 tbsp. onion powder

1 tsp. bold and spicy mustard

½ tsp. chili powder

4 97% fat-free beef franks

4 low-fat hot dog buns

sauerkraut, nonfat shredded cheddar cheese, chopped onion (optional)

Spray inside of slow cooker with cooking spray. Combine chili, tomato paste, bell pepper, onion powder, mustard, and chili powder in slow cooker. Cover and cook on low heat for 3–4 hours. Broil, grill, or boil franks. Split and toast buns. Place hot dog on bun; top with chili mixture and sauerkraut, cheese, or onion, if desired.

Nutrition Facts per serving: 278 cal., 2.1 g total fat, 15 mg chol., 1,340 mg sodium, 44 g carbo., 5 g fiber, 16 g pro.
Exchanges: 3 Starch, 1 Very Lean Meat
Carb Choices: 3

Shopping List

Produce	**Packaged**
small bell pepper	low-fat hot dog buns
Meat	**Condiments**
12-oz. pkg. 97% fat-free beef franks	bold and spicy mustard
	Seasonings
Canned	onion powder
15-oz. can nonfat chili with beans	chili powder
6-oz. can Italian tomato paste with roasted garlic	**Optional**
	sauerkraut, nonfat shredded cheddar cheese, onion

Hot Dogs with Spicy Chili Sauce

Easy | Do Ahead | Serves: 8

2 lbs. extra-lean ground beef
1 cup chopped onion
2 15-oz. cans tomato sauce
1 tsp. ground ginger
½ tsp. ground allspice
1 tbsp. ground cumin
2 tbsp. chili powder
8 97% fat-free beef franks
chopped onion, sweet pickle relish, prepared mustard (optional)

Shopping List

Produce
large onion

Meat
2 lbs. extra-lean ground beef
12-oz. pkg. 97% fat-free beef franks

Canned
2 15-oz. cans tomato sauce

Seasonings
ground ginger
ground allspice
ground cumin
chili powder

Optional
onion, sweet pickle relish, prepared mustard

Spray large nonstick skillet with cooking spray. Add ground beef and onion to skillet. Cook over medium heat, stirring frequently, until beef is browned and crumbled. Drain well. Add remaining ingredients except franks and optional ingredients and mix well. Spoon mixture into slow cooker; cover and cook on low heat for 6–8 hours. Just before serving, broil franks. Serve meat sauce over cooked franks and top with onion, relish, and mustard, if desired.

Nutrition Facts per serving: 244 cal., 4.9 g total fat, 76 mg chol., 732 mg sodium, 16 g carbo., 3 g fiber, 30 g pro.
Exchanges: 3 Vegetable, 3 Lean Meat
Carb Choices: 1

Beef Entrées

Unlike USDA mandatory inspection, mandatory beef grading is used to determine quality and yield. The top three levels of grading are prime, choice, and select. The grade of beef you buy not only makes a difference in tenderness and overall quality but also helps determine the method of cooking.

Cincinnati-Style Chili

Easy | Do Ahead | Serves: 6

1½ lbs. extra-lean ground beef

2 cups frozen seasoning vegetables, *thawed and drained*

3 tsp. minced garlic

2 tbsp. + ¼ tsp. chili powder

1 tbsp. paprika

4½ tsp. dried Italian seasoning

1 tsp. ground cinnamon

½ tsp. cayenne pepper

½ tsp. crushed red pepper

¼ tsp. ground allspice

½ tsp. pepper

2 14½-oz. cans petite-cut diced tomatoes with roasted garlic and sweet onion, *do not drain*

1 8-oz. can tomato sauce

½ cup water

12 oz. spaghetti, *cooked and drained*

1 cup chopped onion (optional)

1½ cups nonfat shredded cheddar cheese (optional)

1 15-oz. can red kidney beans, *heated* (optional)

Spray large nonstick skillet with cooking spray. Add ground beef and seasoning vegetables to skillet. Cook over medium heat, stirring frequently, until beef is browned and crumbled and vegetables are softened. Drain well. Spray inside of slow cooker with cooking spray. Spoon beef mixture into slow cooker. Add remaining ingredients except spaghetti and optional ingredients and mix well. Cover and cook on low heat for 7–9 hours or high heat for 3½–4½ hours. Place 1 cup hot cooked spaghetti on each plate; top with chili, onion, cheese, and beans, if desired.

Nutrition Facts per serving: 285 cal., 5.6 g total fat, 61 mg chol., 483 mg sodium, 29 g carbo., 4 g fiber, 27 g pro.

Exchanges: 2 Vegetable, 1 Starch, 3 Lean Meat

Carb Choices: 2

Shopping List

Meat	8-oz. can tomato	crushed red pepper
1½ lbs. extra-lean	sauce	ground allspice
ground beef		pepper
	Packaged	
Frozen	12-oz. pkg.	**Optional**
10-oz. pkg. frozen	spaghetti	large onion
seasoning		nonfat shredded
vegetables	**Seasonings**	cheddar cheese
	minced garlic	15-oz. can red
Canned	chili powder	kidney beans
2 14½-oz. cans	paprika	
petite-cut diced	dried Italian	
tomatoes with	seasoning	
roasted garlic	ground cinnamon	
and sweet onion	cayenne pepper	

Spectacular Sloppy Joes

Easy | **Do Ahead** | **Serves: 8**

1½ lbs. extra-lean ground beef

1 tbsp. onion powder

1 tsp. minced garlic

¾ cup ketchup

½ cup chopped green bell pepper

½ cup chopped celery

¼ cup water

2 tbsp. brown sugar

2 tbsp. prepared mustard

2 tbsp. Worcestershire sauce

1½ tsp. chili powder

8 whole wheat pita breads

Spray large nonstick skillet with cooking spray. Add ground beef, onion powder, and minced garlic to skillet. Cook over medium heat, stirring frequently, until beef is browned and crumbled. Drain well. Spray inside of slow cooker with cooking spray. Combine ketchup, bell pepper, celery, water, brown sugar, mustard, Worcestershire sauce, and chili powder in slow cooker; add meat mixture and stir. Cover and cook on low heat for 6–8 hours or high heat for 3–4 hours. Spoon mixture into whole wheat pita breads.

Nutrition Facts per serving: 259 cal., 4.1 g total fat, 46 mg chol., 430 mg sodium, 32 g carbo., 1 g fiber, 20 g pro.
Exchanges: 1 Vegetable, 1 Starch, ½ Other Carbo., 2 Lean Meat
Carb Choices: 2

Beef Entrées

Shopping List

Produce
small green bell pepper
small bunch celery

Meat
1½ lbs. extra-lean ground beef

Packaged
12-oz. pkg. whole wheat pita breads

Baking Goods
brown sugar

Condiments
ketchup
prepared mustard
Worcestershire sauce

Seasonings
onion powder
minced garlic
chili powder

Beef Fajitas

1½ lbs. beef flank steak, *cut into 6 portions*

1 cup chopped onion

1 large green bell pepper, *cut into ½-inch pieces*

2 tbsp. diced canned jalapeño peppers, *drained*

1 tbsp. chopped fresh cilantro

1½ tsp. minced garlic

1½ tsp. chili powder

1 tsp. ground coriander

1 14½-oz. can stewed tomatoes with bell pepper and onion, *do not drain*

6 98% fat-free flour tortillas

nonfat shredded cheddar cheese, salsa (optional)

Spray inside of slow cooker with cooking spray. Combine steak, onion, bell pepper, jalapeños, cilantro, minced garlic, chili powder, and coriander in slow cooker and stir; add undrained tomatoes. Cover and cook on low heat for 8–10 hours or high heat for 4–5 hours. Remove meat from slow cooker and shred. Return to cooker and keep warm. Wrap tortillas in foil and place in 350° oven for 10–15 minutes until warm. Using a slotted spoon, fill warm tortillas with meat mixture. Garnish with cheese and salsa, if desired.

Nutrition Facts per serving: 312 cal., 5.8 g total fat, 48 mg chol., 548 mg sodium, 30 g carbo., 3 g fiber, 31 g pro.
Exchanges: 1 Vegetable, 1½ Starch, 3 Lean Meat
Carb Choices: 2

Shopping List

Produce	Canned	Seasonings
large onion	4-oz. can diced	minced garlic
large green bell	jalapeño peppers	chili powder
pepper	14½-oz. can	ground coriander
fresh cilantro	stewed tomatoes	
	with bell pepper	**Optional**
Meat	and onion	nonfat shredded
1½ lbs. beef flank		cheddar cheese,
steak	**Packaged**	salsa
	17.5-oz. pkg.	
	98% fat-free	
	flour tortillas	

Tamale Pie

Easy | Do Ahead | Serves: 6

1 lb. extra-lean ground beef

¾ cup yellow cornmeal

¾ cup skim milk

¾ cup nonfat half and half

¼ cup egg substitute

1 1.25-oz. packet chili seasoning mix

1 tsp. Mrs. Dash seasoning

1 14½-oz. can petite-cut tomatoes with green chiles, *do not drain*

1 16-oz. can whole kernel corn, *drained*

1¼ cups nonfat shredded cheddar cheese

Spray large nonstick skillet with cooking spray. Add ground beef to skillet and cook over medium heat, stirring frequently, until browned and crumbled. Drain well. Combine cornmeal, milk, half and half, and egg substitute in a large bowl and mix well. Add meat, chili seasoning mix, Mrs. Dash seasoning, undrained tomatoes, and corn. Spray inside of slow cooker with cooking spray. Pour mixture into cooker; cover and cook on high heat for 3–4 hours. Sprinkle cheese on top; cover and cook 5–10 minutes longer.

Nutrition Facts per serving: 316 cal., 4 g total fat, 41 mg chol., 1,295 mg sodium, 39 g carbo., 6 g fiber, 26 g pro.
Exchanges: 2 Vegetable, 2 Starch, 2 Lean Meat
Carb Choices: 3

Beef
Entrées

Shopping List

Meat
1 lb. extra-lean ground beef

Dairy
6 oz. skim milk
6 oz. nonfat half and half
egg substitute
6 oz. nonfat shredded cheddar cheese

Canned
14½-oz. can petite-cut diced tomatoes with green chiles
16-oz. can whole kernel corn

Packaged
yellow cornmeal

Seasonings
1.25-oz. packet chili seasoning mix
Mrs. Dash seasoning

Calico Casserole

1½ lbs. extra-lean ground beef

1 tsp. garlic powder

½ cup frozen chopped onions, *thawed and drained*

1 15-oz. can tomato sauce with roasted garlic

¼ cup water

½ tsp. chili powder

⅛ tsp. pepper

⅔ cup uncooked long grain rice

1 cup Mexicorn, *drained*

¼ cup frozen chopped green bell peppers, *thawed and drained*

Spray large nonstick skillet with cooking spray. Add ground beef and garlic powder to skillet. Cook over medium heat, stirring frequently, until browned and crumbled. Drain well. Spray inside of slow cooker with cooking spray. Spoon ground beef into slow cooker; top with chopped onions. Combine tomato sauce, water, chili powder, and pepper in medium bowl and mix well. Pour half the sauce mixture over beef; sprinkle rice over sauce. Top with Mexicorn, bell peppers, and remaining sauce. Cover and cook on low heat for 5–6 hours.

Nutrition Facts per serving: 408 cal., 7.5 g total fat, 91 mg chol., 847 mg sodium, 45 g carbo., 3 g fiber, 37 g pro.
Exchanges: 3 Vegetable, 2 Starch, 3½ Lean Meat
Carb Choices: 3

Shopping List

Meat
1½ lbs. extra-lean ground beef

Frozen
12-oz. pkg. frozen chopped onions
10-oz. pkg. frozen chopped green bell peppers

Canned
15-oz. can tomato sauce with roasted garlic
11-oz. can Mexicorn

Packaged
8-oz. pkg. long grain rice

Seasonings
garlic powder
chili powder
pepper

Mexican-Style Pot Roast

Easy | **Do Ahead** | **Serves: 6**

1½ lbs. boneless beef chuck shoulder pot roast

1 tbsp. Cajun seasoning

1 11-oz. can Mexicorn, *drained*

½ cup frozen chopped onions, *thawed and drained*

½ cup chopped green bell pepper

½ tsp. Tabasco sauce

1 14½-oz. can petite-cut diced tomatoes with green chiles, *do not drain*

Spray inside of slow cooker with cooking spray. Rub pot roast with Cajun seasoning and place roast in slow cooker. Top with Mexicorn, onions, and bell pepper. Mix Tabasco sauce into undrained tomatoes; pour over roast and vegetables. Cover and cook on low heat for 8–10 hours.

Nutrition Facts per serving: 297 cal., 10.2 g total fat, 101 mg chol., 657 mg sodium, 15 g carbo., 2 g fiber, 36 g pro.
Exchanges: 2 Vegetable, ½ Starch, 4 Lean Meat
Carb Choices: 1

Beef Entrées

Shopping List

Produce
small bell pepper

Condiments
Tabasco sauce

Meat
1½ lbs. boneless beef chuck shoulder pot roast

Seasonings
Cajun seasoning

Frozen
12-oz. pkg. frozen chopped onions

Canned
11-oz. can Mexicorn
14½-oz. can petite-cut diced tomatoes with green chiles

Beef Enchiladas

1 lb. extra-lean ground beef

¾ cup frozen chopped onions, *thawed and drained*

1½ cups chopped bell peppers

1 cup chopped mushrooms

2 tbsp. canned diced jalapeño peppers

1½ tsp. minced garlic

3 cups chunky-style salsa

6 98% fat-free flour tortillas

¾ cup nonfat shredded cheddar cheese

nonfat sour cream, chopped green onions (optional)

Spray large nonstick skillet with cooking spray. Add ground beef to skillet. Cook over medium heat, stirring frequently, until beef is browned and crumbled. Drain well and set aside. Add onions, bell peppers, mushrooms, jalapeño peppers, and garlic to skillet. Cook, stirring frequently, until onions are translucent. Remove skillet from heat and return meat to skillet. Add ¾ cup salsa to meat mixture and mix well. Spoon ¾ cup meat mixture down the center of each tortilla; sprinkle with 1–2 tablespoons cheese. Roll tortillas and secure with wooden toothpicks. Spray inside of slow cooker with cooking spray. Pour 1 cup salsa in bottom of slow cooker. Place 3 tortillas in slow cooker; top with ¾ cup salsa. Place remaining tortillas on top and pour remaining salsa over top. Cover and cook on low heat 3–4 hours. Just before serving, garnish with sour cream and green onions, if desired.

Shopping List

Produce
2 medium bell peppers
4 oz. mushrooms

Meat
1 lb. extra-lean ground beef

Dairy
3 oz. nonfat shredded cheddar cheese

Frozen
12-oz. pkg. frozen chopped onions

Canned
4-oz. can diced jalapeño peppers

Packaged
17.5-oz. pkg. 98% fat-free flour tortillas

Condiments
24 oz. chunky-style salsa

Seasonings
minced garlic

Optional
nonfat sour cream, green onions

Nutrition Facts per serving:
309 cal., 3.6 total fat, 41 mg chol., 1,294 mg sodium, 36 g carbo., 3 g fiber, 28 g pro.
Exchanges: 4 Vegetable, 1 Starch, 2½ Lean Meat
Carb Choices: 2

Stuffed Peppers

Easy | **Do Ahead** | **Serves: 4**

1 lb. extra-lean ground beef

¾ tsp. garlic powder

½ tsp. onion powder

2 cups instant rice

2 cups V-8 juice

4 large green bell peppers,
   cored and seeded

2 14-oz. cans Mexican-style
   stewed tomatoes, *drained*

Spray inside of slow cooker with cooking spray. Combine ground beef, garlic powder, onion powder, rice, and vegetable juice in medium bowl and mix well. Stuff mixture into cored bell peppers. Arrange bell peppers in slow cooker. Spoon tomatoes on top of and around bell peppers. Cover and cook on low heat for 8–9 hours or high heat for 4–5 hours. To serve, cut peppers in half and spoon tomatoes over top.

Nutrition Facts per serving: 390 cal., 5.3 g total fat, 61 mg chol., 1,274 mg sodium, 56 g carbo., 5 g fiber, 28 g pro.
Exchanges: 2 Vegetable, 3 Starch, 2 Lean Meat
Carb Choices: 4

Beef
Entrées

Shopping List

Produce
4 large green bell peppers

Meat
1 lb. extra-lean ground beef

Canned
16-oz. can V-8 juice
2 14½-oz. cans Mexican-style
   stewed tomatoes

Packaged
8-oz. pkg. instant rice

Seasonings
garlic powder
onion powder

Spanish Rice with Beef

Easy | Do Ahead | Serves: 6

- 2 lbs. extra-lean ground beef
- ¾ cup chopped onion
- ¾ cup chopped green bell pepper
- 2 14½-oz. cans stewed tomatoes with bell pepper and onion, *do not drain*
- 1 16-oz. can tomato sauce
- 1½ cups water
- 2½ tsp. chili powder
- 2 tsp. Mrs. Dash seasoning
- 2 tbsp. Worcestershire sauce
- 2 cups uncooked converted rice
- 1 tbsp. dried celery flakes
- 1½ cups nonfat shredded cheddar cheese (optional)

Spray large nonstick skillet with cooking spray. Add ground beef to skillet and cook over medium heat, stirring frequently, until beef is browned and crumbled. Drain well. Spray inside of slow cooker with cooking spray. Add all ingredients except cheese to slow cooker and mix well. Cover and cook on low heat for 6–8 hours or high heat for 3–4 hours. Sprinkle each serving with 2–4 tablespoons cheese, if desired.

Nutrition Facts per serving: 360 cal., 6.9 g total fat, 81 mg chol., 422 mg sodium, 31 g carbo., 4 g fiber, 37 g pro.
Exchanges: 3 Vegetable, 1 Starch, 4 Lean Meat
Carb Choices: 2

Shopping List

Produce	Packaged
large onion	8-oz. pkg. converted rice
medium green bell pepper	
	Condiments
Meat	Worcestershire sauce
2 lbs. extra-lean ground beef	
	Seasonings
	chili powder
Canned	Mrs. Dash seasoning
2 14½-oz. cans stewed tomatoes with bell pepper and onion	celery flakes
16-oz. can tomato sauce	**Optional**
	6 oz. nonfat shredded cheddar cheese

Pork Dinners 2

Pork and Black Bean Chili

Boneless Pork Chops with Vegetables

2 cups low-fat cream of
  mushroom soup

¼ cup nonfat chicken broth

1 lb. boneless pork chops

1 tsp. pepper

1 10-oz. pkg. frozen cut
  green beans, *thawed and
  drained*

3 large potatoes, *cut into
  chunks*

Spray inside of slow cooker with cooking spray. Combine mushroom soup and chicken broth in bowl and mix well; pour into slow cooker. Place pork chops on top of soup; sprinkle with pepper. Add green beans and potatoes. Cover and cook on low heat for 4–5 hours or high heat for 2–2½ hours. Stir mixture and serve hot.

Nutrition Facts per serving: 452 cal., 9.2 g total fat, 110 mg chol., 1,043 mg sodium, 51 g carbo., 6 g fiber, 39 g pro.
Exchanges: 1 Vegetable, 3 Starch, ½ Other Carbo., 3 Lean Meat
Carb Choices: 3

Shopping List

Produce
3 large potatoes

Meat
1 lb. boneless pork chops

Frozen
10-oz. pkg. frozen cut green
  beans

Canned
2 10¾-oz. cans low-fat cream
  of mushroom soup
14-oz. can nonfat chicken
  broth

Seasonings
pepper

Meatball and Sauerkraut Supper

Easy | **Do Ahead** | **Serves: 6**

1½ lbs. ground pork

¾ cup chopped onion

¾ cup uncooked white rice (not instant)

¼ cup egg substitute

½ tsp. pepper

1 22-oz. jar sauerkraut with juice

Combine pork, onion, rice, egg substitute, and pepper in medium bowl and mix well. Form mixture into 2-inch balls. Place half the sauerkraut in the bottom of slow cooker; top with meatballs and add remaining sauerkraut. Cover and cook on low heat for 8–10 hours or high heat for 4–5 hours.

Nutrition Facts per serving: 261 cal., 4.5 g total fat, 81 mg chol., 777 mg sodium, 25 g carbo., 3 g fiber, 29 g pro.
Exchanges: 1 Vegetable, 1 Starch, 3 Lean Meat
Carb Choices: 2

Pork Dinners

Shopping List

Produce
large onion

Meat
1½ lbs. ground pork

Dairy
egg substitute

Canned
22-oz. jar sauerkraut

Packaged
white rice (not instant)

Seasonings
pepper

When buying pork, look for cuts with a relatively small amount of fat on the outside and with meat that is firm and a grayish pink in color.

Pork and Cabbage

2 medium onions, *sliced thin*

2 cups shredded cabbage

2 tsp. red pepper flakes

2 tsp. minced garlic

1 3-lb. pork loin roast, *trimmed*

2 cups barbecue sauce

¼ cup cold water

2 tbsp. cornstarch

Shopping List

Produce
2 medium onions
8-oz. pkg. shredded cabbage

Meat
3-lb. pork loin roast

Baking Goods
cornstarch

Condiments
16-oz. bottle barbecue sauce

Seasonings
crushed red pepper flakes
minced garlic

Spray inside of slow cooker with cooking spray. Place onions and cabbage on bottom of slow cooker; sprinkle with 1 teaspoon red pepper flakes and 1 teaspoon minced garlic. Place pork roast on top of vegetables and sprinkle with remaining red pepper flakes and minced garlic. Pour barbecue sauce over top. Cover and cook on low heat for 6–8 hours or high heat for 3–4 hours. Remove pork from slow cooker; shred with 2 forks and set aside. Combine water and cornstarch in small bowl and mix until smooth. Add to slow cooker and mix to blend. Cook, stirring occasionally, 15–20 minutes until thickened. Return meat to slow cooker, mix with sauce, and heat through.

Nutrition Facts per serving: 444 cal., 9.5 g total fat, 161 mg chol., 1,452 mg sodium, 38 g carbo., 1 g fiber, 52 g pro.
Exchanges: 2 Vegetable, 2 Other Carbo., 7 Very Lean Meat
Carb Choices: 3

Although meat inspection is mandatory, grading for quality is voluntary, and a plant pays to have its pork graded. USDA grades for pork reflect only two levels: Acceptable and Utility. Pork that's acceptable quality is the only fresh pork sold in supermarkets and has a high proportion of lean meat to fat and bone. Pork graded as utility is used only in processed products.

German-Style Pork and Sauerkraut

Easy | Do Ahead | Serves: 4

4 boneless pork chops, *about 1 inch thick*

1 tsp. Mrs. Dash seasoning

½ tsp. pepper

1 large onion, *sliced thick*

2 medium turnips, *peeled and sliced*

2 medium Granny Smith apples, *cored, peeled, and sliced*

16 baby carrots

1 16-oz. can sauerkraut, *do not drain*

1 10¾-oz. can low-fat cream of celery soup

⅔ cup nonfat chicken broth

Spray large nonstick skillet with cooking spray. Sprinkle pork chops with Mrs. Dash seasoning and pepper and cook in skillet over medium heat until browned on both sides. Spray inside of slow cooker with cooking spray. Combine sliced onion, turnips, apples, and carrots in bottom of slow cooker; spoon undrained sauerkraut over vegetables. Place pork chops on top. Combine celery soup and broth; pour over all ingredients. Cover and cook on low heat for 7–8 hours or high heat for 3½–4 hours.

Nutrition Facts per serving: 340 cal., 9.7 g total fat, 46 mg chol., 1,291 mg sodium, 37 g carbo., 10 g fiber, 28 g pro.
Exchanges: 4 Vegetable, 1 Other Carbo., 3 Lean Meat
Carb Choices: 2

Pork Dinners

Shopping List

Produce	Canned
large onion	16-oz. can sauerkraut
2 medium turnips	10¾-oz. can low-fat cream of celery soup
2 medium Granny Smith apples	14-oz. can nonfat chicken broth
8-oz. pkg. baby carrots	

Meat	Seasoning
4 boneless pork chops	Mrs. Dash seasoning
	pepper

Slow Cooker Pork and Potatoes

2 16-oz. pkgs. potato cubes

2 lbs. boneless pork loin, *trimmed and cut into 1-inch cubes*

1 tbsp. prepared mustard

2 cups barbecue sauce, *divided*

pepper to taste

Spray inside of slow cooker with cooking spray. Place potatoes in slow cooker; top with pork cubes. Combine mustard and 1 cup barbecue sauce; spoon over pork and potatoes. Cover and cook on low heat for 8–9 hours. Stir in remaining barbecue sauce; add pepper. Heat through.

Nutrition Facts per serving: 396 cal., 7.1 g total fat, 108 mg chol., 1,082 mg sodium, 42 g carbo., 4 g fiber, 38 g pro.
Exchanges: 1 Starch, 1½ Other Carbo., 4 Lean Meat
Carb Choices: 3

Shopping List

Produce
2 16-oz. pkgs. potato cubes

Meat
2 lbs. boneless pork loin

Condiments
prepared mustard
16-oz. bottle barbecue sauce

Seasonings
pepper

Pork Chops and Stuffing

Easy | Do Ahead | Serves: 6

2 lbs. boneless pork loin chops

1 tsp. Mrs. Dash seasoning

1 16-oz. pkg. corn bread stuffing mix

1 cup frozen seasoning vegetables, *thawed and patted dry*

½ tsp. dried thyme

2 cups water

½ cup nonfat chicken broth

1 cup nonfat shredded cheddar cheese

Spray nonstick skillet with cooking spray. Sprinkle pork chops with Mrs. Dash seasoning and cook in skillet 5–6 minutes, turning several times, until browned on both sides. Spray inside of slow cooker with cooking spray. Combine corn bread stuffing mix, seasoning vegetables, thyme, water, and broth and mix well. Place in slow cooker and top with pork chops. Cover and cook on low heat for 5–6 hours. Remove pork chops from cooker. Add cheese to stuffing mix and cook, stirring frequently, until melted. Serve pork chops with stuffing.

Pork Dinners

Nutrition Facts per serving: 491 cal., 10.4 g total fat, 45 mg chol., 1,595 mg sodium, 58 g carbo., 1 g fiber, 37 g pro.
Exchanges: 4 Starch, 3 Lean Meat
Carb Choices: 4

Shopping List

Meat
2 lbs. boneless pork loin chops

Canned
14-oz. can nonfat chicken broth

Dairy
4 oz. nonfat shredded cheddar cheese

Packaged
16-oz. pkg. corn bread stuffing mix

Frozen
10-oz. pkg. frozen seasoning vegetables

Seasonings
Mrs. Dash seasoning
dried thyme

Creamy Pork Chops

Easy | Do Ahead | Serves: 6

- 6 pork chops, *about ¾ inch thick*
- ¾ cup frozen chopped onions, *thawed and drained*
- 3 tbsp. ketchup
- 1 10¾-oz. can low-fat cream of celery soup
- 2 tsp. low-sodium soy sauce

Spray large nonstick skillet with cooking spray. Add pork chops to skillet and cook over medium heat until browned on both sides. Spray inside of slow cooker with cooking spray. Place pork chops in bottom of slow cooker. Combine remaining ingredients in small bowl and pour over pork chops. Cover and cook on low heat for 4–5 hours.

Nutrition Facts per serving: 518 cal., 22.2 g total fat, 126 mg chol., 465 mg sodium, 9 g carbo., 1 g fiber, 66 g pro.
Exchanges: 2 Vegetable, 8½ Lean Meat
Carb Choices: 1

Shopping List

Meat
6 pork chops

Frozen
12-oz. pkg. frozen chopped onions

Canned
10¾-oz. can low-fat cream of celery soup

Condiments
ketchup
low-sodium soy sauce

Pork Chops with Mushroom Gravy

Easy | **Do Ahead** | **Serves: 8**

8 boneless pork chops, *about ¾ inch thick*

4 large Granny Smith apples, *peeled, cored, and sliced*

2 large onions, *sliced*

2 10¾-oz. cans low-fat cream of mushroom soup

½ cup water

1 tbsp. brown sugar

1 tbsp. steak sauce

¾ tsp. dried basil

Shopping List

Produce
4 large Granny Smith apples
2 large onions

Meat
8 boneless pork chops

Canned
2 10¾-oz. cans low-fat cream of mushroom soup

Baking Goods
brown sugar

Condiments
steak sauce

Seasonings
dried basil

Spray inside of slow cooker with cooking spray. Place pork, apples, and onions in bottom of slow cooker. Combine remaining ingredients in medium bowl and mix well; Add to slow cooker. Cover and cook on low heat for 8–9 hours or high heat for 4–4½ hours.

Nutrition Facts per serving: 299 cal., 9.4 g total fat, 46 mg chol., 381 mg sodium, 28 g carbo., 1 g fiber, 25 g pro.
Exchanges: 1 Fruit, 1 Other Carbo., 3 Lean Meat
Carb Choices: 2

Pork Dinners

Pork's four basic cuts are shoulder, loin, side, and leg. You'll find them further cut into steaks, roasts, chops, spare/back ribs, bacon, and ham.

Pork Chops with Mushroom-Wine Sauce

Easy | Do Ahead | Serves: 4

1 10¾-oz. can low-fat cream of mushroom soup

¼ cup dry white wine

¼ cup Dijon mustard

¾ tsp. dried basil

1 tsp. minced garlic

½ tsp. pepper

5 medium potatoes, *sliced ¼ inch thick*

1 medium onion, *sliced thin*

4 pork loin chops, *¾ inch thick*

Spray inside of slow cooker with cooking spray. Combine soup, wine, Dijon mustard, basil, minced garlic, and pepper in small bowl and mix well. Place potatoes and onion in slow cooker; pour soup mixture over top and toss to coat. Arrange pork chops on top. Cover slow cooker and cook on low heat for 6–7 hours until pork chops and vegetables are tender.

Nutrition Facts per serving: 466 cal., 10.7 g total fat, 46 mg chol., 582 mg sodium, 62 g carbo., 6 g fiber, 29 g pro.
Exchanges: 3 Starch, 1 Other Carbo., 3 Lean Meat
Carb Choices: 4

Shopping List

Produce
5 medium potatoes
medium onion

Meat
4 pork loin chops

Canned
10¾-oz. can low-fat cream
  of mushroom soup

Condiments
Dijon mustard

Seasonings
dried basil
minced garlic
pepper

Canned
dry white wine

Pork and Noodles

Easy | **Do Ahead** | **Freeze** | **Serves: 6**

1½ lbs. pork tenderloin, *cut into ½-inch cubes*

1 cup frozen chopped onions, *thawed and drained*

2 cups sliced fresh mushrooms

1 tsp. garlic powder

3 cups nonfat chicken broth

1 12-oz. pkg. no-yolk egg noodles, *uncooked*

1 cup nonfat sour cream

Spray inside of slow cooker with cooking spray. Combine pork, onions, mushrooms, garlic powder, and broth in slow cooker and mix well. Cover and cook on low heat for 4–6 hours or high heat for 2–3 hours. If cooking on low heat, increase to high. Add noodles and stir to mix. Cover and cook about 30 minutes until noodles are tender. Stir in sour cream; heat through.

Nutrition Facts per serving: 452 cal., 6.1 g total fat, 105 mg chol., 529 mg sodium, 48 g carbo., 3 g fiber, 47 g pro.
Exchanges: 3 Vegetable, 2 Starch, 4½ Lean Meat
Carb Choices: 3

Pork Dinners

Shopping List

Produce
½ lb. mushrooms

Meat
1½ lbs. pork tenderloin

Dairy
8 oz. nonfat sour cream

Frozen
12-oz. pkg. frozen chopped onions

Canned
2 14-oz. cans nonfat chicken broth

Packaged
12-oz. pkg. no-yolk egg noodles

Seasonings
garlic powder

Three-Ingredient Pork Chops

4 pork chops, ½ inch thick

1 15-oz. can 99% fat-free vegetarian chili

1 14½-oz. can stewed tomatoes with bell pepper and onion, *do not drain*

¾ cup water

Spray inside of slow cooker with cooking spray. Combine all ingredients in slow cooker and mix well. Cover and cook on low heat for 7–8 hours or high heat for 3½–4 hours.

Nutrition Facts per serving: 267 cal., 7.8 g total fat, 45 mg chol., 518 mg sodium, 18 g carbo., 3 g fiber, 30 g pro.
Exchanges: 4 Vegetable, 3 Lean Meat
Carb Choices: 1

Shopping List

Meat
4 pork chops

Canned
15-oz. can 99% fat-free vegetarian chili
14½-oz. can stewed tomatoes with bell pepper and onion

Pork Chops with Pepper-Tomato Sauce

Easy | Do Ahead | Serves: 4

- 4 pork chops, *about ½ inch thick*
- 3 cups frozen seasoning vegetables, *thawed and drained*
- 1 14½-oz. can stewed tomatoes with bell pepper and onion, *do not drain*
- ½ cup ketchup
- 2 tbsp. cider vinegar
- 2 tbsp. brown sugar
- 2 tbsp. Worcestershire sauce
- 1 tbsp. lemon juice
- 1 tsp. beef bouillon granules
- 2 tbsp. cornstarch
- 2 tbsp. cold water

Spray inside of slow cooker with cooking spray. Combine all ingredients except cornstarch and water in slow cooker and mix well. Cover and cook on low heat for 5–6 hours. Combine cornstarch and water in small bowl and mix until smooth. Add to slow cooker and stir to mix. Cover and cook about 30 minutes until sauce is thickened.

Nutrition Facts per serving: 295 cal., 7.8 g total fat, 45 mg chol., 790 mg sodium, 32 g carbo., 3 g fiber, 26 g pro.
Exchanges: 3 Vegetable, 1 Other Carbo., 3 Lean Meat
Carb Choices: 2

Pork Dinners

Shopping List

Meat
4 pork chops

Frozen
16-oz. pkg. frozen seasoning vegetables

Canned
14½-oz. can stewed tomatoes with bell pepper and onion

Baking Goods
brown sugar
cornstarch

Condiments
ketchup
cider vinegar
Worcestershire sauce
lemon juice

Seasonings
beef bouillon granules

Provençal Pork Chops with Artichokes

Easy | Do Ahead | Serves: 4

- 4 pork chops, *about ½ inch thick*
- 2 cups frozen pepper stir-fry, *thawed and drained*
- 1 13¾-oz. can artichoke hearts, *drained and chopped*
- 2 8-oz. cans tomato sauce with roasted garlic
- 1½ tsp. dried Italian seasoning
- 1 tsp. minced garlic
- ½ tsp. crushed red pepper
- 2 tbsp. cooking sherry
- 1 tbsp. brown sugar
- ¼ tsp. pepper

Spray large nonstick skillet with cooking spray. Add pork chops to skillet and cook over medium heat until browned on both sides. Spray inside of slow cooker with cooking spray. Place pork chops in bottom of slow cooker; cover pork chops with pepper stir-fry and artichoke hearts. Combine remaining ingredients in small bowl and mix well; pour mixture over vegetables and pork chops. Cover and cook on low heat for 7–8 hours or high heat for 3½–4 hours.

Nutrition Facts per serving: 278 cal., 8.2 g total fat, 45 mg chol., 823 mg sodium, 25 g carbo., 2 g fiber, 29 g pro.
Exchanges: 3 Vegetable, ½ Other Carbo., 3 Lean Meat
Carb Choices: 2

Shopping List

Meat
4 pork chops

Frozen
16-oz. pkg. frozen pepper stir-fry

Canned
13¾-oz. can artichoke hearts
2 8-oz. cans tomato sauce with roasted garlic

Baking Goods
brown sugar

Condiments
cooking sherry

Seasonings
dried Italian seasoning
minced garlic
crushed red pepper
pepper

Curried Pork and Pineapple

2 tbsp. + 1¼ cups nonfat chicken broth, *divided*

3 tbsp. flour

½ tsp. pepper

2¼ lbs. boneless pork, *cut into 1-inch cubes*

¾ cup frozen chopped onions, *thawed and drained*

1 tbsp. curry powder

1 tbsp. paprika

1–2 tsp. cayenne pepper

1 tbsp. mango chutney

1 16-oz. can pineapple chunks in light syrup, *do not drain*

Spray large nonstick skillet with cooking spray. Add 2 tablespoons broth to skillet and heat over medium-high heat. Combine flour and pepper in zip-top bag and shake to mix. Drop pork cubes in bag and shake to coat with flour mixture. Add pork to skillet; cook over medium heat, stirring frequently, until pork is browned on all sides. Spray inside of slow cooker with cooking spray. Transfer pork to slow cooker. Add 1¼ cups chicken broth and remaining ingredients to skillet; bring to a boil. Pour broth mixture over pork. Cover and cook on low heat for 6–8 hours.

Pork Dinners

Nutrition Facts per serving: 294 cal., 6.8 g total fat, 121 mg chol., 272 mg sodium, 18 g carbo., 1 g fiber, 39 g pro.
Exchanges: 1½ Fruit, 6 Very Lean Meat
Carb Choices: 1

Shopping List

Meat	Baking Goods
2¼ lbs. boneless pork	flour

Frozen	Condiments
12-oz. pkg. frozen chopped onions	mango chutney

	Seasonings
Canned	pepper
14-oz. can nonfat chicken broth	curry powder
	paprika
16-oz. can pineapple chunks in light syrup	cayenne pepper

Oriental Shredded Pork

Easy | Do Ahead | Serves: 6

2½ lbs. pork shoulder, *trimmed and cut into chunks*

1 cup apple cider

2 tbsp. low-sodium soy sauce

2 tbsp. hoisin sauce

1½ tsp. five-spice powder

6 nonfat whole wheat pita breads, *split in half*

Shopping List

Produce
8 oz. apple cider

Meat
2½ lbs. pork shoulder

Packaged
12-oz. pkg. whole wheat pita breads

Condiments
low-sodium soy sauce
hoisin sauce

Seasonings
five-spice powder

Spray inside of slow cooker with cooking spray. Place pork chunks in slow cooker. Combine remaining ingredients except pita breads; mix well and pour over pork. Cover and cook on low heat for 7–8 hours. Remove meat from slow cooker and shred with 2 forks. Return meat to slow cooker and heat through. Serve in whole wheat pita breads.

Nutrition Facts per serving: 585 cal., 28.9 g total fat, 184 mg chol., 759 mg sodium, 21 g carbo., 1 g fiber, 53 g pro.
Exchanges: 1 Starch, ½ Other Carbo., 6 High-Fat Meat
Carb Choices: 1

What is five-spice powder? One of the basics in Chinese cooking, this sweet, sour, bitter, pungent, and salty spice blend is a mixture of star anise, fennel, cloves, cinnamon, and Szechwan pepper. Use it in marinades or as a rub for meat, poultry, or fish. Five-spice powder is great added to rice or vegetable dishes. A dash or two goes a long way.

Sweet and Sour Pork

Easy | Do Ahead | Serves: 6

2 lbs. pork tenderloin, *cut into 1-inch cubes*

1 20-oz. can pineapple chunks packed in juice, *drained well*

1 red bell pepper, *cut into 1-inch chunks*

1 medium onion, *cut into ¼-inch slices*

½ cup canned water chestnuts, *drained*

1 10-oz. jar sweet and sour sauce

2 tbsp. flour

5 tbsp. water

hot cooked rice (optional)

Spray inside of slow cooker with cooking spray. Combine pork, pineapple, bell pepper, onion, water chestnuts, and sweet and sour sauce in slow cooker and mix well. Cover and cook on low heat for 7–9 hours or high heat for 3½–4½ hours. Remove pork, pineapple, bell pepper, onion, and water chestnuts from cooker. Combine flour and water in small bowl. If cooking on low heat, increase to high. Add flour mixture to cooker; cover and cook for 5 minutes until mixture is thickened. Return pork and other ingredients and heat through. Serve over cooked rice, if desired.

Pork Dinners

Nutrition Facts per serving: 322 cal., 5.7 g total fat, 108 mg chol., 199 mg sodium, 32 g carbo., 1 g fiber, 35 g pro.
Exchanges: 1 Vegetable, 1 Fruit, ½ Other Carbo., 4 Lean Meat
Carb Choices: 2

Shopping List

Produce	Baking Goods
medium red bell pepper	flour
medium onion	
	Condiments
Meat	10-oz. jar sweet and sour
2 lbs. pork tenderloin	sauce
Canned	**Optional**
6-oz. can water chestnuts	rice
20-oz. can pineapple chunks in juice	

Pink is okay! Even when pork has reached a safe internal temperature (160°F), it may still have a pink tinge due to the cooking method or added ingredients.

Teriyaki Pork Chops

Easy | Do Ahead | Serves: 4

⅓ cup teriyaki sauce
1 tbsp. brown sugar
½ tsp. ground ginger
4 pork chops, *about 1 inch thick*

Spray inside of slow cooker with cooking spray. Combine teriyaki sauce, brown sugar, and ginger in small bowl and mix well. Place pork chops in bottom of slow cooker; pour teriyaki mixture over top. Cover and cook on low heat for 7–8 hours.

Nutrition Facts per serving: 238 cal., 7.7 g total fat, 45 mg chol., 684 mg sodium, 16 g carbo., 0 g fiber, 25 g pro.
Exchanges: 1 Other Carbo., 3 Lean Meat
Carb Choices: 1

Shopping List

Meat
4 pork chops

Baking Goods
brown sugar

Condiments
teriyaki sauce

Seasonings
ground ginger

Safety Tip: Never brown or partially cook pork, then refrigerate it to finish cooking later. The brief browning of the meat may not destroy all bacteria, and the meat could become contaminated.
On the other hand, it is safe to partially precook or microwave pork IMMEDIATELY before transferring it to a hot grill to finish cooking.

Saucy Pork Chops

Easy | Do Ahead | Serves: 6

1 28-oz. can crushed tomatoes with garlic, *do not drain*

½ cup frozen chopped onions, *thawed and drained*

½ cup + 2 tbsp. brown sugar

2 tbsp. vinegar

2 tbsp. dark corn syrup

2 tsp. garlic powder

1 tsp. chili powder

1½ lbs. pork chops, *trimmed and boned*

3 cups cooked rice

Spray inside of slow cooker with cooking spray. Combine undrained tomatoes, onions, brown sugar, vinegar, corn syrup, garlic powder, and chili powder in slow cooker and mix well. Add pork chops and toss to coat. Cover and cook on low heat for 6–7 hours. Add cooked rice during last 30 minutes of cooking; stir to mix and heat through.

Nutrition Facts per serving: 552 cal., 13.4 g total fat, 75 mg chol., 299 mg sodium, 63 g carbo., 2 g fiber, 43 g pro.
Exchanges: 3 Vegetable, 2 Starch, 1 Other Carbo., 4½ Lean Meat
Carb Choices: 4

Pork Dinners

Shopping List

Meat
1½ lbs. pork chops

Frozen
12-oz. pkg. frozen chopped onions

Canned
28-oz. can crushed tomatoes with garlic

Packaged
rice

Baking Goods
brown sugar
dark corn syrup

Condiments
vinegar

Seasonings
garlic powder
chili powder

Festive Pork Dinner

Easy | Do Ahead | Serves: 8

1 cup chunky-style cinnamon applesauce

2 29-oz. cans sweet potatoes, *drained and sliced*

2 tbsp. brown sugar

2 lbs. boneless pork loin chops

1 16-oz. can whole cranberry sauce

Spray inside of slow cooker with cooking spray. Spread applesauce in slow cooker; add sweet potato slices and sprinkle with brown sugar. Top with pork chops and spoon cranberry sauce over top. Cover and cook on low heat for 7–9 hours or high heat for 3½–4½ hours.

Nutrition Facts per serving: 155 cal., 13.4 g total fat, 75 mg chol., 368 mg sodium, 62 g carbo., 5 g fiber, 46 g pro.
Exchanges: 2 Fruit, 1 Starch, 1 Other Carbo., 5 Lean Meat
Carb Choices: 4

Shopping List

Meat
2 lbs. boneless pork loin chops

Canned
8-oz. jar chunky-style cinnamon applesauce
2 29-oz. cans sweet potatoes
16-oz. can whole cranberry sauce

Baking Goods
brown sugar

Roast Pork with Apple Glaze

Easy | **Do Ahead** | **Serves: 8**

6 Granny Smith apples,
cored and quartered

1 4-lb. pork loin roast,
trimmed

2 tsp. Mrs. Dash seasoning

1 tsp. pepper

¼ cup apple juice

3 tbsp. brown sugar

1 tsp. ground ginger

Spray inside of slow cooker with cooking spray. Place apples in bottom of slow cooker. Rub pork roast with Mrs. Dash seasoning and pepper; place roast on top of apples. Combine apple juice, brown sugar, and ginger and mix well; pour juice mixture over roast and apples, spreading to coat. Cover and cook on low heat for 10–12 hours or high heat for 5–6 hours.

Nutrition Facts per serving: 372 cal., 8.7 g total fat, 161 mg chol., 119 mg sodium, 22 g carbo., 2 g fiber, 50 g pro.
Exchanges: 1 Fruit, ½ Other Carbo., 7 Very Lean Meat
Carb Choices: 1

Pork
Dinners

Shopping List

Produce
6 Granny Smith apples

Meat
4-lb. pork loin roast

Canned
4 oz. apple juice

Baking Goods
brown sugar

Seasonings
Mrs. Dash seasoning
pepper
ground ginger

Orange-Lime Pork

Easy | **Do Ahead** | **Freeze** | **Serves: 6**

1½ lbs. pork tenderloin

½ tsp. garlic powder

¼ cup + 2 tbsp. lime juice

3 tbsp. orange juice

½ tsp. dried basil

nonfat chicken broth (optional)

Spray inside of slow cooker with cooking spray. Combine all ingredients in slow cooker; cover and cook on low heat for 7–8 hours or high heat for 3½–4 hours. If too much liquid evaporates while pork is still cooking, add a little nonfat chicken broth. Serve pork with a fruit salsa (see pages 340 and 341).

Nutrition Facts per serving: 196 cal., 5.5 g total fat, 105 mg chol., 76 mg sodium, 2 g carbo., 0 g fiber, 33 g pro.
Exchanges: 4 Lean Meat
Carb Choices: 0

Shopping List

Produce
lime juice
orange juice

Meat
1½ lbs. pork tenderloin

Seasonings
garlic powder
dried basil

Optional
nonfat chicken broth

Peach-Glazed Pork Roast

Easy | Do Ahead | Serves: 8

1 14-oz. can nonfat chicken broth

1 18-oz. jar peach preserves

¾ cup frozen chopped onions, *thawed and drained*

2 tbsp. Dijon mustard

1 4-lb. boneless pork loin roast

Spray inside of slow cooker with cooking spray. Combine broth, preserves, onions, and mustard in slow cooker; add pork and turn to coat. Cover and cook on low heat for 8–9 hours or high heat for 4–4½ hours.

Nutrition Facts per serving: 484 cal., 8.8 g total fat, 161 mg chol., 355 mg sodium, 48 g carbo., 1 g fiber, 51 g pro.
Exchanges: 3 Other Carbo., 7 Very Lean Meat
Carb Choices: 3

Pork Dinners

Shopping List

Meat
4-lb. boneless pork loin roast

Frozen
12-oz. pkg. frozen chopped onions

Canned
14-oz. can nonfat chicken broth

Condiments
18-oz. jar peach preserves
Dijon mustard

Substitution Tip: Use apricot, pineapple, or red raspberry preserves instead of peach.

Autumn Pork Roast

1 2-lb. boneless pork loin roast

1½ tsp. garlic powder

1 6-oz. pkg. dried medley fruit mix

½ cup apple or cranberry juice

¼ tsp. pepper

Shopping List

Meat
2-lb. boneless pork loin roast

Canned
4 oz. apple or cranberry juice

Packaged
6-oz. pkg. dried medley fruit mix

Seasonings
garlic powder
pepper

Spray inside of slow cooker with cooking spray. Place pork roast in slow cooker and sprinkle with garlic powder. Top roast with fruit; pour juice over roast and sprinkle with pepper. Cover and cook on low heat for 7–9 hours.

Nutrition Facts per serving: 293 cal., 4.4 g total fat, 81 mg chol., 60 mg sodium, 36 g carbo., 2 g fiber, 26 g pro.
Exchanges: 2½ Fruit, 3 Lean Meat
Carb Choices: 2

While product dating is not required by federal regulations, many stores voluntarily label packages of raw pork with "sell by" or "use by" dates. For safety's sake, use these products within 3–5 days of purchase and always buy a product before the expiration date.

Pork Roast with Pineapple Sauce

Easy | Do Ahead | Serves: 8

- 1 4-lb. pork loin roast
- 1 large onion, *sliced thin*
- 3 tbsp. white wine vinegar
- 1 tbsp. ketchup
- 2 tbsp. Worcestershire sauce
- ¼ cup brown sugar
- ½ tsp. ground ginger
- 1 tsp. crushed garlic
- 1 cup frozen chopped bell peppers, *thawed and drained*
- ½ tsp. pepper
- 2 tbsp. cornstarch
- 1 tbsp. cold water
- 1 8-oz. can crushed pineapple, *do not drain*

Spray large nonstick skillet with cooking spray and heat over medium-high heat. Add pork roast to skillet and cook 3–5 minutes per side. Remove roast from skillet. Spray inside of slow cooker with cooking spray. Place sliced onion in bottom of slow cooker. Place roast on top of onion. Combine vinegar, ketchup, Worcestershire sauce, brown sugar, ginger, garlic, bell peppers, and pepper in small bowl and mix well. Spoon vinegar mixture over roast and onions. Combine cornstarch and water in small bowl and mix until smooth; pour over top and mix. Cover and cook on low heat for 8–9 hours. Add undrained pineapple, stir to mix, and cook 1 hour.

Pork Dinners

Nutrition Facts per serving: 352 cal., 8.4 g total fat, 161 mg chol., 177 mg sodium, 16 g carbo., 1 g fiber, 51 g pro.
Exchanges: 1 Vegetable, 1 Fruit, 7 Very Lean Meat
Carb Choices: 1

Shopping List

Produce	**Baking Goods**
large onion	brown sugar
	cornstarch
Meat	
4-lb. pork loin roast	**Condiments**
	white wine vinegar
Frozen	ketchup
10-oz. pkg. frozen chopped green bell peppers	Worcestershire sauce
	Seasonings
Canned	ground ginger
8-oz. can crushed pineapple	crushed garlic
	pepper

Peachy Pork Chops

1 lb. pork chops
1 29-oz. can cling peach halves
¼ cup brown sugar
¾ tsp. ground cinnamon
¼ tsp. ground allspice
1 8-oz. can tomato sauce
¼ cup vinegar

Spray large nonstick skillet with cooking spray and heat over medium-high heat. Add pork chops to skillet and cook until brown on both sides. Drain well. Drain peaches, reserving ¼ cup syrup. Combine peaches, reserved syrup, brown sugar, cinnamon, allspice, tomato sauce, and vinegar in bowl and mix well. Spray inside of slow cooker with cooking spray. Place pork chops in slow cooker; pour peach mixture over top. Cover and cook on low heat for 4–6 hours.

Nutrition Facts per serving: 500 cal., 9.2 g total fat, 68 mg chol., 105 mg sodium, 73 g carbo., 1 g fiber, 36 g pro.
Exchanges: 4 Fruit, 1 Other Carbo., 4 Lean Meat
Carb Choices: 5

Shopping List

Meat
1 lb. pork chops

Canned
29-oz. can cling peach halves
8-oz. can tomato sauce

Baking Goods
brown sugar

Condiments
vinegar

Seasonings
ground cinnamon
ground allspice

Pork products labeled "natural" do not contain artificial flavoring, coloring, chemical preservatives, or any other artificial or synthetic ingredients, and the products that are labeled as such are not more than minimally processed.

Apple-Glazed Pork Tenderloins

Easy | **Do Ahead** | **Serves: 4**

2 pork tenderloins, ¾ *pound each*

1½ tsp. Mrs. Dash seasoning

1 tsp. pepper

2 tbsp. apple jelly

1 tbsp. cider vinegar

2 Granny Smith apples, *peeled, cored, and chopped*

1 large onion, *sliced thin*

Spray large nonstick skillet with cooking spray. Rub pork tenderloins with Mrs. Dash seasoning and pepper. Add tenderloins to skillet and cook over medium heat until browned on both sides. Spray inside of slow cooker with cooking spray. Place pork tenderloins in slow cooker; add remaining ingredients and mix. Cover and cook on low heat for 7–9 hours or high heat for 3½–4½ hours.

Nutrition Facts per serving: 299 cal., 6.6 g total fat, 121 mg chol., 90 mg sodium, 21 g carbo., 2 g fiber, 38 g pro.
Exchanges: 1½ Fruit, 6 Very Lean Meat
Carb Choices: 1

Pork Dinners

Shopping List

Produce
2 Granny Smith apples
large onion

Meat
2 pork tenderloins (¾ pound each)

Condiments
apple jelly
cider vinegar

Seasonings
Mrs. Dash seasoning
pepper

Safety Tip: Consume cooked pork within 2 hours (1 hour if air temperature is above 90°F) or refrigerate at 40°F or less in shallow, covered containers. Eat within 3–4 days, either cold or reheated to 165°F (hot and steaming). It is safe to freeze prepared pork dishes. For best quality, use within 3 months.

Sweet and Sassy Pork Roast

2 lbs. pork tenderloin

1½ tsp. garlic powder

¼ cup whole-berry cranberry sauce

¼ cup peach preserves

Spray inside of slow cooker with cooking spray. Sprinkle pork tenderloin with garlic powder. Combine cranberry sauce and peach preserves in small bowl and mix well; spread cranberry mixture over pork tenderloin. Place pork in slow cooker. Cover and cook on low heat for 8–10 hours.

Nutrition Facts per serving: 230 cal., 5.4 g total fat, 105 mg chol., 80 mg sodium, 11 g carbo., 0 g fiber, 33 g pro.
Exchanges: ½ Other Carbo., 4 Lean Meat
Carb Choices: 1

Shopping List

Meat
2 lbs. pork tenderloin

Condiments
16-oz. can whole-berry cranberry sauce
8-oz. jar peach preserves

Seasonings
garlic powder

Orange-Cranberry Pork

Easy | **Do Ahead** | **Serves: 4**

1½ lbs. pork tenderloin
¾ cup chopped onion
1 cup fresh cranberries
¼ tsp. ground cinnamon
¼ tsp. ground ginger
¼ cup brown sugar
1 cup orange juice
3 tbsp. flour
2 tbsp. cold water

Spray inside of slow cooker with cooking spray. Combine pork tenderloin, onion, cranberries, cinnamon, ginger, brown sugar, and orange juice in cooker. Cover and cook on low heat for 6–7 hours. Combine flour and cold water in small bowl and mix until smooth. Add flour mixture to cooker and stir. Cover and cook until mixture thickens.

Nutrition Facts per serving: 407 cal., 8.4 g total fat 158 mg chol., 120 mg sodium, 30 g carbo., 1 g fiber, 50 g pro.
Exchanges: 1 Fruit, 1 Other Carbo., 5½ Lean Meat
Carb Choices: 2

Pork
Dinners

Shopping List

Produce
large onion
8-oz. pkg. fresh cranberries
8 oz. orange juice

Meat
1½ lbs. pork tenderloin

Baking Goods
brown sugar
flour

Seasonings
ground cinnamon
ground ginger

Holiday Pork Roast

Easy | Do Ahead | Serves: 6

2½ lbs. pork tenderloin
¾ tsp. garlic powder
1 cup Craisins
½ cup nonfat chicken broth
½ cup cranberry juice, *divided*
2 tbsp. cornstarch

Spray inside of slow cooker with cooking spray. Trim fat from pork tenderloin. Sprinkle tenderloin with garlic powder and place in slow cooker. Combine Craisins, broth, and ¼ cup cranberry juice in small bowl; pour mixture over pork. Cover and cook over low heat for 7–9 hours. Remove pork from slow cooker and place on platter; cover with foil to keep warm. Pour juices from slow cooker into saucepan. Combine remaining cranberry juice with cornstarch in small bowl and mix until smooth. Add to saucepan and cook over medium-low heat, stirring constantly, until thickened and bubbly, about 2–3 minutes. Slice pork roast and serve with cranberry sauce.

Nutrition Facts per serving: 330 cal., 7 g total fat, 134 mg chol., 163 mg sodium, 22 g carbo., 1 g fiber, 42 g pro.
Exchanges: 1½ Fruit, 6½ Very Lean Meat
Carb Choices: 1

Shopping List

Meat
2½ lbs. pork tenderloin

Canned
14-oz. can nonfat chicken broth
cranberry juice

Packaged
6-oz. pkg. Craisins

Baking Goods
cornstarch

Seasonings
garlic powder

Apple-Cinnamon Pork Chops

- 2 tbsp. nonfat chicken broth
- 6 pork loin chops, *cut ¾ inch thick*
- 1 21-oz. can apple pie filling, *divided*
- 2 tsp. lemon juice
- ½ tsp. instant chicken bouillon granules
- ¼ tsp. ground cinnamon

Spray large nonstick skillet with cooking spray. Add broth to skillet and heat over medium-high heat. Add pork chops and cook over medium heat until browned on both sides. Remove from skillet. Spray inside of slow cooker with cooking spray. Combine half the apple pie filling, the lemon juice, bouillon granules, and cinnamon in slow cooker and mix well. Place pork chops on top; cover and cook on low heat for 6–7 hours. Spoon remaining apple pie filling into bowl and heat in microwave on high until warm. Serve with pork chops.

Pork Dinners

Nutrition Facts per serving: 270 cal., 7.8 g total fat, 45 mg chol., 12 mg sodium, 26 g carbo., 0 g fiber, 24 g pro.
Exchanges: 1 Fruit, ½ Other Carbo., 3 Lean Meat
Carb Choices: 2

Shopping List

Meat
6 pork loin chops

Canned
14-oz. can nonfat chicken broth
21-oz. can apple pie filling

Condiments
lemon juice

Seasonings
instant chicken bouillon granules
ground cinnamon

Spanish Rice Pork Casserole

2 14½-oz. cans stewed tomatoes with bell pepper and onion, *chopped, do not drain*

2 8-oz. cans tomato sauce with roasted garlic

1 cup chopped onion

1 Granny Smith apple, *peeled and chopped*

¾ cup chopped green bell pepper

⅓ cup raisins

1–2 tbsp. curry powder

1 tsp. garlic powder

½ tsp. ground cinnamon

⅛ tsp. cayenne pepper

1½ cups converted white rice

1½ lbs. boneless pork chops or tenderloin, *cut into strips*

Spray inside of slow cooker with cooking spray. Combine undrained stewed tomatoes, tomato sauce, onion, apple, bell pepper, raisins, curry powder, garlic powder, cinnamon, cayenne pepper, and rice in cooker. Stir pork into tomato mixture and mix lightly. Cover and cook on low heat for 6–8 hours or low heat for 3–4 hours.

Nutrition Facts per serving: 451 cal., 5.1 g total fat, 81 mg chol., 869 mg sodium, 70 g carbo., 5 g fiber, 32 g pro.
Exchanges: 5 Vegetable, 3 Starch, 3 Very Lean Meat
Carb Choices: 5

Shopping List

Produce	Packaged
large onion	6-oz. pkg. raisins
Granny Smith apple	8-oz. pkg. converted white
green bell pepper	rice

Meat	Seasonings
1½ lbs. boneless pork chops or tenderloin	curry powder
	garlic powder
	ground cinnamon
Canned	cayenne pepper
2 14½-oz. cans stewed tomatoes with bell pepper and onion	
2 8-oz. cans tomato sauce with roasted garlic	

Meat Loaf

Easy | **Do Ahead** | **Serves: 8**

- 1 lb. ground pork
- 1 lb. extra-lean ground beef
- ½ cup egg substitute
- ¼ cup nonfat half and half
- ¼ cup quick-cooking oats
- 1 tsp. steak sauce
- ¼ tsp. pepper
- ½ tsp. dried Italian seasoning
- 2 cups frozen chopped onions, *thawed and drained*
- 1 cup nonfat shredded cheddar cheese
- ¼ cup barbecue sauce or ketchup

Spray inside of slow cooker with cooking spray. Combine pork, beef, egg substitute, half and half, oats, steak sauce, pepper, Italian seasoning, and onions in medium bowl and mix thoroughly. Press half of meat mixture into bottom of slow cooker; top with cheese. Press remaining meat mixture on top. Cover and cook on low heat for 10–11 hours or high heat for 5–5½ hours. Spread barbecue sauce or ketchup over top and cook 30 minutes on high heat.

Nutrition Facts per serving: 300 cal., 14.7 g total fat, 76 mg chol., 360 mg sodium, 12 g carbo., 1 g fiber, 27 g pro.
Exchanges: 2 Vegetable, 3 High-Fat Meat
Carb Choices: 1

Pork Dinners

Shopping List

Meat
1 lb. ground pork
1 lb. extra-lean ground beef

Dairy
egg substitute
nonfat half and half
6 oz. nonfat shredded cheddar cheese

Frozen
12-oz. pkg. frozen chopped onions

Packaged
quick-cooking oats

Condiments
steak sauce
barbecue sauce or ketchup

Seasonings
pepper
dried Italian seasoning

Saucy Pork and Sweet Potatoes

1½ lbs. boneless pork loin, *cut into 1-inch cubes*

6 medium sweet potatoes, *cut into 1-inch pieces*

1 large onion, *cut into large wedges*

2 cups barbecue sauce, *divided*

1½ tbsp. prepared mustard

1 tsp. minced garlic

Spray large nonstick skillet with cooking spray. Add pork cubes to skillet and cook over medium heat until browned on all sides. Spray inside of slow cooker with cooking spray. Place pork, potatoes, and onion in slow cooker. Combine 1 cup barbecue sauce, mustard, and minced garlic in small bowl and mix well; pour over pork and vegetables and mix well. Cover and cook on low heat for 6½–7 hours. Serve pork and potatoes with remaining barbecue sauce.

Nutrition Facts per serving: 393 cal., 5.5 g total fat, 81 mg chol., 1,447 mg sodium, 59 g carbo., 4 g fiber, 28 g pro.
Exchanges: 3 Starch, ½ Other Carbo., 3 Very Lean Meat
Carb Choices: 4

Shopping List

Produce
6 medium sweet potatoes
large onion

Meat
1½ lbs. boneless pork loin

Condiments
16-oz. bottle barbecue sauce
prepared mustard

Seasonings
minced garlic

Barbecue Pork

Easy | Do Ahead | Serves: 8

1 tsp. garlic powder

1 tbsp. onion powder

½ tsp. pepper

¼ tsp. red pepper flakes

2 lbs. boneless pork loin roast, *trimmed*

1½ cups ketchup

1 8-oz. can tomato sauce with roasted garlic

2 tbsp. brown sugar

1 tbsp. molasses

1 tbsp. Worcestershire sauce

2 tbsp. barbecue sauce

1 tbsp. apple cider vinegar

½–1 tsp. cayenne pepper

whole wheat buns or pita breads (optional)

Spray inside of slow cooker with cooking spray. Mix garlic powder, onion powder, pepper, and red pepper flakes and rub over pork loin. Place pork loin in slow cooker. Cover and cook on high heat for 45–60 minutes. Reduce heat to low and cook 4½ hours. Remove pork from slow cooker and cut into large chunks; return to slow cooker. Combine remaining ingredients and mix well. Pour sauce over pork and toss to mix. Cook on low heat for 1 hour; remove pork and shred using 2 forks. Return pork to slow cooker and heat through. Serve on buns or in pita breads, if desired.

Pork Dinners

Nutrition Facts per serving: 224 cal., 4.2 g total fat, 81 mg chol., 780 mg sodium, 21 g carbo., 1 g fiber, 25 g pro.
Exchanges: 1 Vegetable, 1 Other Carbo., 3 Very Lean Meat
Carb Choices: 1

Shopping List

Meat	barbecue sauce
2 lbs. boneless pork loin	apple cider vinegar
Canned	**Seasonings**
8-oz. can tomato sauce with roasted garlic	garlic powder
	onion powder
	pepper
Baking Goods	red pepper flakes
brown sugar	cayenne pepper
Condiments	**Optional**
12 oz. ketchup	whole wheat buns or pita breads
molasses	
Worcestershire sauce	

Easy Shredded Barbecue Pork

2 lbs. pork tenderloin

1½ tsp. garlic powder

2 cups barbecue sauce

½ cup frozen chopped onions, *thawed and drained*

toasted bread, whole wheat buns, tortillas, pita breads, or baked potatoes

barbecue sauce (optional)

Spray inside of slow cooker with cooking spray. Place pork tenderloin in slow cooker; sprinkle with garlic powder. Add barbecue sauce and onions and mix lightly. Cover and cook on low heat for 7–9 hours. Remove meat from slow cooker. Shred with 2 forks. Return meat to slow cooker and toss with barbecue sauce until well coated. Heat through and serve on toasted bread, whole wheat buns, tortillas, pita breads, or baked potatoes with additional barbecue sauce.

Nutrition Facts per serving: 131 cal., 3.5 g total fat, 54 mg chol., 379 mg sodium, 6 g carbo., 1 g fiber, 18 g pro.
Exchanges: 1 Vegetable, 3 Very Lean Meat
Carb Choices: 0

Shopping List

Meat
2 lbs. pork tenderloin

Frozen
12-oz. pkg. frozen chopped onions

Condiments
16-oz. bottle barbecue sauce

Seasonings
garlic powder

Optional
bread, whole wheat buns, tortillas, pita breads, or potatoes
barbecue sauce

Pork tenderloin is one of the leanest cuts of pork, containing 139 calories and 4.1 grams of fat per 3-ounce serving. Other lean cuts include boneless pork sirloin chop (164 calories and 5.7 grams of fat), boneless pork loin roast (165 calories and 6.1 grams of fat), and boneless pork top loin chop (173 calories and 6.6 grams of fat).

p. 91 Pork Chops and Stuffing

p. 132 Pork and Black Bean Chili

p. 116 Spanish Rice Pork Casserole

Oriental Shredded Pork p. 100

Sweet and Sour Pork p. 101

Roast Pork with Apple Glaze p. 105

Salsa-Style Pork

Easy | **Do Ahead** | **Serves: 4**

- 1 lb. boneless pork loin, *cut into 1-inch cubes*
- 1 20-oz. jar chunky-style salsa
- 1 4-oz. can diced green chiles, *drained*
- 1 15-oz. can black beans, *drained*
- 1 cup nonfat shredded cheddar cheese
- 4 98% fat-free flour tortillas, *warmed in oven or microwave* (optional)
- nonfat sour cream (optional)
- chopped fresh cilantro (optional)

Spray inside of slow cooker with cooking spray. Combine pork loin, salsa, and chiles in slow cooker and mix well. Cover and cook on low heat for 6–8 hours. Add black beans and stir to mix. Increase heat to high and cook 10–20 minutes until beans are heated. Sprinkle cheese over top and serve. If desired, serve pork on warmed tortillas and garnish with sour cream and cilantro.

Nutrition Facts per serving: 330 cal., 4.5 g total fat, 81 mg chol., 1,821 mg sodium, 28 g carbo., 4 g fiber, 41 g pro.
Exchanges: 3 Vegetable, 1 Starch, 5 Very Lean Meat
Carb Choices: 2

Pork Dinners

Shopping List

Meat
1 lb. boneless pork loin

Dairy
4 oz. nonfat shredded cheddar cheese

Canned
4-oz. can diced green chiles
15-oz. can black beans

Condiments
20-oz. jar chunky-style salsa

Optional
98% fat-free flour tortillas
nonfat sour cream
fresh cilantro

Pepper Pork

Easy | Do Ahead | Serves: 6

2 tbsp. nonfat chicken broth

2 lbs. boneless pork loin chops, *cut into strips*

1 16-oz. pkg. frozen pepper stir-fry, *thawed and drained*

2 cups sliced fresh mushrooms

1 8-oz. can tomato sauce

2 tbsp. brown sugar

1½ tsp. white vinegar

2 tbsp. Worcestershire sauce

Spray large nonstick skillet with cooking spray. Add broth to skillet and heat over medium-high heat. Add pork strips and cook until browned. Drain well. Combine browned pork, pepper stir-fry, mushrooms, tomato sauce, brown sugar, white vinegar, and Worcestershire sauce in slow cooker and mix well. Cover and cook on low heat for 6–8 hours or high heat for 3–4 hours.

Nutrition Facts per serving: 196 cal., 4.3 g total fat, 81 mg chol., 284 mg sodium, 12 g carbo., 1 g fiber, 27 g pro.
Exchanges: 1 Vegetable, ½ Other Carbo., 3 Very Lean Meat
Carb Choices: 1

Shopping List

Produce
½ lb. mushrooms

Meat
2 lbs. boneless pork loin chops

Frozen
16-oz. pkg. frozen pepper stir-fry

Canned
14-oz. can nonfat chicken broth
8-oz. can tomato sauce

Baking Goods
brown sugar

Condiments
white vinegar
Worcestershire sauce

Slow Cooker Pork Special

Easy | **Do Ahead** | **Serves: 6**

- 2 lbs. boneless pork loin, *cut into 1-inch cubes*
- 1 16-oz. pkg. frozen pepper stir-fry, *thawed and drained*
- 2 15-oz. cans black beans, *drained and divided*
- 1 14¾-oz. can creamed corn, *do not drain*
- 1 14½-oz. can stewed tomatoes with bell pepper and onion, *do not drain*
- 1 4-oz. can diced green chiles, *do not drain*
- 1¼ tsp. chili powder

Shopping List

Meat
2 lbs. boneless pork loin

Frozen
16-oz. pkg. frozen pepper stir-fry

Canned
2 15-oz. cans black beans
14¾-oz. can creamed corn
14½-oz. can stewed tomatoes with bell pepper and onion
4-oz. can diced green chiles

Seasonings
chili powder

Spray large nonstick skillet with cooking spray. Add pork to skillet and cook over medium heat, stirring frequently, until browned on all sides. Spray inside of slow cooker with cooking spray. Combine pork, pepper stir-fry, 1 can of beans, undrained creamed corn, tomatoes, green chiles, and chili powder in slow cooker and mix well. Blend remaining can of beans in food processor or blender until smooth; add to mixture in slow cooker and mix well. Cover and cook on low heat for 4–6 hours or high heat for 2–3 hours.

Nutrition Facts per serving: 416 cal., 6.4 g total fat, 108 mg chol., 1,221 mg sodium, 46 g carbo., 7 g fiber, 45 g pro.
Exchanges: 3 Vegetable, 2 Starch, 5 Very Lean Meat
Carb Choices: 3

Pork Dinners

Selecting and storing pork: Select pork just before checking out at the supermarket. Store packages of raw pork in disposable plastic bags (if available) to contain any leakage, which could cross-contaminate cooked foods or produce. Take pork home immediately and refrigerate it at 40°F; use within 3–5 days or freeze (0°F).

Pork and Black Bean Chili

Easy | **Do Ahead** | **Serves: 6**

1 lb. pork tenderloin, *cut into 1-inch cubes*

1 16-oz. jar chunky-style salsa

3 15-oz. cans black beans, *rinsed and drained*

½ cup nonfat chicken broth

1 tbsp. onion powder

2½ tsp. chili powder

1 tsp. dried oregano

¼ cup nonfat sour cream (optional)

Shopping List

Meat
1 lb. pork tenderloin

Canned
3 15-oz. cans black beans
14-oz. can nonfat chicken broth

Condiments
16-oz. jar chunky-style salsa

Seasonings
onion powder
chili powder
dried oregano

Optional
nonfat sour cream

Spray inside of slow cooker with cooking spray. Combine all ingredients except sour cream in slow cooker and mix well. Cover and cook on low heat for 8–9 hours. Serve with a dollop of sour cream, if desired.

Nutrition Facts per serving: 325 cal., 3.6 g total fat, 54 mg chol., 1,335 mg sodium, 41 g carbo., 7 g fiber, 31 g pro.
Exchanges: 2 Vegetable, 2 Starch, 3 Very Lean Meat
Carb Choices: 3

Chicken and Turkey 3

Chicken Fajitas

Superb Chicken Dinner

3½ lbs. boneless, skinless chicken breasts

2 tsp. garlic powder

2 tsp. paprika

pepper to taste

1 10-oz. can low-fat cream of mushroom soup

½ cup dry white wine

Spray inside of slow cooker with cooking spray. Sprinkle chicken with garlic powder, paprika, and pepper. Combine mushroom soup and wine in a small bowl and mix well. Place half the chicken in the slow cooker; pour half the soup mixture over the chicken and repeat. Cover and cook on low heat for 6 hours or high heat for 4 hours.

Nutrition Facts per serving: 288 cal., 2.4 g total fat, 97 mg chol., 257 mg sodium, 4 g carbo., 1 g fiber, 39 g pro.
Exchanges: ½ Other Carbo., 5 Very Lean Meat
Carb Choices: 0

Shopping List

Poultry
3½ lbs. boneless, skinless chicken breasts

Canned
10-oz. can low-fat cream of mushroom soup

Seasonings
garlic powder
paprika
pepper

Other
dry white wine

Slow Cooker Chicken and Vegetables

Easy | **Do Ahead** | **Serves: 6**

- 2 lbs. small red potatoes, *cut in half*
- 1 8-oz. pkg. baby carrots
- ¾ cup chopped onion
- 2 lbs. bone-in chicken breasts, *skin removed*
- 1 14-oz. can nonfat chicken broth
- 1 cup nonfat sour cream
- 3 tbsp. flour

Spray inside of slow cooker with cooking spray. Place potatoes, carrots, and onion in cooker; top with chicken breasts. Pour broth over top. Cover and cook on low heat for 10–12 hours or high heat for 5–6 hours. Combine sour cream and flour in small bowl and mix until blended. Stir mixture into slow cooker. If cooking on low heat, increase to high and cook, uncovered, 5–6 minutes. Serve immediately.

Nutrition Facts per serving: 357 cal., 1.7 g total fat, 74 mg chol., 351 mg sodium, 44 g carbo., 5 g fiber, 37 g pro.
Exchanges: 3 Vegetable, 2 Starch, 3 Very Lean Meat
Carb Choices: 3

Chicken and Turkey

Shopping List

Produce
2 lbs. small red potatoes
8-oz. pkg. baby carrots
large onion

Poultry
2 lbs. bone-in chicken breasts

Dairy
8 oz. nonfat sour cream

Canned
14-oz. can nonfat chicken broth

Baking Goods
flour

Saucy Chicken

1 lb. boneless, skinless
   chicken breasts

2 tbsp. flour

½ tsp. pepper

½ tsp. garlic powder

1 10¾-oz. can low-fat cream
   of chicken soup

1¼ cups nonfat half and half

Spray inside of slow cooker with cooking spray. Place chicken breasts in slow cooker. Combine flour, pepper, and garlic powder; sprinkle flour mixture over chicken and turn chicken to coat. Combine chicken soup and half and half and mix until blended. Pour soup mixture over chicken. Cover and cook on low heat for 4–6 hours.

Nutrition Facts per serving: 219 cal., 2.3 g total fat, 56 mg chol., 370 mg sodium, 20 g carbo., 1 g fiber, 24 g pro.
Exchanges: 1½ Other Carbo., 3 Very Lean Meat
Carb Choices: 1

Shopping List

Poultry
1 lb. boneless, skinless
   chicken breasts

Dairy
12 oz. nonfat half and half

Canned
10¾-oz. can low-fat cream of
   chicken soup

Baking Goods
flour

Seasonings
pepper
garlic powder

Chicken Stroganoff

Easy | **Do Ahead** | **Serves: 6**

1½ lbs. boneless, skinless chicken breasts

1 10¾-oz. can low-fat cream of chicken soup

2 cups nonfat sour cream

¼ cup instant minced onion

2 tbsp. chicken bouillon granules

½ tsp. onion powder

3 cups cooked rice or no-yolk egg noodles

Shopping List

Poultry
1½ lbs. boneless, skinless chicken breasts

Dairy
16 oz. nonfat sour cream

Canned
10¾-oz. can low-fat cream of chicken soup

Packaged
rice or no-yolk egg noodles

Seasonings
instant minced onion
chicken bouillon granules
onion powder

Spray inside of slow cooker with cooking spray. Combine all ingredients in slow cooker and mix well. Cover and cook on low heat for 4–6 hours or high heat for 2–3 hours.

Nutrition Facts per serving: 339 cal., 2.1 g total fat, 56 mg chol., 624 mg sodium, 42 g carbo., 1 g fiber, 31 g pro.
Exchanges: 3 Starch, 3 Very Lean Meat
Carb Choices: 3

Chicken and Turkey

It is not necessary to rinse or wash raw chicken before preparation or cooking. The cooking process will destroy any bacteria that are present.

Chicken and Pasta with Mushroom Sauce

Easy | **Do Ahead** | **Serves: 4**

1 cup frozen chopped onions, *thawed and drained*

3 cups sliced fresh mushrooms

1 lb. chicken breast tenderloins, *cubed*

3 tbsp. flour

½ tsp. pepper

1 tbsp. instant chicken bouillon granules

1½ cups water

1 cup nonfat half and half

3 tbsp. sherry

8 oz. uncooked spaghetti, *broken into small pieces*

2 tbsp. nonfat Parmesan cheese

Spray inside of slow cooker with cooking spray. Combine onions, mushrooms, chicken, flour, pepper, and bouillon granules in slow cooker and toss to mix. Combine water, half and half, and sherry in medium bowl and mix well. Pour sauce over chicken mixture. Cover and cook on low heat for 6–8 hours or high heat for 3–4 hours. Add broken spaghetti and stir to mix; sprinkle with cheese. Cover and cook on high heat for 15–20 minutes.

Nutrition Facts per serving: 424 cal., 2.2 g total fat, 55 mg chol., 326 mg sodium, 62 g carbo., 1 g fiber, 32 g pro.
Exchanges: 3 Vegetable, 3 Starch, 3 Very Lean Meat
Carb Choices: 4

Shopping List

Produce	Packaged
¾ lb. mushrooms	8-oz. pkg. spaghetti
Poultry	**Baking Goods**
1 lb. chicken breast tenderloins	flour
	Seasonings
Dairy	pepper
8 oz. nonfat half and half	instant chicken bouillon granules
nonfat Parmesan cheese	
Frozen	**Other**
12-oz. pkg. frozen chopped onions	sherry

Chicken with Creamy Mushroom Gravy

Easy | Do Ahead | Serves: 6

- 1½ lbs. boneless, skinless chicken breasts
- 1 tsp. garlic powder
- ¾ tsp. onion powder
- 1¾ cups nonfat chicken broth
- 1 10¾-oz. can low-fat cream of mushroom soup
- ¾ cup evaporated skim milk

Spray inside of slow cooker with cooking spray. Place chicken breasts in slow cooker; sprinkle with garlic powder and onion powder. Combine broth, mushroom soup, and evaporated skim milk in bowl and mix well. Pour soup mixture over chicken. Cover and cook on low heat for 8–9 hours.

Nutrition Facts per serving: 172 cal., 2 g total fat, 57 mg chol., 538 mg sodium, 9 g carbo., 1 g fiber, 26 g pro.
Exchanges: ½ Starch, 3 Very Lean Meat
Carb Choices: 1

Chicken and Turkey

Shopping List

Poultry
1½ lbs. boneless, skinless chicken breasts

Canned
14-oz. can nonfat chicken broth
10¾-oz. can low-fat cream of mushroom soup
12-oz. can evaporated skim milk

Seasonings
garlic powder
onion powder

Defrosting Frozen Chicken: Choose from three safe ways to defrost chicken: in the refrigerator, in cold water, or in the microwave. The slowest, safest of these methods is the refrigerator. You'll need to defrost boneless chicken breasts overnight and bone-in parts and whole chickens 1–2 days or longer. Once raw chicken is defrosted, you can keep it in the refrigerator 1–2 days before cooking it. If the chicken you've defrosted in the refrigerator is not used, it can be safely refrozen without cooking first.

Chicken Divan

2 6-oz. pkgs. grilled chicken breast strips, *cut into 1-inch pieces*

½ cup frozen chopped onions, *thawed and drained*

1 10¾-oz. can low-fat cream of celery soup

⅓ cup nonfat mayonnaise

2 tbsp. flour

1 cup chopped celery

1 10-oz. pkg. frozen broccoli florets, *thawed and drained*

½ tsp. curry powder

1 tbsp. lemon juice

Spray inside of slow cooker with cooking spray. Combine all ingredients in slow cooker and mix well. Cover and cook on low heat for 6–8 hours or high heat for 3–4 hours.

Nutrition Facts per serving: 222 cal., 2.9 g total fat, 51 mg chol., 991 mg sodium, 25 g carbo., 4 g fiber, 24 g pro.
Exchanges: 2 Vegetable, 1 Starch, 3 Very Lean Meat
Carb Choices: 2

Shopping List

Produce	**Canned**
small bunch celery	10¾-oz. can low-fat cream of celery soup
Poultry	
2 6-oz. pkgs. grilled chicken breast strips	**Baking Goods**
	flour
Frozen	**Condiments**
12-oz. pkg. frozen chopped onions	nonfat mayonnaise
10-oz. pkg. frozen broccoli florets	lemon juice
	Seasonings
	curry powder

Chicken Tetrazzini

3 cups diced, cooked
  chicken breast

2 10¾-oz. cans low-fat
  cream of mushroom soup

1 cup chopped onion

1 tsp. minced garlic

1½ cups nonfat shredded
  cheddar cheese

  pepper to taste

4 cups cooked spaghetti or
  other pasta or rice

Spray inside of slow cooker with cooking spray. Combine chicken, mushroom soup, onion, minced garlic, cheese, and pepper in slow cooker and mix lightly. Cover and cook on low heat for 4–6 hours. Serve over hot cooked spaghetti or other pasta or rice.

Nutrition Facts per serving: 227 cal., 3.2 g total fat, 35 mg chol., 966 mg sodium, 26 g carbo., 2 g fiber, 22 g pro.
Exchanges: 1½ Starch, 3 Very Lean Meat
Carb Choices: 2

Chicken
and
Turkey

Shopping List

Produce
large onion

Canned
2 10¾-oz. cans low-fat
  cream of mushroom soup

Poultry
1 lb. boneless, skinless
  chicken breast (makes
  3 cups cooked)

Packaged
8-oz. pkg. spaghetti or
  other pasta or rice

Dairy
6 oz. nonfat shredded
  cheddar cheese

Seasonings
minced garlic
pepper

Mushroom Wine-Sauced Chicken

Easy | Do Ahead | Freeze | Serves: 4

- 1 lb. boneless, skinless chicken breasts
- 1 10¾-oz. can low-fat cream of chicken soup
- 1 tbsp. skim milk
- 2 cups sliced fresh mushrooms
- ½ cup frozen chopped onions, *thawed and drained*
- 1 tsp. dried parsley
- ¼ cup dry white wine
- ½ tsp. minced garlic
- ¼ tsp. pepper

Spray inside of slow cooker with cooking spray. Place chicken breasts in slow cooker. Combine remaining ingredients in medium bowl and mix well. Pour mixture over chicken and turn to coat. Cover and cook on low heat for 8–10 hours or high heat for 4–5 hours.

Nutrition Facts per serving: 182 cal., 2.4 g total fat, 57 mg chol., 377 mg sodium, 11 g carbo., 1 g fiber, 24 g pro.
Exchanges: 1 Vegetable, ½ Other Carbo., 3 Very Lean Meat
Carb Choices: 1

Shopping List

Produce
½ lb. sliced mushrooms

Poultry
1 lb. boneless, skinless chicken breasts

Dairy
skim milk

Frozen
12-oz. pkg. frozen chopped onions

Canned
10¾-oz. can low-fat cream of chicken soup

Seasonings
dried parsley
minced garlic
pepper

Other
dry white wine

Creamy Chicken and Vegetables

3 carrots, *sliced*

3 stalks celery, *sliced*

1 large onion, *cut into wedges*

2 6-oz. pkgs. grilled chicken breast strips, *cut into 1-inch pieces*

1 10¾-oz. can low-fat cream of chicken soup

¾ cup nonfat chicken broth

Spray inside of slow cooker with cooking spray. Arrange carrots, celery, and onion in bottom of slow cooker; top with chicken. Combine chicken soup and broth and mix well. Pour over chicken and vegetables and toss to mix. Cover and cook on low heat for 4–6 hours or high heat for 2–3 hours.

Nutrition Facts per serving: 200 cal., 3 g total fat, 51 mg chol., 998 mg sodium, 21 g carbo., 3 g fiber, 23 g pro.
Exchanges: 2 Vegetable, 1 Starch, 2 Very Lean Meat
Carb Choices: 2

Chicken and Turkey

Shopping List

Produce
3 carrots
bunch celery
large onion

Poultry
2 6-oz. pkgs. grilled chicken breast strips

Canned
10¾-oz. can low-fat cream of chicken soup
14-oz. can nonfat chicken broth

Substitution Tip: Low-fat cream soups, including cream of chicken, easily substitute for each other in most recipes. If you have cream of mushroom and the recipe calls for cream of celery, never fear.

Honey-Dijon Chicken

Easy | **Do Ahead** | **Freeze** | **Serves: 8**

2 lbs. boneless, skinless
chicken breasts

1½ tsp. garlic powder

1 tsp. onion powder

2 cups nonfat honey-Dijon
salad dressing

Spray inside of slow cooker with cooking spray. Place chicken in cooker and sprinkle with garlic powder and onion powder; pour salad dressing over chicken. Cover and cook on low heat for 8–10 hours or high heat for 4–5 hours.

Nutrition Facts per serving: 181 cal., 1 g total fat, 55 mg chol., 326 mg sodium, 17 g carbo., 1 g fiber, 22 g pro.
Exchanges: 1 Other Carbo., 3 Very Lean Meat
Carb Choices: 1

Shopping List

Poultry
2 lbs. boneless, skinless
chicken breasts

Condiments
16-oz. bottle nonfat honey-
Dijon salad dressing

Seasonings
garlic powder
onion powder

Poultry Refrigerator Storage Guide

Fresh or ground chicken	1–2 days
Cooked chicken	3–4 days
Chicken broth or gravy	1–2 days
Cooked chicken casseroles, dishes, or soup	3–4 days
Cooked chicken pieces covered with broth or gravy	1–2 days
Cooked chicken nuggets, patties	1–2 days
Chicken salad	3–5 days
Deli-sliced chicken luncheon meat	3–5 days
Chicken luncheon meat sealed in package	2 weeks (no longer than 1 week after sell-by date)
Chicken luncheon meat after opening package	3–5 days
Chicken hot dogs	7 days

Lemon-Pepper Chicken

Easy | Do Ahead | Serves: 6

1½ lbs. boneless, skinless
   chicken breasts
3 tbsp. lemon juice
1½ tsp. pepper
   lemon juice (optional)

Spray inside of slow cooker with cooking spray. Place chicken breasts in slow cooker. Pour lemon juice over chicken and sprinkle with pepper. Cover and cook on low heat for 6–8 hours or high heat for 3–4 hours. Add more lemon juice, if desired.

Nutrition Facts per serving: 112 cal., 1 g total fat, 55 mg chol., 65 mg sodium, 1 g carbo., 0 g fiber, 22 g pro.
Exchanges: 3 Very Lean Meat
Carb Choices: 0

Chicken and Turkey

Shopping List

Produce
2 lemons

Poultry
1½ lbs. boneless, skinless
   chicken breasts

Seasonings
pepper

If you use fresh lemons (1 medium lemon yields 1–3 tablespoons juice and 1–2 teaspoons grated peel), you can add some of the fresh peel to the slow cooker during preparation for added flavor.

Reuben-Style Chicken Casserole

Easy | Do Ahead | Serves: 6

1 32-oz. jar sauerkraut,
rinsed and well drained

1 cup nonfat Russian or
Thousand Island salad
dressing

1½ lbs. boneless, skinless
chicken breasts

1½ tbsp. prepared mustard

6 slices low-fat rye bread,
toasted

1½ cups nonfat shredded
Swiss cheese

Shopping List

Poultry
1½ lbs. boneless, skinless
chicken breasts

Dairy
6 oz. nonfat Swiss cheese

Canned
32-oz. jar sauerkraut

Packaged
low-fat rye bread

Condiments
8-oz. bottle Russian or
Thousand Island dressing
prepared mustard

Spray inside of slow cooker with cooking spray. Place half (about 2 cups) of sauerkraut in bottom of slow cooker. Drizzle ⅓ cup salad dressing over sauerkraut. Place 3 chicken breasts on top; spread mustard over chicken. Top with remaining sauerkraut and chicken breasts. Drizzle another ⅓ cup salad dressing over chicken. Refrigerate remaining salad dressing until ready to serve. Cover and cook on low heat for 7–8 hours or high heat for 3½–4 hours. Just before serving, toast bread. Place a bread slice on each plate. Top with chicken breast, sauerkraut, and sauce. Sprinkle with cheese (¼–½ cup) and 1 tablespoon dressing.

Nutrition Facts per serving: 294 cal., 2.2 g total fat, 55 mg chol., 1,684 mg sodium, 30 g carbo., 5 g fiber, 30 g pro.
Exchanges: 2 Vegetable, 1 Starch, ½ Other Carbo., 3 Very Lean Meat
Carb Choices: 2

Cajun-Ranch Chicken

Easy | **Do Ahead** | **Serves: 6**

2 tbsp. nonfat ranch salad dressing

2 tbsp. skim milk

1½ lbs. boneless, skinless chicken breasts

2 tbsp. onion powder

½ tsp. dried thyme

¼ tsp. garlic salt

¼ tsp. white pepper

¼ tsp. pepper

Shopping List

Poultry
1½ lbs. boneless, skinless chicken breasts

Dairy
skim milk

Condiments
nonfat ranch salad dressing

Seasonings
onion powder
dried thyme
garlic salt
white pepper
pepper

Spray inside of slow cooker with cooking spray. Combine salad dressing and milk in small bowl and mix well. Dip chicken breasts in dressing mixture and place in slow cooker. Mix remaining ingredients and sprinkle over chicken. Cover and cook on low heat for 8–10 hours or high heat for 4–5 hours.

Nutrition Facts per serving: 118 cal., 1 g total fat, 55 mg chol., 113 mg sodium, 1 g carbo., 0 g fiber, 22 g pro.
Exchanges: 3 Very Lean Meat
Carb Choices: 0

Chicken and Turkey

Quick and Easy Italian Chicken

1½ lbs. boneless, skinless chicken breasts

1 26-oz. jar nonfat pasta sauce

¼ cup nonfat Parmesan cheese

Spray inside of slow cooker with cooking spray. Place chicken breasts in slow cooker; pour sauce over top and sprinkle with cheese. Cover and cook on low heat for 6–7 hours or high heat for 3–3½ hours.

Nutrition Facts per serving: 164 cal., 1 g total fat, 55 mg chol., 477 mg sodium, 10 g carbo., 0 g fiber, 25 g pro.
Exchanges: 2 Vegetable, 3 Very Lean Meat
Carb Choices: 1

Shopping List

Poultry
1½ lbs. boneless, skinless chicken breasts

Dairy
nonfat Parmesan cheese

Condiments
26-oz. jar nonfat pasta sauce

If you prefer to use fresh Parmesan cheese instead of the kind that's grated and jarred, buy a block of cheese and use a grater or potato peeler to make Parmesan strips.

Potatoes and Chicken Italian-Style

Easy | Do Ahead | Freeze | Serves: 4

- 1 lb. boneless, skinless chicken breasts
- 1 cup nonfat Italian salad dressing
- 2 tsp. dried Italian seasoning
- 1 cup nonfat Parmesan cheese
- 4 baking potatoes, *cut into wedges*

Spray inside of slow cooker with cooking spray. Place chicken breasts in bottom of slow cooker. Sprinkle half the salad dressing, Italian seasoning, and cheese on top of chicken; top with potatoes and repeat with remaining ingredients. Cover and cook on low heat for 6–8 hours or high heat for 3–4 hours.

Nutrition Facts per serving: 355 cal., 1.1 g total fat, 55 mg chol., 493 mg sodium, 50 g carbo., 4 g fiber, 33 g pro.
Exchanges: 2 Starch, 1 Other Carbo., 3 Very Lean Meat
Carb Choices: 3

Chicken and Turkey

Shopping List

Produce
4 baking potatoes

Poultry
1 lb. boneless, skinless chicken breasts

Dairy
4 oz. nonfat Parmesan cheese

Condiments
8 oz. nonfat Italian salad dressing

Seasoning
dried Italian seasoning

Italian Chicken Breasts

Easy | **Do Ahead** | **Serves: 4**

- 1 10-oz. pkg. frozen Italian-style green beans, *thawed and drained*
- 1 cup fresh mushrooms, *cleaned and quartered*
- 1 small onion, *sliced ¼ inch thick*
- ¾ lb. chicken breast tenderloins, *cut into 1-inch pieces*
- 1 14½-oz. can Italian-recipe stewed tomatoes with oregano and basil, *do not drain*
- 1 6-oz. can Italian tomato paste with roasted garlic
- 1 tsp. dried Italian seasoning
- ¾ tsp. garlic powder
- 2 cups cooked hot fettuccine, spaghetti, or linguine
- ¼ cup nonfat Parmesan cheese (optional)

Spray inside of slow cooker with cooking spray. Arrange green beans, mushrooms, and onion in slow cooker; top with chicken pieces. Combine undrained tomatoes, tomato paste, Italian seasoning, and garlic powder in medium bowl and mix well. Pour tomato mixture over chicken. Cover and cook on low heat for 5–6 hours or high heat for 2½–3 hours. Serve over hot cooked fettuccine, spaghetti, or linguine. Top with 1 tablespoon cheese, if desired.

Nutrition Facts per serving: 297 cal., 1.4 g total fat, 41 mg chol., 654 mg sodium, 41 g carbo., 5 g fiber, 26 g pro.
Exchanges: 2 Vegetable, 2 Starch, 2 Very Lean Meat
Carb Choices: 3

Shopping List

Produce
¼ lb. mushrooms
small onion

Poultry
¾ lb. chicken breast tenderloins

Frozen
10-oz. pkg. frozen Italian-style green beans

Canned
14½-oz. can Italian-recipe stewed tomatoes with oregano and basil

6-oz. can Italian tomato paste with roasted garlic

Packaged
8 oz. fettuccine, spaghetti, or linguine

Seasonings
dried Italian seasoning
garlic powder

Optional
nonfat Parmesan cheese

Chicken Italiano

- 1½ lbs. boneless, skinless chicken breasts
- 1 14½-oz. can petite-cut diced tomatoes with roasted garlic and sweet onion, *do not drain*
- 1 6-oz. can Italian tomato paste with roasted garlic
- 2 cups sliced fresh mushrooms
- ½ tsp. pepper
- 1 tsp. onion powder
- 2 tsp. dried parsley
- ¼ tsp. garlic powder
- ½ tsp. dried thyme
- 2 tsp. dried Italian seasoning
- 1 tbsp. sugar

Spray inside of slow cooker with cooking spray. Place chicken breasts in slow cooker. Combine remaining ingredients in medium bowl and mix well. Pour tomato mixture over chicken breasts and turn to coat. Cover and cook on low heat for 7–9 hours or high heat for 3½–4½ hours.

Nutrition Facts per serving: 168 cal., 1.1 g total fat, 55 mg chol., 432 mg sodium, 11 g carbo., 2 g fiber, 24 g pro.
Exchanges: 2 Vegetable, 3 Very Lean Meat
Carb Choices: 1

Chicken and Turkey

Shopping List

Produce	Baking Goods
½ lb. mushrooms	sugar

Poultry	Seasoning
1½ lbs. boneless, skinless chicken breasts	pepper
	onion powder
	dried parsley
Canned	garlic powder
14½-oz. can petite-cut diced tomatoes with roasted garlic and sweet onion	dried thyme
	dried Italian seasoning
6-oz. can Italian tomato paste with roasted garlic	

Chicken Cacciatore

Easy | Do Ahead | Serves: 8

- 3 lbs. bone-in chicken breasts, *skin removed*
- 1 14-oz. can Italian-style petite-cut diced tomatoes, *do not drain*
- 1 6-oz. can tomato paste
- 1½ tsp. minced garlic
- 1 16-oz. pkg. frozen pepper stir-fry, *thawed and drained*
- ¼ cup dry red wine
- hot cooked rice or pasta (optional)

Spray inside of cooker with cooking spray. Combine all ingredients in slow cooker. Cover and cook on low heat for 6–8 hours. Serve over hot cooked rice or pasta, if desired.

Nutrition Facts per serving: 221 cal., 1.6 g total fat, 83 mg chol., 396 mg sodium, 10 g carbo., 2 g fiber, 32 g pro.
Exchanges: 2 Vegetable, 5 Very Lean Meat
Carb Choices: 1

Shopping List

Poultry
3 lbs. bone-in chicken breasts

Frozen
16-oz. pkg. frozen pepper stir-fry mix

Canned
14-oz. can Italian-style petite-cut diced tomatoes
6-oz. can tomato paste

Seasonings
minced garlic

Other
dry red wine

Optional
rice or pasta

Chicken Curry

1 cup frozen chopped onions, *thawed and drained*

2 cups canned petite-cut diced tomatoes, *drained*

¾ cup frozen chopped green bell peppers, *thawed and drained*

4 cups nonfat chicken broth

1–3 tbsp. curry powder

1 tbsp. ketchup

1½ lbs. boneless, skinless chicken breasts

Spray inside of slow cooker with cooking spray. Combine onions, tomatoes, and bell peppers in slow cooker. Combine broth, curry powder, and ketchup in bowl and mix well. Pour broth mixture over vegetables. Place chicken on top. Cover and cook on low heat for 8–10 hours or high heat for 4–5 hours. Remove chicken and vegetables with slotted spoon. Pour broth into separate bowl and serve on side.

Nutrition Facts per serving: 231 cal., 1.5 g total fat, 83 mg chol., 1,116 mg sodium, 10 g carbo., 1 g fiber, 37 g pro.
Exchanges: 2 Vegetable, 5 Very Lean Meat
Carb Choices: 1

Chicken and Turkey

Shopping List

Poultry	Condiments
1½ lbs. boneless, skinless chicken breasts	ketchup
	Seasonings
Frozen	curry powder
12-oz. pkg. frozen chopped onions	
10-oz. pkg. frozen chopped green bell peppers	
Canned	
28-oz. can petite-cut diced tomatoes	
3 14-oz. cans nonfat chicken broth	

153

Almond Chicken and Rice

2 6-oz. pkgs. honey-roasted chicken breast strips, *diced*

2 cups cooked brown rice

2¼ cups nonfat chicken broth

½ cup toasted sliced almonds

Spray inside of slow cooker with cooking spray. Combine chicken, rice, and broth in slow cooker and mix well. Cover and cook on low heat for 6–8 hours. Top with toasted sliced almonds just before serving.

Nutrition Facts per serving: 305 cal., 7.6 g total fat, 50 mg chol., 944 mg sodium, 31 g carbo., 1 g fiber, 28 g pro.
Exchanges: 2 Starch, 3 Very Lean Meat, 1 Fat
Carb Choices: 2

Shopping List

Poultry
2 6-oz. pkgs. honey-roasted chicken breast strips

Canned
2 14-oz. cans nonfat chicken broth

Packaged
brown rice
sliced almonds

Substitution Tip: Prepare your own diced chicken and freeze in ready-to-use packages. Bake, grill, microwave, or stir-fry boneless, skinless chicken breasts. One pound yields about 3 cups diced chicken.

Apricot-Glazed Chicken

Easy | **Do Ahead** | **Freeze** | **Serves: 6**

1½ lbs. boneless, skinless chicken breasts

1 tsp. garlic powder

¾ tsp. onion powder

1 cup nonfat Catalina salad dressing

1 1.1-oz. packet dry onion soup mix

1 10-oz. jar apricot preserves

Spray inside of slow cooker with cooking spray. Place chicken breasts in slow cooker; sprinkle with garlic powder and onion powder. Combine salad dressing, onion soup mix, and preserves in small bowl and mix well. Pour salad dressing mixture over chicken. Cover and cook over low heat for 6–8 hours.

Nutrition Facts per serving: 307 cal., 1.3 g total fat, 56 mg chol., 825 mg sodium, 48 g carbo., 1 g fiber, 23 g pro.
Exchanges: 3 Other Carbo., 3 Very Lean Meat
Carb Choices: 3

Chicken and Turkey

Shopping List

Poultry
1½ lbs. boneless, skinless chicken breasts

Packaged
1.1-oz. packet onion soup mix

Condiments
8-oz. bottle nonfat Catalina salad dressing
10-oz. jar apricot preserves

Seasonings
garlic powder
onion powder

Easy Chicken Stir-Fry

Easy | Do Ahead | Serves: 6

- 2 lbs. chicken breast tenderloins, *cut into 1½-inch pieces*
- 1 26-oz. jar sweet and sour simmer sauce
- 1 16-oz. pkg. frozen broccoli stir-fry (broccoli, carrots, onions, red peppers, celery, water chestnuts, mushrooms), *thawed and drained*
- 3 cups cooked rice (optional)

Shopping List

Poultry
2 lbs. chicken breast tenderloins

Frozen
16-oz. pkg. frozen broccoli stir-fry

Condiments
26-oz. jar sweet and sour simmer sauce

Optional
rice (instant or regular)

Spray inside of slow cooker with cooking spray. Place chicken in slow cooker; pour sauce over top and toss lightly to mix. Cover and cook on low heat for 8–10 hours. Ten minutes before serving, add vegetables. Cover and increase heat to high; cook 10–15 minutes until vegetables are crisp-tender. Serve over cooked rice, if desired.

Nutrition Facts per serving: 197 cal., 1.3 g total fat, 74 mg chol., 390 mg sodium, 11 g carbo., 1 g fiber, 30 g pro.
Exchanges: 1 Vegetable, ½ Other Carbo., 4 Very Lean Meat
Carb Choices: 1

Sweet and Sour Chicken

Easy | **Do Ahead** | **Serves: 6**

1½ lbs. boneless, skinless chicken breasts

1 16-oz. can pineapple chunks in light syrup, *drained and liquid reserved*

1 14-oz. can nonfat chicken broth

¼ cup vinegar

3 tbsp. brown sugar

1 tsp. minced garlic

2 tsp. low-sodium soy sauce

1 large green bell pepper, *cut into 1-inch pieces*

3 tbsp. cornstarch

¼ cup cold water

Spray inside of slow cooker with cooking spray. Place chicken breasts in slow cooker. Combine pineapple syrup, broth, vinegar, brown sugar, minced garlic, and soy sauce in small saucepan. Cook over medium heat, stirring frequently, until sugar dissolves. Pour mixture over chicken. Cover and cook on high heat for 1 hour. Add pineapple chunks and green bell pepper; cover and cook on low heat for 7–8 hours. Combine cornstarch and water in small bowl and mix until smooth. Add mixture to slow cooker and stir to mix. Cover and cook 30 minutes.

Chicken and Turkey

Nutrition Facts per serving: 283 cal., 0.6 g total fat, 76 mg chol., 566 mg sodium, 34 g carbo., 1 g fiber, 35 g pro.
Exchanges: 3 Vegetable, 1 Other Carbo., 4 Very Lean Meat
Carb Choices: 2

Shopping List

Produce	Baking Goods
large green bell pepper	brown sugar
	cornstarch
Poultry	
1½ lbs. boneless, skinless chicken breasts	**Condiments**
	vinegar
	low-sodium soy sauce
Canned	
16-oz. can pineapple chunks in light syrup	**Seasonings**
	minced garlic
14-oz. can nonfat chicken broth	

Chicken Sesame

Easy | Do Ahead | Serves: 8

¾ cup tomato juice

¼ cup + 2 tbsp. low-sodium soy sauce

¾ cup brown sugar

¾ cup nonfat chicken broth

1½ tbsp. minced garlic

2 tbsp. sesame seeds

2 lbs. boneless, skinless chicken breasts

Spray inside of slow cooker with cooking spray. Combine tomato juice, soy sauce, brown sugar, chicken broth, minced garlic, and sesame seeds in a bowl and mix well. Dip chicken breasts in sauce to coat and place in slow cooker. Pour remaining sauce over top. Cover and cook on low heat for 6–8 hours.

Nutrition Facts per serving: 213 cal., 2.1 g total fat, 55 mg chol., 597 mg sodium, 23 g carbo., 1 g fiber, 24 g pro.
Exchanges: 1½ Other Carbo., 3 Very Lean Meat
Carb Choices: 2

Shopping List

Poultry
2 lbs. boneless, skinless chicken breasts

Canned
6-oz. can tomato juice
14-oz. can nonfat chicken broth

Condiments
low-sodium soy sauce

Baking Goods
brown sugar

Seasonings
minced garlic
sesame seeds

Chicken with Pineapple and Orange

Easy | **Do Ahead** | **Serves: 8**

Ingredients

- 3 lbs. boneless, skinless chicken breasts
- 1 16-oz. can pineapple slices packed in juice, *drained*
- 1 15-oz. can mandarin oranges, *drained*
- ¼ cup cornstarch
- ⅓ cup brown sugar
- 2 tbsp. lemon juice
- ½ tsp. ground cinnamon
- ¼ tsp. ground ginger
- hot cooked rice (optional)

Spray inside of slow cooker with cooking spray. Combine all ingredients in slow cooker and mix well. Cover and cook on low heat for 4–5 hours or high heat for 2–3 hours. Serve over hot cooked rice, if desired.

Nutrition Facts per serving: 285 cal., 1.5 g total fat, 83 mg chol., 106 mg sodium, 30 g carbo., 1 g fiber, 33 g pro.
Exchanges: 1 Fruit, 1 Other Carbo., 4 Very Lean Meat
Carb Choices: 2

Chicken and Turkey

Shopping List

Poultry
3 lbs. boneless, skinless
chicken breasts

Canned
16-oz. can pineapple slices
packed in juice
15-oz. can mandarin
oranges

Baking Goods
cornstarch
brown sugar

Condiments
lemon juice

Seasonings
ground cinnamon
ground ginger

Optional
rice

Orange-Teriyaki Chicken

Easy | **Do Ahead** | **Serves: 4**

1 16-oz. pkg. frozen broccoli stir-fry (broccoli, carrots, onions, red peppers, celery, water chestnuts, mushrooms), *thawed and drained*

2 tbsp. quick-cooking tapioca

1 lb. chicken breast tenderloins, *cut into 1-inch pieces*

½ cup nonfat chicken broth

2 tbsp. brown sugar

2 tbsp. teriyaki sauce

1 tbsp. prepared mustard

1 tsp. finely shredded orange peel

½ tsp. ground ginger

2 cups hot cooked brown rice or couscous

Spray inside of slow cooker with cooking spray. Place vegetables in bottom of slow cooker; sprinkle tapioca over top. Place chicken pieces on top. Combine broth, brown sugar, teriyaki sauce, mustard, orange peel, and ginger in bowl and mix well. Pour broth mixture over chicken pieces. Cover and cook on low heat for 4–6 hours or high heat for 2–3 hours. Serve over hot cooked rice or couscous.

Nutrition Facts per serving: 307 cal., 1.9 g total fat, 55 mg chol., 567 mg sodium, 42 g carbo., 1 g fiber, 27 g pro.
Exchanges: 3 Vegetable, 1 Starch, ½ Other Carbo., 3 Very Lean Meat
Carb Choices: 3

Shopping List

Poultry
1 lb. chicken breast tenderloins

Frozen
16-oz. pkg. frozen broccoli stir-fry

Canned
14-oz. can nonfat chicken broth

Packaged
quick-cooking tapioca
8-oz. pkg. brown rice or couscous

Baking Goods
brown sugar

Condiments
teriyaki sauce
prepared mustard

Seasonings
orange peel
ground ginger

Asian Pineapple Chicken

Easy | **Do Ahead** | **Serves: 4**

- 1½ lbs. chicken breast tenderloins, *cut into 1-inch pieces*
- ⅔ cup pineapple preserves
- 1½ tbsp. teriyaki sauce
- 1 tsp. minced garlic
- 1 tsp. onion powder
- 1 tbsp. orange juice
- ½ tsp. ground ginger
- 1 10-oz. pkg. frozen sugar snap peas, *thawed and drained*
- 1 10-oz. pkg. frozen broccoli florets, *thawed and drained*
- hot cooked rice (optional)

Spray inside of slow cooker with cooking spray. Place chicken pieces in cooker. Combine remaining ingredients except snap peas and broccoli in bowl and mix well. Pour teriyaki mixture over chicken and toss to coat. Cover and cook on low heat for 6–7 hours or high heat for 3–3½ hours. Add snap peas and broccoli during last 30 minutes of cooking. Serve over hot cooked rice, if desired.

Nutrition Facts per serving: 354 cal., 0.6 g total fat, 85 mg chol., 422 mg sodium, 47 g carbo., 2 g fiber, 40 g pro.
Exchanges: 3 Vegetable, 2 Other Carbo., 4 Very Lean Meat
Carb Choices: 3

Chicken and Turkey

Shopping List

Poultry	Condiments
1½ lbs. chicken breast tenderloins	8-oz. jar pineapple preserves
	teriyaki sauce
Frozen	
10-oz. pkg. frozen sugar snap peas	**Seasonings**
10-oz. pkg. frozen broccoli florets	minced garlic
	onion powder
	ground ginger
Refrigerated	**Optional**
orange juice	rice

Variety: For a change of pace, try peach or apricot preserves with broccoli or sliced carrots.

Orange-Pineapple Glazed Chicken

Easy | Do Ahead | Serves: 6

1 6-oz. can frozen orange-pineapple juice concentrate, *thawed*
¼ tsp. dried basil
⅛ tsp. ground nutmeg
⅛ tsp. garlic powder
1½ lbs. boneless, skinless chicken breasts
2 tbsp. cornstarch
¼ cup water

Spray inside of slow cooker with cooking spray. Combine juice concentrate, basil, nutmeg, and garlic powder and mix well. Dip chicken breasts in juice mixture, tossing to coat, and place in slow cooker. Pour remaining juice mixture over chicken. Cover and cook on low heat for 7–9 hours or high heat for 3½–4½ hours. Remove chicken from slow cooker; pour sauce into saucepan. Combine cornstarch and water in small bowl and mix until smooth. Stir cornstarch mixture into saucepan and cook over medium heat, stirring constantly, until sauce becomes thick and bubbly. Serve sauce over chicken.

Nutrition Facts per serving: 185 cal., 1 g total fat, 55 mg chol., 66 mg sodium, 18 g carbo., 0 g fiber, 23 g pro.
Exchanges: 1 Fruit, 3 Very Lean Meat
Carb Choices: 1

Shopping List

Poultry
1½ lbs. boneless, skinless chicken breasts

Frozen
6-oz. can frozen orange-pineapple juice concentrate

Baking Goods
cornstarch

Seasonings
dried basil
ground nutmeg
garlic powder

Orange Chicken with Sweet Potatoes

Easy | Do Ahead | Freeze | Serves: 4

- 3 large sweet potatoes, *cut into ¼-inch slices*
- ⅔ cup flour
- ¾ tsp. ground cinnamon
- 2 tsp. brown sugar
- ⅛ tsp. pepper
- ⅛ tsp. garlic powder
- 1 lb. boneless, skinless chicken breasts
- 1 10¾-oz. can low-fat cream of chicken soup
- ½ cup orange juice

Spray inside of slow cooker with cooking spray. Arrange potato slices in bottom of slow cooker. Combine flour, cinnamon, brown sugar, pepper, and garlic powder in zip-top bag and shake until mixed. Drop chicken breasts in bag and shake to coat with flour mixture; arrange chicken on top of potato slices. Combine chicken soup and orange juice in medium bowl and mix well; pour over chicken and potatoes. Cover and cook on low heat for 8–10 hours or high heat for 4–5 hours.

Nutrition Facts per serving: 341 cal., 2.6 g total fat, 56 mg chol., 380 mg sodium, 49 g carbo., 4 g fiber, 27 g pro.
Exchanges: 2 Starch, 1 Other Carbo., 3 Very Lean Meat
Carb Choices: 3

Chicken and Turkey

Shopping List

Produce
3 large sweet potatoes

Poultry
1 lb. boneless, skinless chicken breasts

Canned
10¾-oz. can low-fat cream of chicken soup

Refrigerated
orange juice

Baking Goods
flour
brown sugar

Seasonings
ground cinnamon
pepper
garlic powder

Ginger Chicken

1 lb. boneless, skinless
chicken breasts

1 cup low-sodium soy sauce

1 cup water

½ cup brown sugar

1½ tsp. ground ginger

Spray inside of slow cooker with cooking spray. Place chicken breasts in slow cooker. Combine remaining ingredients and mix until sugar is dissolved; pour over chicken. Cover and cook on low heat for 4–6 hours.

Nutrition Facts per serving: 249 cal., 1 g total fat, 55 mg chol., 2,474 mg sodium, 33 g carbo., 0 g fiber, 26 g pro.
Exchanges: 2 Other Carbo., 3 Very Lean Meat
Carb Choices: 2

Shopping List

Poultry
1 lb. boneless, skinless chicken
breasts

Baking Goods
brown sugar

Condiments
8 oz. low-sodium soy sauce

Seasonings
ground ginger

Honey-Soy Chicken

Easy | Do Ahead | Serves: 6

1½ lbs. boneless, skinless chicken breasts

½ cup low-sodium soy sauce

¼ cup dry white wine

½ cup water

½ cup chopped green onions

½ cup honey

Spray inside of slow cooker with cooking spray. Place chicken in slow cooker. Combine soy sauce, wine, water, and green onions in small bowl and pour over chicken. Cover and cook on low heat for 4–6 hours. Remove chicken from slow cooker and brush with honey. Top with sauce from slow cooker.

Nutrition Facts per serving: 217 cal., 1 g total fat, 55 mg chol., 867 mg sodium, 25 g carbo., 1 g fiber, 23 g pro.
Exchanges: 1½ Other Carbo., 3 Very Lean Meat
Carb Choices: 2

Chicken and Turkey

Shopping List

Produce
green onions

Poultry
1½ lbs. boneless, skinless chicken breasts

Condiments
low-sodium soy sauce
honey

Other
dry white wine

For crisper glazed chicken, preheat broiler on high heat; line broiler pan with foil and spray with cooking spray. Remove chicken from slow cooker, brush with honey, and place on broiler pan. Broil 3–5 minutes until golden brown. Top with sauce from slow cooker.

165

Garlic-Soy Chicken

1 small onion, *sliced*

2 tsp. garlic powder

¾ cup low-sodium soy sauce

½ cup vinegar

2 lbs. bone-in chicken breasts, *skin removed*

Spray inside of slow cooker with cooking spray. Combine onion, garlic powder, soy sauce, and vinegar in small bowl and mix well. Place chicken breasts in slow cooker and pour soy mixture over chicken. Cover and cook on low heat for 6–8 hours.

Nutrition Facts per serving: 390 cal., 9.8 g total fat, 170 mg chol., 1,917 mg sodium, 10 g carbo., 1 g fiber, 65 g pro.
Exchanges: ½ Other Carbo., 10 Very Lean Meat
Carb Choices: 1

Shopping List

Produce
small onion

Poultry
2 lbs. bone-in chicken breasts

Condiments
low-sodium soy sauce
vinegar

Seasonings
garlic powder

Curry-Dijon Chicken

Easy | **Do Ahead** | **Serves: 6**

1½ lbs. boneless, skinless chicken breasts

¾ cup honey

¾ cup Dijon-style mustard

3 tbsp. low-sodium soy sauce

¼ tsp. + ⅛ tsp. curry powder

3 cups cooked white or brown rice

Shopping List

Poultry
1½ lbs. boneless, skinless chicken breasts

Packaged
12-oz. pkg. white or brown rice

Condiments
honey
Dijon-style mustard
low-sodium soy sauce

Seasonings
curry powder

Spray inside of slow cooker with cooking spray. Combine all ingredients except rice in cooker and turn chicken to coat. Cover and cook on low heat for 8–9 hours. Serve over hot cooked rice.

Nutrition Facts per serving: 467 cal., 4.3 g total fat, 55 mg chol., 819 mg sodium, 81 g carbo., 1 g fiber, 25 g pro.
Exchanges: 2 Starch, 3 Other Carbo., 3 Very Lean Meat
Carb Choices: 5

Chicken and Turkey

You can marinate chicken in the refrigerator for up to 2 days prior to cooking. Boil any used marinade before brushing it on cooked chicken and discard any uncooked leftover marinade.

Apricot-Orange Chicken

Easy | Do Ahead | Serves: 6

1½ lbs. boneless, skinless chicken breasts

1 tsp. garlic powder

½ cup sugar-free apricot preserves

½ cup orange juice

¼ cup dry red wine

2 tbsp. cornstarch

2 tbsp. brown sugar

2 tbsp. lemon juice

3 cups cooked rice or couscous

Spray inside of slow cooker with cooking spray. Place chicken breasts in slow cooker; sprinkle with garlic powder. Combine remaining ingredients in medium bowl and pour over chicken. Cover and cook on low heat for 6–8 hours or high heat for 3–4 hours. Serve over cooked rice or couscous.

Nutrition Facts per serving: 321 cal., 1.3 g total fat, 55 mg chol., 359 mg sodium, 47 g carbo., 2 g fiber, 25 g pro.
Exchanges: 2 Starch, 1 Other Carbo., 3 Very Lean Meat
Carb Choices: 3

Shopping List

Poultry
1½ lbs. boneless, skinless chicken breasts

Canned
4-oz. can orange juice

Packaged
rice or couscous

Baking Goods
cornstarch
brown sugar

Condiments
sugar-free apricot preserves
lemon juice

Seasonings
garlic powder

Other
dry red wine

Catalina-Style Chicken

Easy | **Do Ahead** | **Serves: 4**

1 lb. boneless, skinless
  chicken breasts

1 20-oz. can pineapple
  slices, *drained, juice
  reserved*

1 8-oz. bottle nonfat Catalina
  salad dressing

¼ cup instant minced onion

2 tbsp. instant chicken
  bouillon granules

½ tsp. onion powder

⅛ tsp. lemon pepper

1 medium green bell pepper,
  cut into thin strips

1 tbsp. cornstarch (optional)

1 tbsp. cold water (optional)

Spray inside of slow cooker with cooking spray. Place chicken breasts in slow cooker. Combine reserved pineapple juice, salad dressing, minced onion, bouillon granules, onion powder, and lemon pepper in a medium bowl and mix well. Pour juice mixture over chicken. Cover and cook on low heat for 6–7 hours or high heat for 3–4 hours. Arrange pineapple and bell pepper strips on top of chicken; cook on high heat for 20 minutes until heated through. Remove chicken, pineapple, and bell pepper from slow cooker and arrange on serving platter. If desired, combine cornstarch and water in small bowl and mix until smooth. Add to slow cooker and cook, stirring frequently, until sauce is thickened. Pour sauce over chicken and serve.

Chicken and Turkey

Nutrition Facts per serving: 285 cal., 1.1 g total fat, 55 mg chol., 765 mg sodium, 43 g carbo., 1 g fiber, 23 g pro.
Exchanges: 2 Fruit, 1 Other Carbo., 3 Very Lean Meat
Carb Choices: 3

Shopping List

Produce
medium green bell pepper

Poultry
1 lb. boneless, skinless
  chicken breasts

Canned
20-oz. can pineapple slices

Condiments
8-oz. bottle nonfat Catalina
  salad dressing

Seasonings
instant minced onion
chicken bouillon granules
onion powder
lemon pepper

Optional
cornstarch

Substitution Tip: You can use any nonfat French salad dressing in place of Catalina. Simply add 1 teaspoon garlic powder and increase onion powder to 1 teaspoon.

Turkey and Rice

- 1 lb. extra-lean ground turkey, *browned and drained*
- 1 small onion, *sliced thin*
- ½ cup chopped celery
- 1 tsp. teriyaki sauce
- 1 10¾-oz. can low-fat cream of chicken soup
- 1 cup cooked rice

Spray inside of slow cooker with cooking spray. Combine all ingredients except rice in slow cooker and mix well; cover and cook on low heat for 6 hours or high heat for 3 hours. Add cooked rice, mix, and cook 25–30 minutes.

Nutrition Facts per serving: 247 cal., 3 g total fat, 47 mg chol., 427 mg sodium, 25 g carbo., 2 g fiber, 29 g pro.
Exchanges: 1 Vegetable, 1½ Starch, 3 Very Lean Meat
Carb Choices: 2

Shopping List

Produce
small onion
celery

Poultry
1 lb. extra-lean ground turkey

Canned
10¾-oz. can low-fat cream of chicken soup

Packaged
rice (white or brown)

Condiments
teriyaki sauce

Storing Ground Poultry: Safely store uncooked ground poultry in the refrigerator for 1–2 days or in the freezer for 3–4 months. Cooked ground poultry stays fresh in the refrigerator for 3–4 days and in the freezer for 2–3 months.

Spicy Chicken and Rice

Easy | Do Ahead | Serves: 6

- 2 14-oz. cans nonfat chicken broth
- 1 14½-oz. can stewed tomatoes with bell pepper and onion, *diced*
- 1 cup chopped bell pepper
- ¾ cup chopped sweet onion (Vidalia or Walla Walla)
- 1 14½-oz. can petite-cut diced tomatoes with green chiles, *drained and patted dry*
- 1⅓ cups uncooked rice (not instant)
- 1½ lbs. chicken breast tenderloins, *cut into 1-inch pieces*
- 1 tbsp. minced garlic
- 1 tsp. ground turmeric
- 1 tbsp. paprika
- 1 tsp. dried parsley
- pepper to taste

Spray inside of slow cooker with cooking spray. Combine all ingredients in cooker and mix lightly. Cover and cook on low heat for 6–8 hours.

Nutrition Facts per serving: 312 cal., 1.3 g total fat, 57 mg chol., 1,091 mg sodium, 44 g carbo., 2 g fiber, 31 g pro.
Exchanges: 2 Vegetable, 2 Starch, 3 Very Lean Meat
Carb Choices: 3

What is turmeric? This yellow spice related to ginger has a warm, mellow flavor and is commonly used to prepare mustard, curry powder, and Middle Eastern dishes.

Chicken and Turkey

Shopping List

Produce
large bell pepper
sweet onion (Vidalia or Walla Walla)

Poultry
1½ lbs. chicken breast tenderloins

Canned
2 14-oz. cans nonfat chicken broth
14½-oz. can stewed tomatoes with bell pepper and onion

14½-oz. can petite-cut diced tomatoes with green chiles

Packaged
8 oz. rice (not instant)

Seasonings
minced garlic
ground turmeric
paprika
dried parsley
pepper

Southwest Chicken

Easy | Do Ahead | Serves: 4

1 lb. chicken breast tenderloins, *cut into thin strips*

2 11-oz. cans Mexicorn, drained

1 15-oz. can black beans, *rinsed and well drained*

1 tsp. ground cumin

2 tsp. chili powder

1 large onion, *cut into thin wedges*

1 large green bell pepper, *cut into thin strips*

1 14½-oz. can petite-cut diced tomatoes with green chiles, *do not drain*

1 6-oz. can Italian tomato paste with roasted garlic

Spray inside of slow cooker with cooking spray. Combine all ingredients in slow cooker and mix well. Cover and cook on low heat for 4½–5 hours.

Nutrition Facts per serving: 417 cal., 2 g total fat, 57 mg chol., 1,705 mg sodium, 64 g carbo., 10 g fiber, 38 g pro.
Exchanges: 3 Vegetable, 3 Starch, 3 Very Lean Meat
Carb Choices: 4

Serving Tip: Serve Southwest Chicken in warmed tortillas, tossed with mixed greens, or as a topping for baked potatoes, sweet potatoes, cooked rice, couscous, or pasta.

Shopping List

Produce
large onion
large green bell pepper

Poultry
1 lb. chicken breast tenderloins

Canned
2 11-oz. cans Mexicorn
15-oz. can black beans
14½-oz. can petite-cut diced tomatoes with green chiles

6-oz. can Italian tomato paste with roasted garlic

Seasonings
ground cumin
chili powder

Chicken Tacos

Easy | Do Ahead | Serves: 4

1 lb. boneless, skinless
   chicken breasts

1 1.25-oz. pkg. taco
   seasoning mix

1 cup water
   low-fat corn or flour tortillas

   shredded lettuce,
   tomatoes, nonfat
   shredded cheddar cheese,
   nonfat sour cream, and/or
   salsa (optional)

Spray inside of slow cooker with cooking spray. Combine chicken, taco seasoning mix, and water and mix well. Cover and cook on low heat for 6–8 hours or high heat for 3–4 hours. Remove chicken and shred with 2 forks. Serve in hard or soft tortillas and garnish with lettuce, tomatoes, cheese, sour cream, and/or salsa, as desired.

Nutrition Facts per serving: 144 cal., 1 g total fat, 55 mg chol., 859 mg sodium, 4 g carbo., 0 g fiber, 22 g pro.
Exchanges: 4 Very Lean Meat
Carb Choices: 0

Chicken
and
Turkey

Shopping List

Poultry
1 lb. boneless, skinless
   chicken breasts

Packaged
low-fat corn or flour tortillas

Seasonings
1.25-oz. pkg. taco seasoning
   mix

Optional
shredded lettuce
tomatoes
nonfat shredded cheddar
   cheese
nonfat sour cream
salsa

Soft Chicken Tacos

Easy | Do Ahead | Serves: 6

1¼ lbs. boneless, skinless chicken breasts

1 1.25-oz. pkg. taco seasoning mix

1 tbsp. brown sugar

1 4-oz. can diced green chiles, *do not drain*

1 cup canned Mexicorn, *drained*

1 10-oz. can enchilada sauce, *divided*

6 98% fat-free flour tortillas

3 cups shredded lettuce

¾ cup chopped tomato

¾ cup nonfat shredded cheddar cheese

Spray inside of slow cooker with cooking spray. Place chicken breasts in slow cooker; sprinkle with taco seasoning mix and brown sugar and toss to coat. Combine undrained green chiles, Mexicorn, and ½ cup enchilada sauce (refrigerate remaining sauce) in medium bowl and mix well. Pour chile mixture over chicken. Cover and cook on low heat for 6–7 hours or high heat for 3–3½ hours. Remove chicken from cooker; shred chicken with 2 forks. Return chicken to cooker. If cooking on high heat, decrease to low. Cover and cook on low heat for 15–20 minutes. Heat reserved enchilada sauce in microwave or on stovetop. Wrap tortillas in foil and bake in 350° oven for 5–8 minutes until heated through, or wrap in paper towels and microwave 45–60 seconds until warm. Fill tortillas with chicken mixture and garnish with lettuce, tomato, and cheese. Drizzle with warmed enchilada sauce and serve.

Shopping List

Produce
8-oz. pkg. shredded lettuce
large tomato

Poultry
1¼ lbs. boneless, skinless chicken breasts

Dairy
nonfat shredded cheddar cheese

Canned
4-oz. can diced green chiles

11-oz. can Mexicorn
10-oz. can enchilada sauce

Packaged
17.5-oz. pkg. 98% fat-free flour tortillas

Baking Goods
brown sugar

Seasonings
1.25-oz. pkg. taco seasoning mix

Nutrition Facts per serving: 320 cal., 1.7 g total fat, 46 mg chol., 1,713 mg sodium, 42 g carbo., 4 g fiber, 28 g pro.
Exchanges: 1 Vegetable, 2 Starch, ½ Other Carbo., 3 Very Lean Meat
Carb Choices: 3

Chicken Fajitas

- 4 large bell peppers, *cut into thin strips*
- 2 medium onions, *peeled and cut into thin wedges*
- 1½ lbs. chicken breast tenderloins, *cut into thin strips*
- 1 tsp. ground cumin
- 2½ tsp. chili powder
- ¾ tsp. garlic powder
- ½ tsp. paprika
- ¼ tsp. pepper
- ⅛ tsp. cayenne pepper
- ¼ cup + 2 tbsp. lime juice, *divided*
- 4 98% fat-free flour tortillas
- shredded lettuce, chopped tomato, nonfat shredded cheddar cheese, nonfat sour cream, salsa (optional)

Spray inside of slow cooker with cooking spray. Combine pepper strips and onions in bottom of slow cooker. Combine chicken strips, cumin, chili powder, garlic powder, paprika, pepper, cayenne pepper, and ¼ cup lime juice in zip-top bag and shake to mix. Pour chicken mixture into slow cooker, scraping any remaining seasonings from bag over chicken. Cover and cook on low heat for 2 hours. Stir mixture; cover and cook 1 hour longer. Stir in remaining lime juice and heat through. Just before serving, wrap tortillas in foil and warm in 350° oven for about 10 minutes or until heated through, or wrap in paper towels and microwave for 45–60 seconds until warm. Fill tortillas with chicken mixture and garnish with lettuce, tomato, cheese, sour cream, and salsa, as desired.

Chicken and Turkey

Nutrition Facts per serving: 339 cal., 2.4 g total fat, 83 mg chol., 442 mg sodium, 37 g carbo., 4 g fiber, 39 g pro.
Exchanges: 4 Vegetable, 1 Starch, 4 Very Lean Meat
Carb Choices: 2

Shopping List

Produce	Packaged	pepper
4 large bell peppers	17.5-oz. pkg. 98%	cayenne pepper
2 medium onions	fat-free flour	
lime juice	tortillas	**Optional**
		lettuce, tomato,
Poultry	**Seasonings**	nonfat shredded
1½ lbs. chicken	ground cumin	cheddar cheese,
breast tenderloins	chili powder	nonfat sour cream,
	garlic powder	salsa
	paprika	

Chicken Enchiladas

Easy | **Do Ahead** | **Freeze** | **Serves: 8**

2 10-oz. cans low-fat enchilada sauce

4 6-oz. pkgs. cooked chicken breast cuts, *chopped*

1 tsp. Mexican seasoning

1 cup nonfat sour cream

3 tbsp. diced green chiles, *drained*

2 cups nonfat shredded cheddar cheese

8 98% fat-free flour tortillas, *torn into quarters*

low-fat enchilada sauce (optional)

Spray inside of slow cooker with cooking spray. Combine enchilada sauce, chicken, Mexican seasoning, sour cream, and green chiles and mix well. Spread a quarter of the chicken mixture on bottom of slow cooker; top with a quarter of the cheese and 2–3 tortillas. Repeat process, ending with chicken mixture on top. Cover and cook on low heat for 2–2½ hours. Serve warm with additional enchilada sauce, if desired.

Nutrition Facts per serving: 315 cal., 3.1 g total fat, 60 mg chol., 1,858 mg sodium, 31 g carbo., 3 g fiber, 36 g pro.
Exchanges: 1 Starch, 1 Other Carbo., 5 Very Lean Meat
Carb Choices: 2

Shopping List

Poultry
4 6-oz. pkgs. cooked chicken breast cuts

Dairy
8 oz. nonfat sour cream
8 oz. nonfat shredded cheddar cheese

Canned
2 10-oz. cans low-fat enchilada sauce
4-oz. can diced green chiles

Packaged
17.5-oz. pkg. 98% fat-free flour tortillas

Seasonings
Mexican seasoning

Optional
low-fat enchilada sauce

Tex-Mex Chicken

Easy | Do Ahead | Freeze | Serves: 6

- 1 15-oz. can black beans, *rinsed and drained*
- 2 11-oz. cans Mexicorn, *drained*
- 1 cup thick and chunky salsa
- 1½ lbs. boneless, skinless chicken breasts
- 1 cup nonfat shredded cheddar cheese

Spray inside of slow cooker with cooking spray. Combine beans, Mexicorn, and ½ cup salsa in slow cooker and mix well. Top with chicken breasts and pour remaining salsa over top. Cover and cook on low heat for 5–6 hours or high heat for 2½–3 hours. If cooking on low heat, increase to high. Sprinkle cheese on top; cover and cook about 5–10 minutes until cheese is melted.

Nutrition Facts per serving: 293 cal., 1.7 g total fat, 55 mg chol., 1,094 mg sodium, 34 g carbo., 5 g fiber, 35 g pro.
Exchanges: 2 Starch, 4 Very Lean Meat
Carb Choices: 2

Chicken and Turkey

Shopping List

Poultry
1½ lbs. boneless, skinless chicken breasts

Dairy
4 oz. nonfat shredded cheddar cheese

Canned
15-oz. can black beans
2 11-oz. cans Mexicorn

Condiments
8-oz. jar thick and chunky salsa

Any poultry labeled "Fresh" means the product has not been in conditions below 26°F. Raw poultry held at 0°F or below must be labeled "Frozen" or "Previously Frozen." According to the USDA, no specific labeling is required on raw poultry stored at temperatures between 0°F and 25°F.

Chipotle Chicken and Rice

Easy | Do Ahead | Serves: 4

- 1¼ lbs. boneless, skinless chicken breasts
- 1 tsp. garlic powder
- ½ tsp. Mexican seasoning
- 1 16-oz. pkg. frozen pepper stir-fry, *thawed and drained*
- 1 cup Mexicorn, *drained*
- 1 14½-oz. can stewed tomatoes with bell pepper and onion, *do not drain*
- 1 14-oz. can nonfat chicken broth
- 2 tbsp. canned chipotle chiles in adobo sauce, *chopped*
- 2 cups hot cooked rice

Spray nonstick skillet with cooking spray and heat over medium heat. Sprinkle chicken breasts with garlic powder and Mexican seasoning. Cook chicken breasts in skillet over medium heat, turning frequently, until browned on both sides. Spray inside of slow cooker with cooking spray. Combine chicken, pepper stir-fry, Mexicorn, undrained tomatoes, broth, and chopped chiles in cooker and mix well. Cover and cook on low heat for 5–6 hours. Serve with hot cooked rice.

Nutrition Facts per serving: 372 cal., 2.1 g total fat, 69 mg chol., 952 mg sodium, 51 g carbo., 5 g fiber, 35 g pro.
Exchanges: 4 Vegetable, 2 Starch, 3 Very Lean Meat
Carb Choices: 3

Shopping List

Poultry
1¼ lbs. boneless, skinless chicken breasts

Frozen
16-oz. pkg. frozen pepper stir-fry

Canned
11-oz. can Mexicorn
14½-oz. can stewed tomatoes with bell pepper and onion
14-oz. can nonfat chicken broth

7-oz. can chipotle chiles in adobo sauce

Packaged
rice (instant or regular)

Seasonings
garlic powder
Mexican seasoning

Chicken Tortilla Strata

Easy | Do Ahead | Serves: 6

- 1½ lbs. chicken breast tenderloins, *cut into bite-size pieces*
- 1 10¾-oz. can low-fat cream of chicken soup
- ½ cup Pace Mexican Creations Verde with Tomatillos and Jalapeños Sauce or other green chile salsa or other salsa
- 1 tbsp. cornstarch
- 1 8.5-oz. pkg. low-fat white corn tortillas, *torn into bite-size pieces*
- ¾ cup chopped onion
- 1½ cups nonfat shredded cheddar cheese

Spray inside of slow cooker with cooking spray. Combine chicken, chicken soup, salsa, and cornstarch in large bowl and mix well. Line bottom of cooker with a third of tortillas; top with a third of chicken mixture. Sprinkle with ¼ cup onion and ½ cup cheese. Repeat layers, ending with cheese. Cover and cook on low heat for 6–8 hours.

Nutrition Facts per serving: 287 cal., 1.3 g total fat, 58 mg chol., 780 mg sodium, 31 g carbo., 3 g fiber, 37 g pro.
Exchanges: 2 Starch, 4 Very Lean Meat
Carb Choices: 2

Chicken and Turkey

Shopping List

Produce	Packaged
large onion	8.5-oz. pkg. low-fat white corn tortillas
Poultry	
1½ lbs. chicken breast tenderloins	**Baking Goods**
	cornstarch
Dairy	**Condiments**
6 oz. nonfat shredded cheddar cheese	14-oz. jar Pace Mexican Creations Verde with Tomatillos and Jalapeños Sauce, green chile salsa, or other salsa
Canned	
10¾-oz. can low-fat cream of chicken soup	

Santa Fe Chicken

1 15-oz. can black beans, *rinsed and drained*

3 11-oz. cans Mexicorn, *drained*

1 cup thick and chunky salsa

2 lbs. boneless, skinless chicken breasts

½ tsp. Mexican seasoning

1½ cups nonfat shredded cheddar cheese

Spray inside of slow cooker with cooking spray. Combine beans, Mexicorn, and ½ cup salsa in cooker and mix well. Top with chicken breasts; sprinkle with Mexican seasoning and pour remaining salsa over chicken. Cover and cook on high heat for 2½–3 hours. Sprinkle cheese over top; cover and cook about 5 minutes.

Nutrition Facts per serving: 385 cal., 2.4 g total fat, 74 mg chol., 1,409 mg sodium, 44 g carbo., 6 g fiber, 46 g pro.
Exchanges: 1 Vegetable, 2½ Starch, 5 Very Lean Meat
Carb Choices: 3

Shopping List

Poultry
2 lbs. boneless, skinless chicken breasts

Dairy
6 oz. nonfat shredded cheddar cheese

Canned
15-oz. can black beans
3 11-oz. cans Mexicorn

Condiments
8-oz. bottle thick and chunky salsa

Seasonings
Mexican seasoning

Southwest-Style Turkey Loaf

Easy | Do Ahead | Serves: 6

1 cup chunky-style salsa

¼ cup + 2 tbsp. egg
  substitute

¼ tsp. pepper

½ tsp. Mrs. Dash seasoning

1¾ lbs. extra-lean ground
  turkey

Spray inside of slow cooker with cooking spray; place rack on bottom of cooker. Combine all ingredients in medium bowl and mix well. Shape into a 6- or 8-inch round loaf. Place turkey loaf on rack. Cover and cook on low heat for 4–5 hours.

Nutrition Facts per serving: 160 cal., 1.7 g total fat, 53 mg chol., 349 mg sodium, 2 g carbo., 1 g fiber, 33 g pro.
Exchanges: ½ Vegetable, 4 Very Lean Meat
Carb Choices: 0

Chicken
and
Turkey

Shopping List

Poultry
1¾ lbs. extra-lean ground
  turkey

Dairy
egg substitute

Condiments
8 oz. chunky-style salsa

Seasonings
pepper
Mrs. Dash seasoning

Substitution Tip: For many recipes, it's perfectly acceptable to substitute ground poultry for ground beef or use a combination of both. Always make sure it is cooked safely. Patties and loaves made of ground poultry or a combination of poultry and beef or pork must reach a temperature of 165°F. After cooking, refrigerate leftovers immediately. Divide into small portions for fast cooling.

Barbecue Chicken

- 2 lbs. boneless, skinless chicken breasts
- 1½ tsp. garlic powder
- 1 tsp. onion powder
- 1 18-oz. bottle barbecue sauce

Spray inside of slow cooker with cooking spray. Place chicken breasts in cooker and sprinkle with garlic powder and onion powder. Pour barbecue sauce over chicken. Cover and cook on low heat for 7–8 hours.

Nutrition Facts per serving: 215 cal., 2.8 g total fat, 74 mg chol., 779 mg sodium, 12 g carbo., 1 g fiber, 31 g pro.
Exchanges: 1 Other Carbo., 4 Very Lean Meat
Carb Choices: 1

Shopping List

Poultry
2 lbs. boneless, skinless chicken breasts

Condiments
18-oz. bottle barbecue sauce

Seasonings
garlic powder
onion powder

Serving Tip: Need a quick fix after work? Toss a package of garden salad with your favorite nonfat salad dressing. Microwave a package of frozen corn on the cob in minutes and dinner's ready!

Honey Barbecue Chicken Tenders

Easy | Do Ahead | Serves: 6

2 lbs. chicken breast
   tenderloins
1½ cups bottled barbecue
   sauce
¼ cup honey
2 tsp. prepared mustard
1½ tsp. Worcestershire sauce

Spray inside of slow cooker with cooking spray. Arrange chicken breast tenderloins in slow cooker. Combine remaining ingredients in medium bowl and mix well. Pour barbecue mixture over chicken. Cover and cook on low heat for 4–5 hours or high heat for 2–2½ hours.

Nutrition Facts per serving: 238 cal., 1.7 g total fat, 76 mg chol., 794 mg sodium, 21 g carbo., 1 g fiber, 35 g pro.
Exchanges: 1½ Other Carbo., 4 Very Lean Meat
Carb Choices: 1

Chicken
and
Turkey

Shopping List

Poultry
2 lbs. chicken breast
   tenderloins

Condiments
12-oz. bottle barbecue sauce
honey
prepared mustard
Worcestershire sauce

Orange-Pineapple Barbecue Chicken

2 lbs. boneless, skinless chicken breasts
1 tsp. garlic powder
¾ tsp. onion powder
1 cup barbecue sauce
¼ cup orange-pineapple juice

Spray inside of slow cooker with cooking spray. Place chicken breasts in cooker; sprinkle with garlic powder and onion powder. Combine barbecue sauce and juice and mix well. Pour barbecue mixture over chicken. Cover and cook on low heat for 8–9 hours.

Nutrition Facts per serving: 140 cal., 1.5 g total fat, 55 mg chol., 320 mg sodium, 5 g carbo., 1 g fiber, 23 g pro.
Exchanges: ½ Other Carbo., 3 Very Lean Meat
Carb Choices: 0

Shopping List

Poultry
2 lbs. boneless, skinless chicken breasts

Refrigerated
orange-pineapple juice

Condiments
8 oz. barbecue sauce

Seasonings
garlic powder
onion powder

Hot and Spicy Tenders

Easy | **Do Ahead** | **Freeze** | **Serves: 16**

4 lbs. chicken breast
   tenderloins

½ cup cider vinegar

1 tbsp. Tabasco sauce

1 cup barbecue sauce

nonfat ranch salad dressing

celery sticks

Spray inside of slow cooker with cooking spray. Place chicken tenderloins in slow cooker. Top with cider vinegar, Tabasco sauce, and barbecue sauce. Cover and cook on low heat for 6 hours or high heat for 3 hours. Serve with nonfat ranch salad dressing and celery sticks.

Nutrition Facts per serving: 121 cal., 0.7 g total fat, 57 mg chol., 319 mg sodium, 3 g carbo., 1 g fiber, 26 g pro.
Exchanges: 4 Very Lean Meat
Carb Choices: 0

Chicken
and
Turkey

Shopping List

Produce
bunch celery

Poultry
4 lbs. chicken breast
   tenderloins

Condiments
cider vinegar
Tabasco sauce
barbecue sauce
nonfat ranch salad dressing

Turkey Joes

1½ lbs. extra-lean ground turkey

1 tsp. onion powder

1 tsp. minced garlic

2 cups frozen seasoning vegetables, *thawed and drained*

⅓ cup ketchup

4 tsp. tomato paste with roasted garlic

1 tsp. cider vinegar

2 tsp. molasses

1 tsp. Worcestershire sauce

1 tsp. chili powder

¼ tsp. paprika

1 cup water

6 whole wheat buns or whole wheat pita breads

Spray large nonstick skillet with cooking spray. Add ground turkey, onion powder, minced garlic, and seasoning vegetables to skillet. Cook over medium heat, stirring frequently, until turkey is browned and crumbled and vegetables are softened. Drain well. Spray inside of slow cooker with cooking spray. Combine ketchup, tomato paste, vinegar, molasses, Worcestershire sauce, chili powder, and paprika in slow cooker and mix well. Add turkey mixture and water; toss to mix. Cover and cook on low heat for 6–8 hours or high heat for 3–4 hours. Serve on whole wheat buns or whole wheat pita breads.

Nutrition Facts per serving: 153 cal., 1.5 g total fat, 46 mg chol., 270 mg sodium, 8 g carbo., 1 g fiber, 27 g pro.
Exchanges: 2 Vegetable, 3 Very Lean Meat
Carb Choices: 1

Shopping List

Poultry
1½ lbs. extra-lean ground turkey

Frozen
10-oz. pkg. frozen seasoning vegetables

Canned
6-oz. can tomato paste with roasted garlic

Packaged
6 whole wheat buns or whole wheat pita breads

Condiments
ketchup
cider vinegar
molasses
Worcestershire sauce

Seasonings
onion powder
minced garlic
chili powder
paprika

Sweet and Sour Turkey Meatballs

Easy | Do Ahead | Serves: 6

- 1 lb. extra-lean ground turkey
- ¼ cup egg substitute
- ½ cup seasoned bread crumbs
- 2 tbsp. skim milk
- 1 10-oz. bottle sweet and sour sauce
- ⅓ cup unsweetened pineapple juice
- ⅓ cup brown sugar
- ¼ tsp. ground ginger
- ⅛ tsp. ground cinnamon

Combine turkey, egg substitute, bread crumbs, and milk in medium bowl and mix well; shape into 1-inch meatballs. Spray nonstick skillet with cooking spray and heat over medium-high heat. Add turkey meatballs to skillet and cook until browned on all sides. Combine remaining ingredients in slow cooker and mix well. Add browned turkey meatballs; stir to coat with sauce. Cover and cook on low heat for 4–5 hours or high heat for 2–2½ hours.

Nutrition Facts per serving: 218 cal., 1.4 g total fat, 30 mg chol., 269 mg sodium, 31 g carbo., 1 g fiber, 20 g pro.
Exchanges: 2 Other Carbo., 2 Very Lean Meat
Carb Choices: 2

Chicken and Turkey

Shopping List

Poultry
1 lb. extra-lean ground turkey

Dairy
egg substitute
skim milk

Canned
6 oz. unsweetened pineapple juice

Packaged
seasoned bread crumbs

Baking Goods
brown sugar

Condiments
10-oz. bottle sweet and sour sauce

Seasonings
ground ginger
ground cinnamon

Cranberry Chicken

Easy | Do Ahead | Serves: 6

1 cup sliced onion

1½ lbs. boneless, skinless chicken breasts

1 cup whole-berry cranberry sauce

1 tbsp. beef bouillon granules

1 tsp. white vinegar

1 tsp. prepared mustard

Spray inside of slow cooker with cooking spray. Place onion on bottom of slow cooker; place chicken breasts on top. Combine remaining ingredients and mix well. Spoon cranberry mixture over chicken and onion and coat well. Cover and cook on low heat for 6–8 hours or high heat for 3–4 hours.

Nutrition Facts per serving: 159 cal., 1.1 g total fat, 55 mg chol., 371 mg sodium, 9 g carbo., 1 g fiber, 25 g pro.
Exchanges: 1 Fruit, 3 Very Lean Meat
Carb Choices: 1

Shopping List

Produce
large onion

Poultry
1½ lbs. boneless, skinless chicken breasts

Canned
16-oz. can whole-berry cranberry sauce

Condiments
white vinegar
prepared mustard

Seasonings
beef bouillon granules

You can defrost frozen chicken in the microwave oven, but it MUST be cooked immediately after thawing, as some areas may become warm and begin to cook during microwaving. The time required to thaw chicken in the microwave depends on the quantity. Any foods you defrost in the microwave must be cooked before refreezing.

Festive Stuffed Turkey Breast

Easy | **Do Ahead** | **Serves: 10**

1 5-lb. boneless turkey breast

1½ tsp. Mrs. Dash seasoning

4 cups cooked wild rice

¾ cup chopped onion

½ cup Craisins

2 apples, *cored, peeled, and chopped*

Spray inside of slow cooker with cooking spray. Place turkey breast in slow cooker and sprinkle with Mrs. Dash seasoning. Combine wild rice, onion, Craisins, and apples in large bowl and mix well. Spoon wild rice mixture around turkey. Cover and cook on low heat for 8–9 hours or high heat for 4–5 hours.

Nutrition Facts per serving: 346 cal., 1.1 g total fat, 136 mg chol., 106 mg sodium, 24 g carbo., 2 g fiber, 59 g pro.
Exchanges: ½ Fruit, 1 Starch, 7 Very Lean Meat
Carb Choices: 2

Chicken and Turkey

Shopping List

Produce
large onion
2 apples

Poultry
5-lb. boneless turkey breast

Packaged
8-oz. pkg. wild rice
6-oz. pkg. Craisins

Seasonings
Mrs. Dash seasoning

Vegetable-Stuffed Turkey Breast

Easy | **Do Ahead** | **Serves: 10**

- 1 6½-lb. bone-in turkey breast
- 1¼ cups frozen seasoning vegetables, *thawed and drained*
- 1 bay leaf
- ½ tsp. pepper
- ½ cup nonfat chicken broth

Spray inside of slow cooker with cooking spray. Remove any packets or parts from turkey breast cavity. Place seasoning vegetables and bay leaf in body cavity of turkey. Place turkey breast in slow cooker; sprinkle with pepper. Drizzle chicken broth over turkey. Cover and cook on low heat for 7–8 hours or high heat for 3–4 hours.

Nutrition Facts per serving: 402 cal., 2.1 g total fat, 245 mg chol., 196 mg sodium, 1 g carbo., 1 g fiber, 89 g pro.
Exchanges: 12 Very Lean Meat
Carb Choices: 0

Shopping List

Poultry
6½-lb. bone-in turkey breast

Frozen
12-oz. pkg. frozen seasoning vegetables

Canned
14-oz. can nonfat chicken broth

Seasonings
bay leaf
pepper

What's the difference between fresh and frozen turkey? Frozen turkeys are flash-frozen immediately after processing and held at that temperature until they are packaged. Fresh turkeys are deep-chilled after packaging. Since they have a shorter shelf life, they are generally more expensive.

Herbed Turkey Breast

- 2 onions, *thinly sliced*
- 2 cups chopped celery
- 12 baby carrots
- 2 tbsp. chopped garlic
- 1 4-lb. boneless turkey breast
- 1 14-oz. can nonfat chicken broth
- ½ cup dry white wine
- 1 tbsp. dried rosemary
- ⅛ tsp. dried sage
- ⅛ tsp. dried thyme
- ⅛ tsp. dried marjoram
- ⅛ tsp. dried oregano
- ⅛ tsp. pepper

Spray inside of slow cooker with cooking spray. Place onions, celery, carrots, and garlic on bottom of cooker. Place turkey breast on top of vegetables. Combine broth, wine, and seasonings in medium bowl and mix well. Pour broth mixture over turkey breast. Cover and cook on low heat for 5–7 hours or high heat for 3–4 hours.

Nutrition Facts per serving: 346 cal., 1.9 g total fat, 188 mg chol., 314 mg sodium, 6 g carbo., 2 g fiber, 70 g pro.
Exchanges: 1 Vegetable, 9½ Very Lean Meat
Carb Choices: 0

Chicken and Turkey

Shopping List

Produce	Seasonings
2 onions	dried rosemary
small bunch celery	dried sage
8-oz. pkg. baby carrots	dried thyme
4-oz. jar chopped garlic	dried marjoram
	dried oregano
Poultry	pepper
4-lb. boneless turkey breast	
	Other
	dry white wine
Canned	
14-oz. can nonfat chicken broth	

Some of the most popular seasonings for poultry are basil, rosemary, sage, tarragon, and thyme.

Cranberry Turkey

- 1 1½-lb. boneless turkey breast portion
- 1 16-oz. can cranberry sauce
- ¼ cup dried minced onion
- 2 tbsp. instant beef bouillon granules
- ½ tsp. onion powder

Spray inside of slow cooker with cooking spray. Place turkey breast in cooker. Combine remaining ingredients and pour over turkey. Cover and cook on high heat for 2 hours. Reduce heat to low and cook for 4–5 hours. Remove turkey breast; thinly slice and serve with cranberry mixture.

Nutrition Facts per serving: 281 cal., 0.9 g total fat, 94 mg chol., 382 mg sodium, 33 g carbo., 1 g fiber, 35 g pro.
Exchanges: 2 Other Carbo., 5 Very Lean Meat
Carb Choices: 2

Shopping List

Poultry
1½-lb. boneless turkey breast portion

Canned
16-oz. can cranberry sauce

Seasonings
dried minced onion
instant beef bouillon granules
onion powder

Are you unsure how big your holiday turkey should be? When buying a whole turkey, purchase 1 lb. of turkey per person to be served. This allows for ample portions of the holiday meal and enough for a leftover meal, too.

Marinated Turkey Roast

Easy | Do Ahead | Serves: 6

1 2½-lb. boneless turkey breast portion

⅓ cup lemon juice

1 tbsp. grated lemon peel

1 tsp. dried rosemary

1 tsp. dried oregano

2 tbsp. Dijon mustard

½ cup dry white wine

2 tsp. minced garlic

pepper to taste

Shopping List

Produce
2 lemons

Poultry
2½-lb. boneless turkey breast portion

Condiments
Dijon mustard

Seasonings
dried rosemary
dried oregano
minced garlic
pepper

Other
dry white wine

Place turkey skin side down in a nonmetallic dish. Combine remaining ingredients in small bowl and mix well; pour mixture over turkey. Cover and refrigerate several hours or overnight. Spray inside of slow cooker with cooking spray. Place turkey in slow cooker and pour marinade over top. Cover and cook on low heat for 6–8 hours.

Nutrition Facts per serving: 288 cal., 1.8 g total fat, 157 mg chol., 174 mg sodium, 5 g carbo., 1 g fiber, 57 g pro.
Exchanges: 8 Very Lean Meat
Carb Choices: 0

Chicken and Turkey

Handling Raw Turkey: Cook fresh turkey within 2 days or freeze it!

Turkey and Stuffing

Easy | Do Ahead | Serves: 6

- 1 tbsp. + ¼ cup nonfat chicken broth, *divided*
- ¾ cup frozen chopped onions, *thawed and drained*
- 2 tbsp. apple jelly
- 1 6-oz. pkg. one-step seasoned stuffing mix
- ½ cup water
- 1 2-lb. boneless turkey breast portion
- ½ tsp. pepper

Spray medium nonstick skillet with cooking spray. Add 1 tablespoon broth and heat over medium-high heat. Add onions to skillet and cook, stirring frequently, until onions are lightly browned. Add jelly and cook, stirring constantly, about 1 minute. Spray inside of slow cooker with cooking spray. Spread stuffing mix in bottom of slow cooker. Combine ¼ cup broth and water; pour over stuffing mix. Top with turkey breast and sprinkle with pepper. Spoon onion mixture on top. Cover and cook on low heat for 5–6 hours.

Nutrition Facts per serving: 291 cal., 1.6 g total fat, 91 mg chol., 491 mg sodium, 27 g carbo., 1 g fiber, 41 g pro.
Exchanges: 1½ Starch, 5 Very Lean Meat
Carb Choices: 2

Shopping List

Poultry
2-lb. boneless turkey breast portion

Frozen
12-oz. pkg. frozen chopped onions

Canned
14-oz. can nonfat chicken broth

Packaged
6-oz. pkg. one-step seasoned stuffing mix

Condiments
apple jelly

Seasonings
pepper

Soups and Chowders 4

Turkey Soup

Beef Vegetable Soup

Easy | Do Ahead | Freeze | Serves: 6

1 lb. extra-lean ground beef

2 cups frozen seasoning vegetables, *thawed and drained*

2 14½-oz. cans ready-cut Italian diced tomatoes with garlic, oregano, and basil

2 16-oz. pkgs. rosemary and garlic diced potatoes

1 16-oz. can cut green beans, *drained*

2 tsp. chili powder

⅛ tsp. cayenne pepper

3½ cups nonfat beef broth

1 cup sliced carrots

1 tsp. Worcestershire sauce

Spray large nonstick skillet with cooking spray. Add ground beef and seasoning vegetables to skillet. Cook, stirring frequently, until beef is browned and crumbled and vegetables are softened. Spray inside of slow cooker with cooking spray. Place meat and vegetables in slow cooker; add remaining ingredients and mix well. Cover and cook on low heat for 8–10 hours.

Nutrition Facts per serving: 273 cal., 3.6 g total fat, 41 mg chol., 939 mg sodium, 35 g carbo., 8 g fiber, 20 g pro.
Exchanges: 4 Vegetable, 1 Starch, 1½ Lean Meat
Carb Choices: 2

Shopping List

Produce	**Canned**
2 16-oz. pkgs. rosemary and garlic diced potatoes	2 14½-oz. cans ready-cut Italian diced tomatoes with garlic, oregano, and basil
2 carrots	
Meat	16-oz. can cut green beans
1 lb. extra-lean ground beef	2 14-oz. cans nonfat beef broth
Frozen	**Condiments**
10-oz. pkg. frozen seasoning vegetables	Worcestershire sauce
	Seasonings
	chili powder
	cayenne pepper

Italian Burger Soup

2 lbs. extra-lean ground beef

1 tsp. garlic powder

1½ tsp. onion powder

1 small zucchini, *cut into ½-inch pieces*

2¾ cups potato cubes

1 11-oz. can whole kernel corn, *drained*

1 16-oz. can tomato sauce

2 tbsp. dried Italian seasoning

3 bay leaves

Spray large nonstick skillet with cooking spray. Add ground beef, garlic powder, and onion powder to skillet. Cook over medium heat, stirring frequently, until meat is browned and crumbled. Place meat and remaining ingredients in slow cooker and mix well. Cover and cook on low heat for 6–8 hours. Remove bay leaves before serving.

Nutrition Facts per serving: 321 cal., 6.4 g total fat, 81 mg chol., 282 mg sodium, 30 g carbo., 5 g fiber, 33 g pro.
Exchanges: 1 Vegetable, 1½ Starch, 3 Lean Meat
Carb Choices: 2

Soups and Chowders

Shopping List

Produce
small zucchini
3 medium potatoes (or 16-oz. pkg. potato cubes)

Meat
2 lbs. extra-lean ground beef

Canned
11-oz. can whole kernel corn
16-oz. can tomato sauce

Seasonings
garlic powder
onion powder
dried Italian seasoning
bay leaves

197

Beefy Minestrone Soup

Easy | Do Ahead | Serves: 8

1 lb. beef stew meat, *cut into 1-inch pieces*

2 14-oz. cans petite-cut diced tomatoes with roasted garlic and sweet onion, *do not drain*

1 cup chopped onion

6 cups nonfat beef broth

1½ tsp. dried Italian seasoning

1 zucchini, *cut into ¼-inch slices*

2 cups shredded cabbage

1 16-oz. can garbanzo beans, *drained*

1 cup uncooked shell macaroni

nonfat Parmesan cheese (optional)

Spray inside of slow cooker with cooking spray. Combine stew meat, undrained tomatoes, onions, broth, and Italian seasoning in slow cooker and mix well. Cover and cook on low heat for 8–10 hours or high heat for 4–5 hours. Add zucchini, cabbage, garbanzo beans, and macaroni to cooker. Cover and cook on high heat for 1 hour. Sprinkle each serving with cheese, if desired.

Nutrition Facts per serving: 234 cal., 4 g total fat, 36 mg chol., 1,000 mg sodium, 26 g carbo., 5 g fiber, 21 g pro.
Exchanges: 2 Vegetable, 1 Starch, 2 Lean Meat
Carb Choices: 2

Shopping List

Produce
large onion
8-oz. pkg. shredded cabbage
medium zucchini

Meat
1 lb. beef stew meat

Canned
2 14-oz. cans petite-cut diced tomatoes with roasted garlic and sweet onion

4 14-oz. cans nonfat beef broth
16-oz. can garbanzo beans

Packaged
8-oz. pkg. shell macaroni

Seasonings
dried Italian seasoning

Optional
nonfat Parmesan cheese

Stewing is a method of cooking beef by immersing it completely in liquid. The liquid becomes part of the soup. Unlike a roast, stew meat is cut into small chunks before cooking.

Beef Barley Soup

Easy | Do Ahead | Freeze | Serves: 4

1 lb. beef stew meat, *cut into ½-inch cubes*

¾ cup chopped onion

1 cup chopped celery

1½ cups chopped carrots

¾ cup barley

1 bay leaf

6 cups nonfat beef broth

pepper to taste

Spray inside of slow cooker with cooking spray. Combine all ingredients in slow cooker and mix well. Cover and cook on low heat for 6–8 hours, stirring occasionally. Remove bay leaf before serving.

Nutrition Facts per serving: 357 cal., 6.6 g total fat 72 mg chol., 128 mg sodium, 37 g carbo., 9 g fiber, 36 g pro.
Exchanges: 3 Vegetable, 1 Starch, 4 Lean Meat
Carb Choices: 2

Soups and Chowders

Shopping List

Produce
large onion
small bunch celery
2 carrots

Meat
1 lb. beef stew meat

Canned
4 14-oz. cans nonfat beef broth

Packaged
barley (not quick-cooking)

Seasonings
bay leaf
pepper

Season your soups or stews with fresh herbs. Try anise, caraway, chives, cumin, dill, fennel, marjoram, mint, tarragon, and/or thyme in your favorite soup recipes for a variety of flavors.

Vegetable Beef Stew

Easy | Do Ahead | Serves: 4

2 tbsp. nonfat beef broth

1 lb. beef stew meat, *cut into 1-inch pieces*

2 tbsp. flour

2¼ cups peeled and cubed potatoes

2 cups sliced carrots

1 cup sliced celery

½ cup chopped onion

2 tsp. instant beef bouillon granules

1½ tsp. minced garlic

1½ tsp. dried Italian seasoning

2½ cups V-8 juice

Spray large nonstick skillet with cooking spray. Add broth and heat over medium-high heat. Roll stew meat in flour to coat and cook in skillet, stirring frequently, until browned on all sides. Drain well. Spray inside of slow cooker with cooking spray. Layer potatoes, carrots, celery, and onion in cooker; sprinkle with bouillon granules, minced garlic, and Italian seasoning. Add meat and V-8 juice. Cover and cook on low heat for 7–8 hours or high heat for 3½–4 hours.

Nutrition Facts per serving: 292 cal., 5.6 g total fat, 72 mg chol., 863 mg sodium, 29 g carbo., 7 g fiber, 31 g pro.
Exchanges: 2 Vegetable, 1 Starch, 3 Lean Meat
Carb Choices: 2

Shopping List

Produce	Baking Goods
½–¾ lb. potatoes	flour
¾ lb. carrots	
small bunch celery	**Seasonings**
medium onion	instant beef bouillon granules
Meat	minced garlic
1 lb. beef stew meat	dried Italian seasoning
Canned	
14-oz. can nonfat beef broth	
3 8-oz. bottles V-8 juice	

Orzo Beef Soup

Easy | **Do Ahead** | **Serves: 6**

1 medium zucchini, *cut into ½-inch pieces*

1 medium yellow squash, *cut into ½-inch pieces*

1 sweet onion, *cut into 6 wedges*

½ tsp. ground cinnamon

¾ lb. round steak, *cut into ½-inch cubes*

2 14½-oz. cans ready-cut Italian diced tomatoes with garlic, oregano, and basil, *do not drain*

½ tsp. pepper

3½ cups hot cooked orzo

Spray inside of slow cooker with cooking spray. Combine all ingredients except orzo in slow cooker and mix well. Cover and cook on high heat for 1 hour. Reduce heat to low and cook 7–8 hours. Add orzo and toss to mix. Serve immediately.

Nutrition Facts per serving: 293 cal., 4.2 g total fat, 48 mg chol., 254 mg sodium, 37 g carbo., 2 g fiber, 25 g pro.
Exchanges: 1 Vegetable, 2 Starch, 2 Lean Meat
Carb Choices: 2

Soups and Chowders

Shopping List

Produce
medium zucchini
medium yellow squash
medium sweet onion (Vidalia, Walla Walla)

Meat
¾ lb. round steak

Canned
2 14½-oz. cans ready-cut Italian diced tomatoes with garlic, oregano, and basil

Packaged
8-oz. pkg. orzo

Seasonings
ground cinnamon
pepper

Substitution Tip: You can use any cooked small pasta, rice, or couscous in place of the orzo.

Beef-Vegetable Stew

Easy | Do Ahead | Freeze | Serves: 10

2½ lbs. boneless beef round, *cut into 1-inch cubes*

1 16-oz. pkg. frozen mixed vegetables, *thawed and drained*

1 15-oz. can tomato sauce

1 tbsp. steak sauce

¼ cup frozen chopped onions, *thawed and drained*

1 1.5-oz. packet beef stew seasoning mix

Shopping List

Meat
2½ lbs. boneless beef round

Frozen
16-oz. pkg. frozen mixed vegetables
10-oz. pkg. frozen chopped onions

Canned
15-oz. can tomato sauce

Condiments
steak sauce

Seasonings
1.5-oz. packet beef stew seasoning mix

Spray inside of slow cooker with cooking spray. Combine all ingredients in slow cooker and mix well. Cover and cook on low heat for 6 hours or high heat for 3 hours.

Nutrition Facts per serving: 264 cal., 7 g total fat, 5 mg chol., 329 mg sodium, 9 g carbo., 1 g fiber, 37 g pro.
Exchanges: 2 Vegetable, 4 Lean Meat
Carb Choices: 1

Prepare your own stew seasoning mix:

Combine 2 cups flour, 4 teaspoons dried oregano, 2 tablespoons dried basil, 4 tablespoons salt, 4 tablespoons black pepper, 4 tablespoons garlic powder, 4 tablespoons paprika, 1 teaspoon cayenne pepper, 2 tablespoons celery seed, 4 tablespoons onion powder, and 4 teaspoons dried rosemary in a zip-top bag. Shake well and store in the freezer. Use 1–1½ tbsp. per 1 lb. of meat.

Southwest Chicken Stew

Easy | **Do Ahead** | **Serves: 6**

- 2 lbs. chicken breast tenderloins, *cut into 1½-inch pieces*
- 1 18-oz. pkg. refrigerated shredded potatoes
- 1 15-oz. jar Southwest-style mild salsa with corn and beans
- 1 4-oz. can diced green chiles, *do not drain*
- 1 1¼-oz. pkg. taco seasoning mix
- 6 tbsp. Italian tomato paste with roasted garlic
- ½ cup water
- 1 16-oz. pkg. frozen cut green beans, *thawed and drained*

Spray inside of slow cooker with cooking spray. Combine chicken and potatoes in slow cooker. Combine salsa, undrained chiles, and taco seasoning mix in medium bowl and mix well. Pour salsa mixture over chicken and mix. Combine tomato paste and water and mix well; pour over top and spread evenly but do not mix in. Cover and cook on low heat for 5½–6 hours or high heat for 2¾–3 hours. Mix lightly. If cooking on low heat, increase to high. Add green beans and mix gently. Cook, uncovered, 15–25 minutes.

Nutrition Facts per serving: 274 cal., 1.4 g total fat, 74 mg chol., 1,364 mg sodium, 25 g carbo., 3 g fiber, 33 g pro.
Exchanges: 2 Vegetable, 1 Starch, 4 Very Lean Meat
Carb Choices: 2

Soups and Chowders

Shopping List

Produce	Canned
18-oz. pkg. refrigerated shredded potatoes	4-oz. can diced green chiles
	6-oz. can Italian tomato paste with roasted garlic
Poultry	
2 lbs. chicken breast tenderloins	**Condiments**
	15-oz. jar Southwest-style mild salsa (with corn and beans)
Frozen	
16-oz. pkg. frozen cut green beans	**Seasonings**
	1¼-oz. pkg. taco seasoning mix

Substitution Tip: You can substitute your favorite salsa for the Southwest-style variety, but a chunky-style salsa will work best in this recipe.

Brunswick Stew

- 2 12-oz. pkgs. frozen chopped onions, *thawed and drained*
- 1½ lbs. chicken breast tenderloins
- 2 14¾-oz. cans cream-style corn
- 2 14½-oz. cans petite-cut diced tomatoes with green chiles, *do not drain*
- 1 14-oz. can nonfat chicken broth
- 1½ cups ketchup
- ¼ cup + 2 tbsp. horseradish
- ¼ cup + 2 tbsp. lemon juice
- 2 tbsp. Worcestershire sauce
- 2 tbsp. cider vinegar
- 2 tbsp. prepared mustard
- ½ tsp. pepper
- ½ tsp. Tabasco sauce

Spray inside of slow cooker with cooking spray. Place onions in bottom of slow cooker; top with chicken. Add remaining ingredients and mix well. Cover and cook on high heat for 1 hour. Reduce heat to low and cook 5–6 hours. Remove chicken from slow cooker and shred with 2 forks. Return chicken to slow cooker, toss to mix, and keep warm or serve immediately.

Nutrition Facts per serving: 264 cal., 1 g total fat, 43 mg chol., 1,454 mg sodium, 43 g carbo., 2 g fiber, 23 g pro.
Exchanges: 2 Vegetable, 1 Starch, 1 Other Carbo., 2 Very Lean Meat
Carb Choices: 3

Shopping List

Poultry
1½ lbs. chicken breast tenderloins

Frozen
2 12-oz. pkgs. frozen chopped onions

Canned
2 14¾-oz. cans cream-style corn
2 14½-oz. cans petite-cut diced tomatoes with green chiles

14-oz. can nonfat chicken broth

Condiments
12-oz. bottle ketchup
horseradish
lemon juice
Worcestershire sauce
cider vinegar
prepared mustard
Tabasco sauce

Seasonings
pepper

Chicken Gumbo

Easy | Do Ahead | Serves: 4

¼ cup nonfat chicken broth, *divided*

1 lb. boneless, skinless chicken breasts, *cut into strips*

2 tbsp. flour

1 cup frozen seasoning vegetables, *thawed and drained*

2 cups chopped fresh tomatoes

2 8-oz. cans tomato sauce with roasted garlic

1 10-oz. pkg. frozen whole okra, *thawed and drained*

Spray large nonstick skillet with cooking spray. Add 2 tablespoons broth to skillet and heat over medium-high heat. Add chicken strips and cook until chicken is browned on all sides. Remove chicken and set aside. Mix flour and remaining broth; add to skillet and cook over medium-high heat, stirring constantly, until mixture becomes thick and blended. Add seasoning vegetables, tomatoes, tomato sauce, and okra to skillet; bring to a boil over high heat. Remove skillet from heat. Add chicken to skillet and toss with vegetable mixture. Spray inside of slow cooker with cooking spray. Spoon chicken and vegetable mixture into cooker; cover and cook on low heat for 3–4 hours.

Soups and Chowders

Nutrition Facts per serving: 208 cal., 1.6 g total fat, 55 mg chol., 820 mg sodium, 22 g carbo., 5 g fiber, 27 g pro.
Exchanges: 4 Vegetable, 3 Very Lean Meat
Carb Choices: 1

Shopping List

Produce
2 large tomatoes

Poultry
1 lb. boneless, skinless chicken breasts

Frozen
10-oz. pkg. frozen seasoning vegetables
10-oz. pkg. frozen whole okra

Canned
14-oz. can nonfat chicken broth
2 8-oz. cans tomato sauce with roasted garlic

Baking Goods
flour

What is gumbo?

Gumbo is a robust Southern-style soup made with meat, poultry, fish, shellfish, or vegetables, often thickened with okra or filé, and served over white rice.

Hearty Chicken Stew

Easy | Do Ahead | Freeze | Serves: 8

2 lbs. chicken breast tenderloins, *cut into 1-inch pieces*

3 medium onions, *peeled and quartered*

3 large carrots, *peeled and sliced 1 inch thick*

2 baking potatoes, *cut into 1-inch cubes*

2 14-oz. cans nonfat chicken broth

2 tbsp. finely chopped celery leaves

½ tsp. dried thyme

¼ tsp. dried basil

½ tsp. pepper

½ lb. mushrooms, *cleaned and cut in half*

1 15¼-oz. can whole kernel corn, *drained*

Spray inside of slow cooker with cooking spray. Combine all ingredients in slow cooker and mix lightly. Cover and cook on low heat for 7–8 hours or high heat for 3½–4 hours.

Nutrition Facts per serving: 230 cal., 1.2 g total fat, 57 mg chol., 678 mg sodium, 27 g carbo., 5 g fiber, 30 g pro.
Exchanges: 2 Vegetable, 1 Starch, 3 Very Lean Meat
Carb Choices: 2

Shopping List

Produce	Canned
3 medium onions	2 14-oz. cans nonfat
3 large carrots	chicken broth
2 baking potatoes	15¼-oz. can whole
small bunch celery	kernel corn
½ lb. mushrooms	
	Seasonings
Poultry	dried thyme
2 lbs. chicken breast	dried basil
tenderloins	pepper

Wild Rice-Chicken Soup

Easy | **Do Ahead** | **Freeze** | **Serves: 12**

4 quarts nonfat chicken broth

4 carrots, *thinly sliced*

4 stalks celery, *chopped*

1 cup chopped onion

2 lbs. chicken breast tenderloins, *cut into ½-inch cubes*

½ cup uncooked wild rice

2 tsp. poultry seasoning

Spray inside of slow cooker with cooking spray. Combine all ingredients in slow cooker and mix well. Cover and cook on low heat for 6–7 hours.

Nutrition Facts per serving: 137 cal., 0.3 g total fat, 38 mg chol., 1,192 mg sodium, 10 g carbo., 1 g fiber, 22 g pro.
Exchanges: ½ Starch, 3 Very Lean Meat
Carb Choices: 1

Shopping List

Produce
4 carrots
small bunch celery
large onion

Poultry
2 lbs. chicken breast
tenderloins

Canned
9 14-oz. cans nonfat chicken
broth

Packaged
wild rice

Seasonings
poultry seasoning

Soups
and
Chowders

Chicken Soup with Corn and Rice

Easy | Do Ahead | Serves: 4

- 1 49½-oz. can nonfat chicken broth
- 1 16-oz. can whole kernel corn, *drained*
- ½ cup converted white rice
- 1 10-oz. pkg. frozen seasoning vegetables, *thawed and drained*
- 2 tbsp. + 2 tsp. dried tarragon, *divided*
- 2 cups chopped cooked chicken
- pepper to taste

Spray inside of slow cooker with cooking spray. Combine broth, corn, rice, seasoning vegetables, and 2 tablespoons tarragon in slow cooker and mix well. Cover and cook on low heat for 5–5½ hours. Add chicken, pepper, and remaining tarragon. Cover and cook 30–35 minutes until heated through.

Nutrition Facts per serving: 236 cal., 3.2 g total fat, 46 mg chol., 2,131 mg sodium, 31 g carbo., 4 g fiber, 25 g pro.
Exchanges: 2 Vegetable, 1 Starch, 3 Very Lean Meat
Carb Choices: 2

Shopping List

Poultry
¾ lb. boneless, skinless chicken breasts or tenderloins

Frozen
10-oz. pkg. frozen seasoning vegetables

Canned
49½-oz. can nonfat chicken broth
16-oz. can whole kernel corn

Packaged
8-oz. pkg. converted white rice

Seasonings
dried tarragon
pepper

Turkey Soup p. 230

Tex-Mex Chili  p. 237

Mama's Minestrone p. 232

Chicken Cannellini Chili p. 245

p. 201 Orzo Beef Soup

Vegetable Bean Soup   p. 226

Southwest-Style Chicken Soup

Easy | Do Ahead | Serves: 8

- 2 14-oz. cans nonfat chicken broth
- 1 14½-oz. can petite-cut diced tomatoes with jalapeños, *do not drain*
- 1 4-oz. can diced green chiles, *do not drain*
- 1 11-oz. can Mexicorn, *drained*
- 1 16-oz. pkg. frozen pepper strips, *thawed, drained, and diced*
- 1 cup diced onion
- 2 lbs. chicken breast tenderloins, *cut into thin strips*
- ¾ tsp. garlic powder
- ¾ tsp. chili powder
- ½ tsp. Mrs. Dash seasoning

Spray inside of slow cooker with cooking spray. Combine broth, undrained tomatoes, undrained chiles, drained Mexicorn, peppers, onion, chicken, and garlic powder in slow cooker and mix well. Cover and cook on high heat for 1 hour. Reduce heat to low and cook 3–4 hours. Stir in chili powder and Mrs. Dash seasoning. Heat 5 minutes.

Nutrition Facts per serving: 186 cal., 1.1 g total fat, 55 mg chol., 786 mg sodium, 15 g carbo., 3 g fiber, 26 g pro.
Exchanges: 2 Vegetable, ½ Starch, 3 Very Lean Meat
Carb Choices: 1

Soups and Chowders

Shopping List

Produce	Canned
large onion	2 14-oz. cans nonfat chicken broth
Poultry	14½-oz. petite-cut diced tomatoes with jalapeños
2 lbs. chicken breast tenderloins	4-oz. can diced green chiles
	11-oz. can Mexicorn
Frozen	
16-oz. pkg. frozen pepper strips	**Seasonings**
	garlic powder
	chili powder
	Mrs. Dash seasoning

Chicken Soup with Spinach and Rice

Easy | **Do Ahead** | **Serves: 10**

- 2 lbs. chicken breast tenderloins, *cut into 1-inch pieces*
- 8 cups water
- 2 tbsp. + 2 tsp. Chicken Garlic and Herb Flavor Instant Bouillon and Seasoning Shakers
- 1 16-oz. pkg. frozen mixed vegetables with broccoli, water chestnuts, and snap peas, *thawed and drained*
- 1 16-oz. pkg. frozen chopped spinach, *thawed and drained*
- ½ tsp. celery seed
- 1 tbsp. lemon juice
- 1 cup instant rice

Spray inside of slow cooker with cooking spray. Combine chicken, water, bouillon, vegetables, spinach, celery seed, and lemon juice in cooker and mix well. Cover and cook on high heat for 5–6 hours. Stir in rice. Cover and cook on high heat for 30 minutes.

Nutrition Facts per serving: 149 cal., 0.5 g total fat, 45 mg chol., 436 mg sodium, 13 g carbo., 2 g fiber, 23 g pro.
Exchanges: 1 Vegetable, ½ Starch, 3 Very Lean Meat
Carb Choices: 1

Shopping List

Poultry	Packaged
2 lbs. chicken breast tenderloins	3.75-oz. jar Chicken Garlic and Herb Flavor Instant Bouillon and Seasoning Shakers
Frozen	instant rice
16-oz. pkg. frozen mixed vegetables with broccoli, water chestnuts, and snap peas	**Condiments**
	lemon juice
16-oz. pkg. frozen chopped spinach	**Seasonings**
	celery seed

Substitution Tip: In place of the Chicken Garlic and Herb Flavor Instant Bouillon and Seasoning product, you can use 8 chicken bouillon cubes or 8 cups nonfat chicken broth (leave out water if using prepared chicken broth).

Chicken Chowder

Easy | Do Ahead | Serves: 4

½ cup shredded carrots

1 baking potato, *peeled and cut into ½-inch chunks*

½ lb. chicken breast tenderloins, *cut into 1-inch pieces*

1 cup nonfat half and half

½ cup nonfat chicken broth

2 15-oz. cans cream-style corn

¼ tsp. pepper

¼ tsp. onion powder

2 tbsp. chopped green onions

½ cup instant mashed potato flakes

½ cup nonfat shredded cheddar cheese

Spray inside of slow cooker with cooking spray. Combine carrots, potato, and chicken in slow cooker. Combine half and half, chicken broth, cream-style corn, pepper, onion powder, and green onions in medium bowl and mix well. Pour half and half mixture over chicken and vegetables and mix well. Cover and cook on low heat for 5–6 hours. Add potato flakes. Increase heat to high and cook 5–10 minutes until mixture has thickened and flakes have dissolved. Sprinkle with cheese just before serving.

Nutrition Facts per serving: 344 cal., 1.2 g total fat, 28 mg chol., 952 mg sodium, 65 g carbo., 5 g fiber, 22 g pro.
Exchanges: 2 Vegetable, 3½ Starch, 1 Very Lean Meat
Carb Choices: 4

Soups and Chowders

Shopping List

Produce	Canned
8-oz. pkg. shredded carrots	14-oz. can nonfat chicken broth
baking potato	2 15-oz. cans cream-style corn
green onions	
Poultry	**Packaged**
½ lb. chicken breast tenderloins	instant mashed potato flakes
Dairy	**Seasonings**
8 oz. nonfat half and half	pepper
nonfat shredded cheddar cheese	onion powder

New England Clam Chowder

2 10¾-oz. cans low-fat cream of celery soup

1 10¾-oz. can low-fat cream of mushroom soup

2 6½-oz. cans chopped clams, *do not drain*

1 16-oz. pkg. frozen fat-free shredded hash brown potatoes

2 cups nonfat half and half

2 tbsp. low-fat Bacon Crumbles

¼ tsp. pepper

Spray inside of slow cooker with cooking spray. Combine all ingredients in slow cooker and mix well. Cover and cook on low heat for 8–9 hours or high heat for 4–4½ hours.

Nutrition Facts per serving: 131 cal., 2.2 g total fat, 24 mg chol., 433 mg sodium, 21 g carbo., 1 g fiber, 5 g pro.
Exchanges: 1½ Starch, ½ Very Lean Meat
Carb Choices: 1

Shopping List

Dairy
16 oz. nonfat half and half

Frozen
16-oz. pkg. frozen fat-free shredded hash brown potatoes

Canned
2 10¾-oz. cans low-fat cream of celery soup
10¾-oz. can low-fat cream of mushroom soup
2 6½-oz. cans chopped clams

Packaged
1.3-oz. pkg. low-fat Bacon Crumbles

Seasonings
pepper

Manhattan Clam Chowder

Easy | Do Ahead | Freeze | Serves: 16

1 32-oz. bottle tomato juice

1 6-oz. can tomato paste

6 6½-oz. cans chopped clams, *do not drain*

2 16-oz. pkgs. frozen mixed vegetables, *thawed and drained*

2 16-oz. pkgs. diced potatoes

1 tsp. garlic powder

1 tsp. dried Italian seasoning

Spray inside of slow cooker with cooking spray. Combine all ingredients in slow cooker and mix well. Cover and cook on low heat for 6 hours or high heat for 3 hours.

Nutrition Facts per serving: 129 cal., 0.9 g total fat, 43 mg chol., 380 mg sodium, 23 g carbo., 3 g fiber, 9 g pro.
Exchanges: 1 Vegetable, 1 Starch, 1 Very Lean Meat
Carb Choices: 2

Soups and Chowders

Shopping List

Produce
2 16-oz. pkgs. diced potatoes

Frozen
2 16-oz. pkgs. frozen mixed vegetables

Canned
32-oz. bottle tomato juice
6-oz. can tomato paste
6 6½-oz. cans chopped clams

Seasonings
garlic powder
dried Italian seasoning

Corn and Garlic Potato Chowder

Easy | Do Ahead | Freeze | Serves: 8

3 16-oz. cans low-fat cream-style corn

¼ cup frozen chopped onions *thawed and drained*

¾ cup nonfat half and half

1¾ cups nonfat vegetable broth

1 cup water

1 7.06-oz. box garlic-flavored dry mashed potato mix

Shopping List

Dairy
8 oz. nonfat half and half

Frozen
12-oz. pkg. frozen chopped onions

Canned
3 16-oz. cans low-fat cream-style corn
14-oz. can nonfat vegetable broth

Packaged
7.06-oz. box garlic-flavored dry mashed potato mix

Spray inside of slow cooker with cooking spray. Combine all ingredients in slow cooker and mix well. Cover and cook on low heat for 6 hours or high heat for 3 hours.

Nutrition Facts per serving: 230 cal., 0.8 g total fat, 0 mg chol., 663 mg sodium, 54 g carbo., 4 g fiber, 6 g pro.
Exchanges: 3 Starch
Carb Choices: 4

How does chowder differ from soup or stew? Chowders are thick soups or stews that often contain seafood, potatoes, corn, and milk or cream. The word chowder is derived from the French *chaudière,* a pot in which vegetables or fish are stewed.

Cheesy Corn Chowder

Easy | Do Ahead | Serves: 6

- 1 14-oz. can nonfat chicken broth
- 2 15-oz. cans cream-style corn
- 1 11-oz. can Mexicorn, *drained*
- 1 tbsp. diced green chiles
- 1 tsp. onion powder
- ⅔ cup nonfat shredded cheddar cheese

Spray inside of slow cooker with cooking spray. Combine all ingredients in slow cooker and mix well. Cover and cook on low heat for 6 hours.

Nutrition Facts per serving: 167 cal., 1 g total fat, 0 mg chol., 949 mg sodium, 36 g carbo., 3 g fiber, 8 g pro.
Exchanges: 2 Starch
Carb Choices: 2

Soups and Chowders

Shopping List

Dairy
4 oz. nonfat shredded cheddar cheese

Canned
14-oz. can nonfat chicken broth
2 15-oz. cans cream-style corn
11-oz. can Mexicorn
4-oz. can diced green chiles

Seasonings
onion powder

Asparagus Soup

2 lbs. fresh asparagus, *cut into 1-inch pieces*

5 cups nonfat chicken or vegetable broth

½ cup chopped green onions

2 cups roasted potato cubes

¼ tsp. Mrs. Dash seasoning

¼ tsp. pepper

½ cup nonfat sour cream (optional)

½ cup chopped tomato (optional)

Spray inside of slow cooker with cooking spray. Combine asparagus, broth, green onions, and potatoes in slow cooker. Cover and cook on low heat for 6–7 hours. Increase heat to high. Working in batches, add vegetable mixture to food processor or blender and process until smooth. Return mixture to slow cooker. Add Mrs. Dash seasoning and pepper. Cover and cook on high heat for 30 minutes. Garnish each serving with 2 tablespoons nonfat sour cream and 2 tablespoons tomato, if desired. Serve hot or cold.

Nutrition Facts per serving: 135 cal., 0.7 g total fat, 0 mg chol., 1,114 mg sodium, 24 g carbo., 4 g fiber, 11 g pro.
Exchanges: 2 Vegetable, 1 Starch
Carb Choices: 2

Shopping List

Produce
2 lbs. fresh asparagus
small bunch green onions
16-oz. pkg. roasted potato cubes

Canned
3 14-oz. cans nonfat chicken or vegetable broth

Seasonings
Mrs. Dash seasoning
pepper

Optional
4 oz. nonfat sour cream
medium tomato

One pound of asparagus contains about 12–15 spears (9–10 inches long and ½–¾ inches thick) and serves 2–4 people.

Satiny Vegetable Soup

Easy | **Do Ahead** | **Serves: 6**

2 medium leeks, *white and light green parts chopped*

3 large carrots, *chopped*

3 small zucchini, *chopped*

2 14-oz. cans nonfat chicken or vegetable broth

1 cup water

½ tsp. Mrs. Dash seasoning

pepper to taste

1½ cups chopped tomatoes

Spray inside of slow cooker with cooking spray. Combine leeks, carrots, zucchini, broth, water, Mrs. Dash seasoning, and pepper in slow cooker and mix well. Cover and cook on low heat for 5½–6 hours. Carefully transfer 3 cups of vegetable mixture with some of its liquid to food processor or blender and process until smooth. Return soup to cooker and mix well. Cook until heated through. Garnish servings with tomatoes.

Nutrition Facts per serving: 71 cal., 0.4 g total fat, 0 mg chol., 478 mg sodium, 15 g carbo., 4 g fiber, 4 g pro.
Exchanges: 3 Vegetable
Carb Choices: 1

Soups and Chowders

Shopping List

Produce
2 medium leeks
3 large carrots
3 small zucchini
2 large tomatoes

Canned
2 14-oz. cans nonfat chicken or vegetable broth

Seasonings
Mrs. Dash seasoning
pepper

Vegetable Bean Soup

Easy | **Do Ahead** | **Serves: 6**

- 1 cup chopped onion
- 2 cups sliced celery
- 2 cups shredded carrots
- 1 8-oz. pkg. shredded cabbage
- 2¼ cups roasted onion potato cubes
- 1 14½-oz. can petite-cut diced tomatoes with roasted garlic and sweet onion, *drained*
- 1 medium zucchini, *diced*
- 2 15-oz. cans garbanzo beans, *drained*
- 2 tsp. minced garlic
- 1 tsp. dried basil
- 1 bay leaf
- ½ tsp. dried rosemary
- ¼ tsp. pepper
- 3 14-oz. cans nonfat chicken or vegetable broth
- 1 16-oz. pkg. frozen cut green beans, *thawed and drained*
- ¾ cup nonfat Parmesan cheese (optional)

Spray inside of slow cooker with cooking spray. Combine onion, celery, carrots, cabbage, potatoes, tomatoes, zucchini, garbanzo beans, minced garlic, basil, bay leaf, rosemary, pepper, and chicken broth in cooker and mix well. Cover and cook on low heat for 7–8 hours. Remove bay leaf; add green beans. Cook 10–15 minutes longer. Top with cheese, if desired.

Nutrition Facts per serving: 331 cal., 1.8 g total fat, 0 mg chol., 1,448 mg sodium, 62 g carbo., 9 g fiber, 18 g pro.
Exchanges: 4 Vegetable, 3 Starch
Carb Choices: 4

Shopping List

Produce
- large onion
- small bunch celery
- 2–3 carrots
- 8-oz. pkg. shredded cabbage
- 16-oz. pkg. roasted onion potato cubes
- medium zucchini

Frozen
- 16-oz. pkg. frozen cut green beans

Canned
- 14½-oz. can petite-cut diced tomatoes with roasted garlic and sweet onion

- 2 15-oz. cans garbanzo beans
- 3 14-oz. cans nonfat chicken or vegetable broth

Seasonings
- minced garlic
- dried basil
- bay leaf
- dried rosemary
- pepper

Optional
- nonfat Parmesan cheese

Cabbage Soup

Easy | **Do Ahead** | **Freeze** | **Serves: 12**

- 2 28-oz. cans V-8 juice
- 1 16-oz. pkg. shredded cabbage
- 2 cups frozen seasoning vegetables, *thawed and drained*
- 2 cups frozen French-cut green beans, *thawed and drained*
- ½ tsp. minced garlic
- 6 tsp. Chicken Garlic and Herb Flavor Instant Bouillon and Seasoning Shakers

Spray inside of slow cooker with cooking spray. Combine all ingredients in slow cooker and mix well. Cover and cook on low heat for 7–8 hours or high heat for 3–4 hours. Remove 3–4 cups of soup from pot; process in food processor or blender until smooth. Return to slow cooker and heat through.

Nutrition Facts per serving: 46 cal., 0.2 g total fat, 0 mg chol., 648 mg sodium, 11 g carbo., 3 g fiber, 2 g pro.
Exchanges: 2 Vegetable
Carb Choices: 1

Soups and Chowders

Shopping List

Produce
16-oz. pkg. shredded cabbage

Frozen
10-oz. pkg. frozen seasoning vegetables
16-oz. pkg. frozen French-cut green beans

Canned
2 28-oz. cans V-8 juice

Packaged
3.75-oz. jar Chicken Garlic and Herb Flavor Instant Bouillon and Seasoning Shakers

Seasonings
minced garlic

Chicken Cabbage Soup with Rice

Easy | Do Ahead | Serves: 8

2 8-oz. pkgs. shredded cabbage

½ cup converted white rice

1 16-oz. pkg. sliced carrots

2 14-oz. cans nonfat chicken broth

1 cup water

1 15-oz. can tomato sauce

1 tbsp. celery seed

1 tsp. dried dillweed

½ tsp. Mrs. Dash seasoning

¼ tsp. pepper

1 14½-oz. can petite-cut diced tomatoes, *do not drain*

Spray inside of slow cooker with cooking spray. Combine cabbage, rice, carrots, broth, water, tomato sauce, celery seed, dillweed, Mrs. Dash seasoning, and pepper in slow cooker and mix well. Cover and cook on low heat for 7–8 hours. Stir in undrained tomatoes and heat through. Serve immediately.

Nutrition Facts per serving: 86 cal., 0.4 g total fat, 0 mg chol., 477 mg sodium, 17 g carbo., 5 g fiber, 4 g pro.
Exchanges: 2 Vegetable, ½ Starch
Carb Choices: 1

Shopping List

Produce	Packaged
2 8-oz. pkgs. shredded cabbage	converted white rice
16-oz. pkg. sliced carrots	**Seasonings**
	celery seed
Canned	dillweed
2 14-oz. cans nonfat chicken broth	Mrs. Dash seasoning
15-oz. can tomato sauce	pepper
14½-oz. can petite-cut diced tomatoes	

Mrs. Dash seasonings come in 12 varieties, each a blend of 14 natural herbs and spices without salt or MSG. These spicy blends are a convenient way to add bold, robust flavor. Try different varieties in your favorite soups and stews.

Chicken and Barley Soup

Easy | **Do Ahead** | **Freeze** | **Serves: 6**

- 2 14-oz. cans nonfat chicken broth
- 2 16-oz. pkgs. frozen mixed vegetables
- 1¼ cups pearl barley
- 2 cups sliced fresh mushrooms
- 4 cups water
- 2 lbs. chicken breast tenderloins, *cubed*
- 1 tsp. Mrs. Dash seasoning
- ½ tsp. pepper

Spray inside of slow cooker with cooking spray. Combine all ingredients in slow cooker and mix well. Cover and cook on low heat for 6 hours or high heat for 3 hours.

Nutrition Facts per serving: 142 cal., 0.6 g total fat, 28 mg chol., 344 mg sodium, 18 g carbo., 5 g fiber, 16 g pro.
Exchanges: 2 Vegetable, ½ Starch, 2 Very Lean Meat
Carb Choices: 1

Soups and Chowders

Shopping List

Produce
8 oz. sliced mushrooms

Poultry
2 lbs. chicken breast tenderloins

Frozen
2 16-oz. pkgs. frozen mixed vegetables

Canned
2 14-oz. cans nonfat chicken broth

Packaged
12-oz. pkg. pearl barley

Seasonings
Mrs. Dash seasoning
pepper

Turkey Soup

3 cups frozen seasoning
   vegetables, *thawed and
   drained*

2 carrots, *sliced thin*

6 oz. mushrooms, *sliced thin*

3 cups shredded cooked
   turkey

¼ tsp. pepper

¼ tsp. dried oregano

¼ tsp. dried basil

3 cups nonfat chicken broth

1 14½-oz. can petite-cut
   diced tomatoes, *drained*

1 tbsp. low-sodium
   soy sauce

   fresh oregano leaves
   (optional)

Spray the inside of slow cooker with cooking spray. Combine all ingredients in slow cooker and mix well. Cover and cook on low heat for 6–8 hours. Garnish with fresh oregano leaves, if desired.

Nutrition Facts per serving: 127 cal., .6 g total fat, 42 mg chol., 657 mg sodium, 9 g carbo., 3 g fiber, 21 g pro.
Exchanges: 2 Vegetable, 2 Very Lean Meat
Carb Choices: 1

Shopping List

Produce
2 carrots
6 oz. sliced mushrooms

Poultry
1 lb. turkey breast
   tenderloins

Frozen
10-oz. pkg. frozen
   seasoning vegetables

Canned
2 14-oz. cans nonfat
   chicken broth

14½-oz. can petite-cut
   diced tomatoes

Condiments
low-sodium soy sauce

Seasonings
pepper
dried oregano
dried basil

Optional
fresh oregano

Barley-Bean Vegetable Soup

Easy | **Do Ahead** | **Serves: 8**

- 1 15-oz. can red kidney beans, *drained*
- 1 10-oz. can whole kernel corn, *drained*
- ½ cup medium pearl barley
- 1 14½-oz. can stewed tomatoes with bell pepper and onion, *drained*
- 2 cups sliced fresh mushrooms
- 1 cup chopped onion
- 1½ cups coarsely chopped carrots
- ½ cup chopped celery
- 1½ tsp. garlic powder
- 2 tsp. dried dillweed
- ¼ tsp. pepper
- 1 bay leaf
- 5 cups nonfat chicken or vegetable broth

Spray inside of slow cooker with cooking spray. Combine all ingredients in slow cooker and mix lightly. Cover and cook on low heat for 8–10 hours or high heat for 4–5 hours. Remove bay leaf before serving.

Nutrition Facts per serving: 210 cal., 1 g total fat, 0 mg chol., 1,332 mg sodium, 42 g carbo., 9 g fiber, 11 g pro.
Exchanges: 2 Vegetable, 2 Starch
Carb Choices: 3

Soups and Chowders

Shopping List

Produce	
8 oz. fresh mushrooms	3 14-oz. cans nonfat chicken or vegetable broth
large onion	
2 carrots	
small bunch celery	**Packaged**
	medium pearl barley
Canned	
15-oz. can red kidney beans	**Seasonings**
10-oz. can whole kernel corn	garlic powder
	dried dillweed
14½-oz. can stewed tomatoes with bell pepper and onion	pepper
	bay leaf

Mama's Minestrone

2 15-oz. cans red kidney beans, *drained*

6 cups nonfat beef broth

1 28-oz. can petite-cut diced tomatoes, *do not drain*

¾ lb. baby carrots, *cut in half*

½ lb. fresh green beans, *cut into 1-inch pieces*

1½ cups chopped celery

1 cup frozen chopped onions, *thawed and drained*

¾ lb. red potatoes, *cut into ½-inch cubes*

1 tbsp. dried Italian seasoning

1½ tsp. minced garlic

¼ tsp. pepper

1 cup nonfat Parmesan cheese

Spray inside of slow cooker with cooking spray. Combine all ingredients except cheese in slow cooker and mix well. Cover and cook on low heat for 6–8 hours or high heat for 3–4 hours. Sprinkle with cheese just before serving.

Nutrition Facts per serving: 238 cal., 0.7 g total fat, 0 mg chol., 1,220 mg sodium, 43 g carbo., 9 g fiber, 15 g pro.
Exchanges: 3 Vegetable, 2 Starch
Carb Choices: 3

Did you know that baby carrots are really not babies at all? They are actually fully grown carrots that have been cut into 2-inch sections and whittled down. Baby carrots are storming the marketplace because they offer the convenience that modern consumers demand.

Shopping List

Produce	Canned
¾ lb. baby carrots	2 15-oz. cans red kidney
½ lb. fresh green beans	beans
small bunch celery	4 14-oz. cans nonfat beef
¾ lb. red potatoes	broth
	28-oz. can petite-cut diced
Dairy	tomatoes
nonfat Parmesan cheese	
	Seasonings
Frozen	dried Italian seasoning
12-oz. pkg. frozen chopped	minced garlic
onions	pepper

Cream of Mushroom Soup

- 2 tbsp. + 3 cups nonfat chicken broth, *divided*
- 6 cups sliced fresh mushrooms
- 2 tbsp. chopped onion
- pepper to taste
- 2 tbsp. flour
- 1 cup nonfat sour cream
- 1 cup nonfat half and half

Shopping List

Produce
1 lb. mushrooms
small onion

Dairy
8 oz. nonfat sour cream
8 oz. nonfat half and half

Canned
2 14-oz. cans nonfat chicken broth

Baking Goods
flour

Seasonings
pepper

Spray large nonstick skillet with cooking spray. Add 2 tablespoons broth to skillet and heat over medium-high heat. Add mushrooms and cook, stirring frequently, until softened. Spray inside of slow cooker with cooking spray. Place mushrooms in slow cooker. Add remaining broth, onion, and pepper and mix well. Cover and cook on low heat for 8–10 hours. Thirty minutes before serving, increase heat to high. Mix flour and sour cream in small bowl; add to slow cooker. Add half and half, mix lightly, and cook until mixture is slightly thickened.

Nutrition Facts per serving: 135 cal., 0.9 g total fat, 0 mg chol., 655 mg sodium, 20 g carbo., 2 g fiber, 9 g pro.
Exchanges: 1 Vegetable, 1 Other Carbo.
Carb Choices: 1

Soups and Chowders

If you want to make your cream soup thicker, puree some of the cooked vegetables with a bit of the liquid.

Potato Soup

Easy | Do Ahead | Serves: 6

6 cups peeled and cubed potatoes

2 cups chopped onions

1 cup sliced carrots

1 cup sliced celery

2 14-oz. cans nonfat chicken broth

1 tsp. dried basil

½ tsp. pepper

¼ cup flour

1½ cups nonfat half and half

Shopping List

Produce
6 potatoes
2 large onions
2 carrots
small bunch celery

Dairy
12 oz. nonfat half and half

Canned
2 14-oz. cans nonfat chicken broth

Baking Goods
flour

Seasonings
dried basil
pepper

Spray inside of slow cooker with cooking spray. Combine potatoes, onions, carrots, celery, broth, basil, and pepper in slow cooker and mix well. Cover and cook on high heat for 3–4 hours. Combine flour and half and half and mix until smooth. Stir into slow cooker and mix well. Cover and cook on high heat 30 minutes.

Nutrition Facts per serving: 181 cal., 0.5 g total fat, 0 mg chol., 532 mg sodium, 37 g carbo., 5 g fiber, 5 g pro.
Exchanges: 1 Vegetable, 2 Starch
Carb Choices: 2

Potato Math:

1 pound white potatoes = 3 medium potatoes

= $2\frac{3}{4}$ cups uncooked potato cubes

= $1\frac{1}{2}$–$2\frac{1}{4}$ cups cooked diced or sliced potatoes

= $1\frac{3}{4}$–2 cups mashed potatoes

Spicy Cauliflower Soup

Easy | **Do Ahead** | **Serves: 4**

4 cups cauliflower florets, *chopped*

2 14½-oz. cans petite-cut diced tomatoes with roasted garlic and sweet onion, *do not drain*

1 14-oz. can nonfat vegetable broth

1 cup chopped onion

½ tsp. minced garlic

⅛ tsp. chili powder

2 tsp. curry powder

⅛ tsp. pepper

Shopping List

Produce
1½ lbs. cauliflower (or packaged cauliflower florets)
large onion

Canned
2 14½-oz. cans petite-cut diced tomatoes with roasted garlic and sweet onion
14-oz. can nonfat vegetable broth

Seasonings
minced garlic
chili powder
curry powder
pepper

Spray inside of slow cooker with cooking spray. Combine cauliflower, undrained tomatoes, broth, onion, and minced garlic in cooker and mix well. Cover and cook on low heat for 7–8 hours or high heat for 3½–4 hours. Increase heat to high. Add chili powder, curry powder, and pepper. Cover and cook 30–35 minutes until heated through. Serve soup hot or cold.

Nutrition Facts per serving: 89 cal., 0.4 g total fat, 0 mg chol., 674 mg sodium, 15 g carbo., 5 g fiber, 5 g pro.
Exchanges: 3 Vegetable
Carb Choices: 3

Soups and Chowders

French Onion Soup

Easy | Do Ahead | Freeze | Serves: 6

12¼ cups nonfat beef broth, *divided*

6 large onions, *peeled and sliced thin*

2 tsp. Worcestershire sauce

1 tsp. paprika

pepper to taste

Spray large Dutch oven with cooking spray. Add ¼ cup broth to Dutch oven and heat over medium-high heat. Add onions and cook, stirring frequently, until slightly softened. Spray inside of slow cooker with cooking spray. Place onions in slow cooker; add remaining ingredients and mix lightly. Cover and cook on low heat for 4–6 hours or high heat for 1½–2 hours.

Nutrition Facts per serving: 98 cal., 0.3 g total fat, 0 mg chol., 1,618 mg sodium, 14 g carbo., 2 g fiber, 8 g pro.
Exchanges: 4 Vegetable
Carb Choices: 0

Shopping List

Produce
6 large onions

Canned
7 14-oz. cans nonfat beef broth

Condiments
Worcestershire sauce

Seasonings
paprika
pepper

Before serving, toast slices of crusty French bread to float on top of soup. Then sprinkle with shredded nonfat Parmesan or mozzarella cheese.

Vegetable Soup

Easy | Do Ahead | Freeze | Serves: 8

- 3 cups V-8 juice
- 1 6-oz. can tomato paste
- ½ tsp. garlic powder
- ¼ cup frozen chopped onions, *thawed and drained*
- 1 16-oz. pkg. frozen mixed vegetables, *thawed and drained*
- 1 14-oz. can nonfat vegetable broth
- 1½ cups water
- ½ tsp. dried Italian seasoning
- ½ tsp. Splenda or sugar

Spray inside of slow cooker with cooking spray. Combine all ingredients in slow cooker and mix well. Cover and cook on low heat for 6 hours or high heat for 3 hours.

Nutrition Facts per serving: 82 cal., 0.2 g total fat, 0 mg chol., 701 mg sodium, 18 g carbo., 3 g fiber, 3 g pro.
Exchanges: 3 Vegetable
Carb Choices: 1

Soups and Chowders

Shopping List

Frozen
10-oz. pkg. frozen chopped onions
16-oz. pkg. frozen mixed vegetables

Canned
24 oz. V-8 juice
6-oz. can tomato paste
14-oz. can nonfat vegetable broth

Baking Goods
Splenda or sugar

Seasonings
garlic powder
dried Italian seasoning

Vegetable Minestrone

Easy | Do Ahead | Freeze | Serves: 12

4 cups tomato juice

4 cups nonfat vegetable broth

1 tbsp. dried Italian seasoning

¼ tsp. pepper

1 cup frozen sliced carrots, *thawed and drained*

1 cup frozen seasoning vegetables, *thawed and drained*

1 cup sliced fresh mushrooms

1 tsp. minced garlic

1 28-oz. can petite-cut diced tomatoes, *do not drain*

1½ cups uncooked rotini pasta

¾ cup nonfat Parmesan cheese (optional)

Spray inside of slow cooker with cooking spray. Combine tomato juice, broth, Italian seasoning, pepper, carrots, seasoning vegetables, mushrooms, minced garlic, and undrained tomatoes in slow cooker and mix well. Cover and cook on low heat for 7–8 hours. Add pasta; cover and cook on high heat for 15–20 minutes. Garnish each serving with 1 tablespoon cheese, if desired.

Nutrition Facts per serving: 105 cal., 0.4 g total fat, 0 mg chol., 429 mg sodium, 19 g carbo., 2 g fiber, 6 g pro.
Exchanges: 2 Vegetable, ½ Starch
Carb Choices: 1

Shopping List

Produce
¼ lb. mushrooms

Frozen
10-oz. pkg. frozen sliced carrots
10-oz. pkg. frozen seasoning vegetables

Canned
32-oz. can tomato juice
3 14-oz. cans nonfat vegetable broth

28-oz. can petite-cut diced tomatoes

Packaged
12-oz. pkg. rotini pasta

Seasonings
dried Italian seasoning
pepper
minced garlic

Optional
nonfat Parmesan cheese

Substitution Tip: You can use ½ cup tomato sauce + ½ cup water for each cup of tomato juice in any recipe. In this recipe you would use 2 cups tomato sauce + 2 cups water in place of the tomato juice.

Tex-Mex Chili

Easy | Do Ahead | Serves: 4

1 lb. extra-lean ground beef

1 tsp. minced garlic

3½ tsp. chili powder

½ tsp. ground cumin

1 15½-oz. can red kidney beans, *drained*

2½ cups frozen seasoning vegetables, *thawed and drained*

2 16-oz. cans petite-cut diced tomatoes with green chiles, *do not drain*

¾ cup V-8 juice

1 6-oz. can Italian tomato paste with roasted garlic

1 cup nonfat shredded cheddar cheese (optional)

¼ cup nonfat sour cream (optional)

¼ cup chopped green onions (optional)

Spray large nonstick skillet with cooking spray. Add ground beef and minced garlic to skillet and cook over medium heat, stirring frequently, until meat is browned and crumbled. Drain well. Stir in chili powder and cumin and mix well. Spray inside of slow cooker with cooking spray. Combine beans, seasoning vegetables, undrained tomatoes, V-8 juice, and tomato paste in slow cooker; stir in meat mixture. Cover and cook on low heat for 8–10 hours or high heat for 4–5 hours. Garnish with cheese, sour cream, and green onions, if desired.

Soups and Chowders

Nutrition Facts per serving: 410 cal., 5.6 g total fat, 61 mg chol., 2,155 mg sodium, 45 g carbo., 10 g fiber, 41 g pro.
Exchanges: 3 Vegetable, 2 Starch, 3 Lean Meat
Carb Choices: 3

Shopping List

Meat	8-oz. bottle V-8 juice
1 lb. extra-lean ground beef	6-oz. can Italian tomato paste with roasted garlic
Frozen	
16-oz. pkg. frozen seasoning vegetables	**Seasonings**
	minced garlic
	chili powder
Canned	ground cumin
15½-oz. can red kidney beans	
2 16-oz. cans petite-cut diced tomatoes with green chiles	**Optional**
	4 oz. nonfat shredded cheddar cheese
	nonfat sour cream
	green onions

Cowboy-Style Chili

Easy | Do Ahead | Freeze | Serves: 10

1½ lbs. boneless beef round, *cut into ½-inch cubes*

1 14-oz. can nonfat beef broth

3 15-oz. cans red kidney beans, *drained*

1 15-oz. can tomato sauce

1 cup frozen chopped onions, *thawed and drained*

1 1.25-oz. packet chili seasoning mix

¾ tsp. garlic powder

Shopping List

Meat
1½ lbs. boneless beef round

Frozen
10-oz. pkg. frozen chopped onions

Canned
14-oz. can nonfat beef broth
3 15-oz. cans red kidney beans
15-oz. can tomato sauce

Seasonings
1.25-oz. packet chili seasoning mix
garlic powder

Spray inside of slow cooker with cooking spray. Combine all ingredients in slow cooker and mix well. Cover and cook on low heat for 8–10 hours or high heat for 4–5 hours.

Nutrition Facts per serving: 253 cal., 3.7 g total fat, 43 mg chol., 908 mg sodium, 28 g carbo., 7 g fiber, 25 g pro.
Exchanges: 2 Vegetable, 1 Starch, 2 Very Lean Meat
Carb Choices: 2

Freeze leftover chili in serving-size containers for ready-to-go lunch meals or easy-prep dinners. Thaw overnight in refrigerator or thaw in microwave, then heat and serve.

Southwest Chili

Easy | **Do Ahead** | **Freeze** | **Serves: 6**

- 1 lb. beef eye of round, *cut into ½-inch pieces*
- 1 15-oz. can spicy chili beans
- 1 14½-oz. can petite-cut diced tomatoes with jalapeños, *do not drain*
- 1 16-oz. jar thick and chunky salsa
- 1 8-oz. can whole kernel corn, *drained*
- 1 tbsp. sugar
  nonfat shredded cheddar cheese, chopped green onions, or crumbled baked tortilla chips (optional)

Spray inside of slow cooker with cooking spray. Combine all ingredients in slow cooker and mix well. Cover and cook on low heat for 8–10 hours or high heat for 4–5 hours. Garnish with cheese, green onions, or tortilla chips, if desired.

Nutrition Facts per serving: 245 cal., 3.9 g total fat, 48 mg chol., 913 mg sodium, 27 g carbo., 5 g fiber, 25 g pro.
Exchanges: 2 Vegetable, 1 Starch, 2 Lean Meat
Carb Choices: 2

Soups and Chowders

Shopping List

Meat	Baking Goods
1 lb. beef eye of round	sugar

Canned	Optional
15-oz. can spicy chili beans	nonfat shredded cheddar cheese, green onions, or baked tortilla chips
14½-oz. can petite-cut diced tomatoes with jalapeños	
8-oz. can whole kernel corn	

Condiments
16-oz. jar thick and chunky salsa

Substitution Tip: You can use a 10-ounce package of frozen whole kernel corn (thawed and drained) or an 11-ounce can of Mexicorn (drained) in place of the canned corn.

Hot and Spicy Chili

Easy | **Do Ahead** | **Serves: 6**

1 lb. extra-lean ground beef

2 15½-oz. cans spicy chili beans

2 14½-oz. cans petite-cut diced tomatoes with jalapeños, *do not drain*

1 6-oz. can tomato paste

1 cup chopped onion

3 tbsp. dried celery flakes

1 4-oz. can diced green chiles, *drained*

2 tbsp. sugar

1 bay leaf

¾ tsp. dried basil

½ tsp. garlic powder

pepper to taste

chopped onions, nonfat sour cream, or nonfat shredded cheddar cheese (optional)

Spray large nonstick skillet with cooking spray. Add ground beef to skillet and cook over medium heat, stirring frequently, until browned and crumbled. Drain well. Spray inside of slow cooker with cooking spray. Add browned ground beef and remaining ingredients to slow cooker and mix well. Cover and cook on low heat for 8–10 hours. Remove bay leaf, stir, and serve. Garnish with onions, sour cream, or cheese, if desired.

Nutrition Facts per serving: 308 cal., 4.1 g total fat, 41 mg chol., 1,233 mg sodium, 43 g carbo., 7 g fiber, 26 g pro.
Exchanges: 2 Vegetable, 2 Starch, 2 Lean Meat
Carb Choices: 3

Shopping List

Produce	Baking Goods
large onion	sugar

Meat	Seasonings
1 lb. extra-lean ground beef	celery flakes
	bay leaf
Canned	dried basil
2 15½-oz. cans spicy chili beans	garlic powder
	pepper
2 14½-oz. cans petite-cut diced tomatoes with jalapeños	
	Optional
6-oz. can tomato paste	onions, nonfat sour cream, or nonfat shredded
4-oz. can diced green chiles	cheddar cheese

Chunky Pork Chili with Black Beans

Easy | Do Ahead | Freeze | Serves: 6

1 lb. pork tenderloin strips, *cut into 1-inch pieces*

¾ tsp. garlic powder

1 16-oz. jar chunky-style salsa

3 15-oz. cans black beans, *rinsed and drained*

½ cup nonfat chicken broth

1½ cups frozen pepper stir-fry, *thawed and drained*

¾ cup chopped onion

½ tsp. ground cumin

2½ tsp. chili powder

1 tsp. dried oregano

nonfat shredded cheddar cheese, nonfat sour cream, or chopped green onions (optional)

Spray inside of slow cooker with cooking spray. Place pork tenderloin in slow cooker and sprinkle with garlic powder. Add remaining ingredients and toss to mix. Cover and cook on low heat for 8–9 hours or high heat for 4–4½ hours. Garnish with cheese, sour cream, or green onions, if desired.

Nutrition Facts per serving: 330 cal., 3.7 g total fat 53 mg chol., 1,330 mg sodium, 43 g carbo., 7 g fiber, 31 g pro.
Exchanges: 2 Vegetable, 2 Starch, 3½ Very Lean Meat
Carb Choices: 3

Soups and Chowders

Shopping List

Produce	Condiments
large onion	16-oz. jar chunky-style salsa
Meat	
1 lb. pork tenderloin strips	**Seasonings**
	garlic powder
Frozen	ground cumin
16-oz. pkg. frozen pepper stir-fry	chili powder
	dried oregano
Canned	**Optional**
3 15-oz. cans black beans	nonfat shredded cheddar cheese, nonfat sour cream, or green onions
14-oz. can nonfat chicken broth	

Chili Chicken Stew

Easy | Do Ahead | Serves: 6

- 2 tbsp. nonfat chicken broth
- 2 lbs. chicken breast tenderloins, *cut into 1-inch pieces*
- 1 cup chopped onion
- 1 cup chopped bell pepper
- 1 tsp. minced garlic
- 3 14½-oz. cans petite-cut diced tomatoes with green chiles, *lightly drained*
- 1 16-oz. can chili beans, *drained*
- ⅔ cup picante sauce
- 1 tsp. chili powder
- 1 tsp. ground cumin
- 3 cups cooked rice (optional)

Spray large nonstick skillet with cooking spray. Add broth to skillet and heat over medium-high heat. Add chicken, onion, bell pepper, and minced garlic. Cook, stirring frequently, until vegetables are softened. Spoon mixture into slow cooker; add remaining ingredients and mix lightly. Cover and cook on low heat for 4–6 hours. Serve over cooked rice, if desired.

Nutrition Facts per serving: 403 cal., 2.2 g total fat, 76 mg chol., 1,578 mg sodium, 63 g carbo., 7 g fiber, 42 g pro.
Exchanges: 2 Vegetable, 3 Starch, 3½ Very Lean Meat
Carb Choices: 4

Shopping List

Produce
large onion
large bell pepper

Poultry
2 lbs. chicken breast
  tenderloins

Canned
14-oz. can nonfat chicken
  broth
2 14½-oz. cans petite-cut
  diced tomatoes with green
  chiles

16-oz. can chili beans

Condiments
8-oz. jar picante sauce

Seasonings
minced garlic
chili powder
ground cumin

Optional
rice

Chicken Cannellini Chili

Easy | **Do Ahead** | **Serves: 8**

- 3 15-oz. cans cannellini beans, *drained*
- 3 6-oz. pkgs. refrigerated grilled chicken breast strips, *chopped*
- 1 cup chopped onion
- 1½ cups chopped bell pepper
- 2 tbsp. diced green chiles
- 1 tsp. minced garlic
- 1 tsp. ground cumin
- ½ tsp. chili powder
- ½ tsp. dried oregano
- 3½ cups nonfat chicken broth
- 1 cup nonfat shredded cheddar cheese (optional)
- 4 oz. baked tortilla chips, crushed (optional)

Spray inside of slow cooker with cooking spray. Combine cannellini beans, chicken, onion, bell peppers, chiles, minced garlic, cumin, chili powder, and oregano in slow cooker. Stir in broth and mix well. Cover and cook on low heat for 8–10 hours or high heat for 4–5 hours. Garnish with cheese and tortilla chips, if desired.

Nutrition Facts per serving: 368 cal., 2.4 g total fat, 37 mg chol., 999 mg sodium, 54 g carbo., 1 g fiber, 34 g pro.
Exchanges: 1 Vegetable, 3 Starch, 3 Very Lean Meat
Carb Choices: 4

Soups and Chowders

Shopping List

Produce	Seasonings
large onion	minced garlic
2 medium bell peppers	ground cumin
	chili powder
Poultry	dried oregano
3 6-oz. pkgs. grilled chicken breast strips	
	Optional
	4 oz. nonfat shredded cheddar cheese
Canned	baked tortilla chips
3 15-oz. cans cannellini beans	
4-oz. can diced green chiles	
2 14-oz. cans nonfat chicken broth	

Cannellini Bean Chili

Easy | Do Ahead | Serves: 8

1 16-oz. pkg. frozen pepper stir-fry, *thawed and drained*

1 lb. top sirloin steak, *cut into ¾-inch pieces*

1 cup canned crushed tomatoes with garlic, *do not drain*

1½ tsp. minced garlic

1 tbsp. chili powder

2 tsp. quick-cooking tapioca

1½ tsp. dried oregano

¾ tsp. ground cumin

¼ tsp. pepper

2 tsp. instant beef bouillon granules

1 19-oz. can cannellini beans, *drained*

Spray inside of slow cooker with cooking spray. Combine peppers and steak in slow cooker. Combine remaining ingredients except beans in medium bowl and mix well. Pour tomato mixture over steak and mix well. Top with beans but do not stir. Cover and cook on high for 3–4 hours. Stir mixture and serve.

Nutrition Facts per serving: 223 cal., 5 g total fat, 50 mg chol., 167 mg sodium, 20 g carbo., 1 g fiber, 23 g pro.
Exchanges: 1 Vegetable, 1 Starch, 2 Lean Meat
Carb Choices: 1

Broths are also commonly referred to as stocks, bouillons, or consommés. These are prepared by cooking vegetables, poultry, meat, or fish in water.

Shopping List

Meat	Packaged
1 lb. top sirloin steak	quick-cooking tapioca

Frozen	Seasonings
16-oz. pkg. frozen pepper stir-fry	minced garlic
	chili powder
	dried oregano
Canned	ground cumin
28-oz. can crushed tomatoes with garlic	pepper
19-oz. can cannellini beans	instant beef bouillon granules

Black Bean Chili

Easy | **Do Ahead** | **Freeze** | **Serves: 12**

4 cups water

4 cups nonfat vegetable broth

2 tsp. dried oregano

¼ cup + 2 tbsp. tomato paste

2 tsp. ground cumin

¼ tsp. cayenne pepper

2½ cups chopped onions

1½ tbsp. minced garlic

4 4-oz. cans diced green chiles, *drained*

4 15-oz. cans black beans, *rinsed and drained*

4 red bell peppers, *chopped*

½ cup chopped fresh cilantro

2 cups nonfat shredded cheddar cheese

chopped green onions, nonfat sour cream, and baked totilla chips (optional)

Spray inside of slow cooker with cooking spray. Combine all ingredients except cilantro and cheese in slow cooker and mix well. Cover and cook on low heat for 8–9 hours or high heat for 4–5 hours. Stir in cilantro and cheese just before serving. Garnish with green onions, sour cream, and tortilla chips, if desired.

Nutrition Facts per serving: 204 cal., 0.8 g total fat 0 mg chol., 1,513 mg sodium, 34 g carbo., 6 g fiber, 16 g pro.
Exchanges: 2 Vegetable, 2 Starch
Carb Choices: 2

Soups and Chowders

Shopping List

Produce	Seasonings
3 medium onions	dried oregano
4 red bell peppers	ground cumin
fresh cilantro	cayenne pepper
	minced garlic
Dairy	
8 oz. nonfat shredded cheddar cheese	**Optional**
	green onions, nonfat sour cream, and baked tortilla chips
Canned	
3 14-oz. cans nonfat vegetable broth	
6-oz. can tomato paste	
4 4-oz. cans diced green chiles	
4 15-oz. cans black beans	

Beef Chili

3 lbs. extra-lean ground beef

1¼ cups frozen chopped onions, *thawed and drained*

2 tbsp. chili powder

1 tbsp. seasoned salt

1 tsp. onion powder

2 tsp. ground cumin

½ tsp. garlic powder

1 tsp. dried oregano

2 16-oz. cans red kidney beans, *drained*

1 28-oz. can diced tomatoes, *do not drain*

1 12-oz. can tomato paste

2 14-oz. cans nonfat chicken or vegetable broth

Spray nonstick skillet with cooking spray. Add beef and onions to skillet and cook over medium heat, stirring frequently, until beef is browned and crumbled. Drain well. Spray inside of slow cooker with cooking spray. Place beef mixture in slow cooker; add remaining ingredients and mix well. Cover and cook on low heat for 8 hours or high heat for 4 hours.

Nutrition Facts per serving: 196 cal., 4.1 g total fat, 46 mg chol., 839 mg sodium, 17 g carbo., 4 g fiber, 21 g pro.

Exchanges: 1 Starch, ½ Lean Meat

Carb Choices: 1

Substitution Tip: You can use two ¾-oz. packets of chili seasoning mix in place of the seasonings called for in the recipe.

Shopping List

Meat	12-oz. can tomato paste
3 lbs. extra-lean ground beef	2 14-oz. cans nonfat chicken or vegetable broth
Frozen	
12-oz. pkg. frozen chopped onions	**Seasonings**
	chili powder
	seasoned salt
Canned	onion powder
2 16-oz. cans red kidney beans	ground cumin
	garlic powder
28-oz. can diced tomatoes	dried oregano

Turkey Chili with White Beans

Easy | Do Ahead | Serves: 6

1 lb. extra-lean ground turkey breast

¾ tsp. garlic powder

½ tsp. onion powder

2 tbsp. + 2½ tsp. chili powder

1 tsp. sweet Hungarian paprika

¼ tsp. pepper

1 7-oz. can diced green chiles, *do not drain*

1 16-oz. pkg. dry small white beans, *rinsed, drained, and picked over*

1 14-oz. can nonfat chicken broth, *boiling*

2¼ cups boiling water

2 cups chopped onions

Spray large nonstick skillet with cooking spray. Add turkey, garlic powder, and onion powder to skillet. Cook over medium heat, stirring frequently, until browned and crumbled. Drain well. Spray inside of slow cooker with cooking spray. Combine browned turkey, chili powder, paprika, pepper, undrained chiles, beans, broth, water, and onions in slow cooker. Cover and cook on high heat for 1 hour. Reduce heat to low and cook 8–9 hours.

Nutrition Facts per serving: 217 cal., 2 g total fat, 30 mg chol., 710 mg sodium, 26 g carbo., 3 g fiber, 25 g pro.

Exchanges: 2 Vegetable, 1 Starch, 3 Very Lean Meat

Carb Choices: 2

Soups and Chowders

Shopping List

Produce	Packaged
2 large onions	16-oz. pkg. dry small white beans
Poultry	
1 lb. extra-lean ground turkey breast	**Seasonings**
	garlic powder
	onion powder
Canned	chili powder
7-oz. can diced green chiles	sweet Hungarian paprika
14-oz. can nonfat chicken broth	pepper

Vegetarian Chili with Beans

Easy | **Do Ahead** | **Freeze** | **Serves: 16**

- 2 14-oz. cans nonfat vegetable broth
- 2 cups frozen chopped onions, *thawed and drained*
- 2 ¾-oz. packets chili seasoning mix
- 2 15-oz. cans black beans, *drained*
- 2 15-oz. cans red kidney beans, *drained*
- 2 15-oz. cans chili beans, *drained*
- 2 8-oz. cans tomato sauce

Shopping List

Frozen
2 10-oz. pkgs. frozen chopped onions

Canned
2 14-oz. cans nonfat vegetable broth
2 15-oz. cans black beans
2 15-oz. cans red kidney beans
2 15-oz. cans chili beans
2 8-oz. cans tomato sauce

Seasonings
2 ¾-oz. packets chili seasoning mix

Spray inside of slow cooker with cooking spray. Combine all ingredients in slow cooker and mix well. Cover and cook on low heat for 8 hours or high heat for 4 hours.

Nutrition Facts per serving: 189 cal., 0.7 g total fat, 0 mg chol., 1,036 mg sodium, 34 g carbo., 5 g fiber, 12 g pro.
Exchanges: 1 Vegetable, 2 Starch
Carb Choices: 2

Garnish vegetarian chili with crushed baked tortilla chips; shredded nonfat cheddar cheese; nonfat sour cream; chopped green, red, or yellow onions; or diced green chiles. For a heartier meal, serve with cooked white or brown rice, small pasta, or couscous.

Lentil and Barley Soup

Easy | Do Ahead | Serves: 6

1 cup dry lentils, *rinsed and drained*

⅓ cup pearl barley

1 cup chopped carrots

1 cup chopped celery

1 cup chopped onion

1 tsp. minced garlic

1¼ tsp. dried Italian seasoning

1 bay leaf

3½ cups nonfat vegetable broth

2½ cups water

1 14½-oz. can petite-cut diced tomatoes with roasted garlic and sweet onion, *do not drain*

Spray inside of slow cooker with cooking spray. Combine all ingredients in slow cooker and mix well. Cover and cook on low heat for 10–12 hours or high heat for 5–6 hours. Remove bay leaf before serving.

Nutrition Facts per serving: 99 cal., 0.6 g total fat, 0 mg chol., 599 mg sodium, 19 g carbo., 5 g fiber, 5 g pro.
Exchanges: 1 Vegetable, 1 Starch
Carb Choices: 1

Substitution Tip: You can use vegetable, chicken, and beef broths interchangeably in recipes, but the flavor may vary slightly. Or substitute bouillon cubes or granules and add water accordingly.

Soups and Chowders

Shopping List

Produce	Packaged
2 carrots	8-oz. pkg. dry lentils
small bunch celery	8-oz. pkg. pearl barley
large onion	
	Seasonings
Canned	minced garlic
2 14-oz. cans nonfat vegetable broth	dried Italian seasoning
	bay leaf
14½-oz. can petite-cut diced tomatoes with roasted garlic and sweet onion	

Lentil-Tomato Soup

1 cup dry lentils, *rinsed and drained*

1 cup chopped carrots

1 cup chopped celery

1 cup chopped onion

1 tsp. minced garlic

1¼ tsp. dried Italian seasoning

1 bay leaf

2 14-oz. cans nonfat chicken or vegetable broth

1½ cups water

1 14½-oz. can Italian recipe stewed tomatoes with oregano and basil, *do not drain*

Spray inside of slow cooker with cooking spray. Combine all ingredients in slow cooker and mix lightly. Cover and cook on low heat for 10–12 hours or high heat for 5–6 hours. Remove bay leaf before serving.

Nutrition Facts per serving: 154 cal., 0.4 g total fat, 0 mg chol., 582 mg sodium, 26 g carbo., 2 g fiber, 12 g pro.
Exchanges: 4 Vegetable, ½ Starch
Carb Choices: 2

Shopping List

Produce	Packaged
2 carrots	8-oz. pkg. dry lentils
small bunch celery	
large onion	**Seasonings**
	minced garlic
Canned	dried Italian seasoning
2 14-oz. cans nonfat chicken or vegetable broth	bay leaf
14½-oz. can Italian recipe stewed tomatoes with oregano and basil	

Meatless Meals  5

Stuffed Peppers

Bean Dip or Filling

Easy | Do Ahead | Freeze | Serves: 4

1 15-oz. can nonfat refried beans

1 cup thick and chunky salsa

2 cups nonfat shredded cheddar cheese

¾ cup nonfat sour cream

3 oz. nonfat cream cheese, *softened*

1 tbsp. chili powder

¼ tsp. ground cumin

4 98% fat-free flour tortillas

shredded lettuce, chopped tomatoes, and/or chopped green onions (optional)

baked tortilla chips and salsa (optional)

Spray inside of slow cooker with cooking spray. Combine beans, salsa, cheddar cheese, sour cream, cream cheese, chili powder, and cumin in slow cooker and mix well. Cover and cook on high heat for 2 hours, stirring once or twice while cooking. Spoon mixture into tortillas and top with lettuce, tomatoes, and green onions, if desired, or serve as dip with tortilla chips and additional salsa.

Nutrition Facts per serving: 425 cal., 0.8 g total fat, 0 mg chol., 1,947 mg sodium, 64 g carbo., 6 g fiber, 35 g pro.
Exchanges: 2 Vegetable, 3½ Starch, 3 Very Lean Meat
Carb Choices: 4

Shopping List

Dairy
8 oz. nonfat shredded cheddar cheese
6 oz. nonfat sour cream
3 oz. nonfat cream cheese

Canned
15-oz. can nonfat refried beans

Packaged
17.5-oz. pkg. 98% fat-free flour tortillas

Condiments
8-oz. jar thick and chunky salsa

Seasonings
chili powder
ground cumin

Optional
lettuce, tomatoes, and green onions
baked tortilla chips and salsa

Curried Cauliflower and Potatoes

Easy | **Do Ahead** | **Serves: 4**

3 cups cauliflower florets

3 medium potatoes, *peeled and quartered*

¾ tsp. dry mustard

1¼ tsp. chili powder

½ tsp. sugar

1 14½-oz. can petite-cut diced tomatoes, *do not drain*

1¼ cups water

½ tsp. curry powder

Spray inside of slow cooker with cooking spray. Combine all ingredients in slow cooker and mix well. Cover and cook on low heat for 6–8 hours or high heat for 3–4 hours.

Nutrition Facts per serving: 154 cal., 0.2 g total fat, 0 mg chol., 856 mg sodium, 36 g carbo., 5 g fiber, 5 g pro.
Exchanges: 3 Vegetable, 1 Starch
Carb Choices: 2

Meatless Meals

Shopping List

Produce
1 lb. cauliflower
3 medium potatoes

Canned
14½-oz. can petite-cut diced tomatoes

Baking Goods
sugar

Seasonings
dry mustard
chili powder
curry powder

Curry powder is a blend of many ground spices, including cumin, coriander, turmeric, pepper, cardamom, cloves, cinnamon, and nutmeg. The turmeric gives curried dishes their distinctive yellow color.

Chili Cheese Tortilla Wraps

Easy | **Do Ahead** | **Serves: 4**

- 1 16-oz. can nonfat refried beans
- 1 8-oz. pkg. nonfat cream cheese, *cut into cubes and softened*
- 1 4-oz. can diced green chiles, *drained*
- ¾ cup chopped green onions
- 1 cup nonfat shredded cheddar cheese
- 4 98% fat-free flour tortillas
  baked tortilla chips (optional)

Spray inside of slow cooker with cooking spray. Combine refried beans, cream cheese, chiles, and green onions in slow cooker and mix well. Cover and cook on low heat for 4 hours or high heat for 2 hours, stirring once or twice during cooking. If cooking on low heat, increase to high. Stir in ¾ cup of the cheese and sprinkle ¼ cup cheese over top. Wrap tortillas in foil and warm in 350° oven 5–10 minutes until heated through. Spoon bean mixture into tortillas; roll and serve immediately. If desired, serve bean mixture with tortilla chips instead of tortillas.

Nutrition Facts per serving: 378 cal., 0.9 g total fat, 0 mg chol., 1,907 mg sodium, 62 g carbo., 7 g fiber, 29 g pro.
Exchanges: 4 Starch, 2 Very Lean Meat
Carb Choices: 4

Shopping List

Produce
small bunch green onions

Dairy
8 oz. nonfat cream cheese
4 oz. nonfat shredded cheddar cheese

Canned
16-oz. can nonfat refried beans
4-oz. can diced green chiles

Packaged
17.5-oz. pkg. 98% fat-free flour tortillas

Optional
baked tortilla chips

Vegetarian Cabbage Rolls

Do Ahead | **Serves: 4**

Ingredients

- 1 2-lb. whole green cabbage
- 1 cup cooked brown rice
- 1 15-oz. can black beans, *drained*
- ¾ cup frozen chopped onions, *thawed and drained*
- 1 26-oz. jar nonfat pasta sauce, *divided*

Shopping List

Produce
2-lb. whole green cabbage

Frozen
12-oz. pkg. frozen chopped onions

Canned
15-oz. can black beans
26-oz. jar nonfat pasta sauce

Packaged
8-oz. pkg. brown rice (instant or regular)

Remove 8 large outer leaves from cabbage. Bring 4 cups water to a boil in saucepan. Add cabbage leaves; turn off heat and let leaves soak for 5 minutes. Remove leaves from water, drain, and let cool. Shred 4 cups of the remaining cabbage; wrap and refrigerate unused portion of cabbage for another use. Spray inside of slow cooker with cooking spray. Place shredded cabbage in bottom of cooker. Combine cooked rice, beans, onions, and ½ cup pasta sauce in medium bowl and mix well. Place about ⅓ cup mixture in center of each leaf; fold sides over filling and roll up. Pour half the remaining pasta sauce over shredded cabbage and toss to mix. Place cabbage rolls on shredded cabbage, stacking if necessary, and top with remaining pasta sauce. Cover and cook on low heat for 6–7 hours or high heat for 3–3½ hours. Serve cabbage rolls with shredded cooked cabbage.

Meatless Meals

Nutrition Facts per serving: 283 cal., 1.1 g total fat, 0 mg chol., 1,027 mg sodium, 57 g carbo., 8 g fiber, 12 g pro.
Exchanges: 2 Vegetable, 3 Starch
Carb Choices: 4

Vegetable-Stuffed Peppers

Easy | **Do Ahead** | **Serves: 4**

- 4 large bell peppers
- ½ cup converted white rice
- 1 15¼-oz. can whole kernel corn, *drained*
- ½ cup chopped green onions
- ¼ tsp. Mrs. Dash seasoning
- ⅛ tsp. garlic powder
- ⅛ tsp. pepper
- 1 14½-oz. can petite-cut diced tomatoes, *do not drain*
- ⅓ cup dry red wine
- 1 6-oz. can Italian tomato paste with roasted garlic

Spray inside of slow cooker with cooking spray. Cut off tops of bell peppers and remove stems; chop remaining portion of each top and set aside. Clean out the inside of peppers. Arrange peppers standing upright in slow cooker. Combine chopped pepper, rice, corn, green onions, Mrs. Dash seasoning, garlic powder, pepper, and ¼ cup tomatoes (without juice) and mix well. Stuff mixture into peppers. Combine remaining tomatoes and liquid with wine and tomato paste; mix well. Pour mixture over and around peppers. Cover and cook on low heat for 6–7 hours or high heat for 3–3½ hours.

Nutrition Facts per serving: 259 cal., 1.6 g total fat, 0 mg chol., 908 mg sodium, 53 g carbo., 6 g fiber, 7 g pro.
Exchanges: 4 Vegetable, 2 Starch
Carb Choices: 4

Shopping List

Produce	Packaged
4 large bell peppers (any color)	converted white rice
small bunch green onions	**Seasonings**
	Mrs. Dash seasoning
Canned	garlic powder
15¼-oz. can whole kernel corn	pepper
14½-oz. can petite-cut diced tomatoes	**Other**
6-oz. can Italian tomato paste with roasted garlic	dry red wine

Potato-Stuffed Cabbage

Easy | Do Ahead | Serves: 6

12 large cabbage leaves

5 lbs. potatoes, *peeled and grated*

1½ cups frozen chopped onions, *thawed, drained, and divided*

½ cup converted rice

1 tsp. celery seed

¼ tsp. pepper

¼ cup egg substitute

1 28-oz. can petite-cut diced tomatoes, *do not drain*

Bring 4 cups water to a boil in saucepan. Add cabbage leaves; turn off heat and let leaves soak for 5 minutes. Remove leaves from water, drain, and let cool. Spray inside of slow cooker with cooking spray. Combine potatoes, ¾ cup onions, rice, celery seed, pepper, and egg substitute in a medium bowl and mix well. Place about 2 tablespoons of mixture in the center of each leaf; fold sides over filling and roll up. Arrange cabbage rolls in slow cooker, stacking if necessary. Combine remaining onions with undrained tomatoes and pour over cabbage rolls. Cover and cook on low heat for 4–6 hours or high heat for 2–3 hours.

Meatless Meals

Nutrition Facts per serving: 466 cal., 0.8 g total fat, 0 mg chol., 283 mg sodium, 107 g carbo., 2 g fiber, 12 g pro.
Exchanges: 3 Vegetable, 5 Starch
Carb Choices: 7

Shopping List

Produce	Canned
head cabbage	28-oz. can petite-cut diced
5 lbs. potatoes	tomatoes

Frozen	Packaged
12-oz. pkg. frozen chopped	converted rice
onions	

	Seasonings
Dairy	celery seed
egg substitute	pepper

Ratatouille

1 large eggplant, *peeled and cut into 1-inch cubes*

1–2 tsp. salt

2 cups frozen chopped onions, *thawed, drained, and patted dry*

1 28-oz. can diced tomatoes, *do not drain*

1 large green bell pepper, *cut into ½-inch pieces*

1 large red bell pepper, *cut into ½-inch pieces*

2 medium zucchini, *sliced*

1 yellow squash, *sliced*

3 tbsp. dried basil

1 tsp. minced garlic

3 tbsp. nonfat vegetable broth

1 6-oz. can Italian tomato paste with roasted garlic

3 tbsp. chopped fresh basil

Spray inside of slow cooker with cooking spray. Sprinkle eggplant with salt and let stand in colander 30–60 minutes to drain. Press out any excess moisture; rinse eggplant with water and pat dry with paper towels. Arrange eggplant in bottom of cooker. Top with onions, undrained tomatoes, bell peppers, zucchini, and squash. Add dried basil and minced garlic to broth; pour over vegetables and mix well. Cover and cook on low heat for 6 hours or high heat for 3 hours. Stir in tomato paste and fresh basil.

Nutrition Facts per serving: 126 cal., 0.9 g total fat, 0 mg chol., 487 mg sodium, 27 g carbo., 6 g fiber, 5 g pro.
Exchanges: 5 Vegetable
Carb Choices: 2

Shopping List

Produce	Canned
large eggplant	28-oz. can diced tomatoes
large green bell pepper	14-oz. can nonfat vegetable
large red bell pepper	broth·
2 medium zucchini	6-oz. can Italian tomato
medium yellow squash	paste with roasted garlic
fresh basil	

Frozen	Seasonings
12-oz. pkg. frozen chopped	salt
onions	dried basil
	minced garlic

Macaroni and Cheese

Easy | **Do Ahead** | **Serves: 4**

- 1 12-oz. can evaporated skim milk
- 1½ cups nonfat half and half
- ½ cup egg substitute
- 8 oz. uncooked elbow macaroni
- 4 cups nonfat shredded cheddar cheese, *divided*
- ½ tsp. pepper

Shopping List

Dairy
12 oz. nonfat half and half
egg substitute
16-oz. pkg. nonfat shredded
  cheddar cheese

Canned
12-oz. can evaporated skim
  milk

Packaged
8 oz. elbow macaroni

Seasonings
pepper

Spray inside of slow cooker with cooking spray. Combine evaporated skim milk, half and half, egg substitute, macaroni, 3½ cups cheese, and pepper in slow cooker and mix well. Sprinkle remaining cheese on top. Cover and cook on low heat for 6–8 hours.

Nutrition Facts per serving: 531 cal., 1 g total fat, 3 mg chol., 1,312 mg sodium, 72 g carbo., 0 g fiber, 49 g pro.
Exchanges: 4 Starch, 1 Other Carbo., 4 Very Lean Meat
Carb Choices: 5

Meatless
Meals

For variety, add canned diced green chiles or well-drained tomatoes to the recipe, or substitute mozzarella cheese for half of the cheddar.

Enchilada Casserole

1 28-oz. can crushed tomatoes in tomato puree

1 16-oz. jar thick and chunky salsa

1 6-oz. can roasted garlic tomato paste

2 15-oz. cans black beans, *drained*

1 16-oz. can whole kernel corn, *drained*

1 4-oz. can diced green chiles, *drained*

2¼ tsp. chili powder

½ tsp. garlic powder

1 8.5-oz. pkg. low-fat white corn tortillas

1 cup nonfat shredded cheddar cheese

Spray inside of slow cooker with cooking spray. Combine tomatoes, salsa, tomato paste, beans, corn, chiles, chili powder, and garlic powder in medium bowl and mix well. Spoon about 1 cup of mixture into bottom of slow cooker and spread evenly. Top with 1½ tortillas (cutting as necessary to fit). Top with a third of remaining tomato mixture and another layer of tortillas. Repeat layers, ending with tomato mixture. Cover and cook on low heat for 5–6 hours. Just before serving, sprinkle cheese on top and cook 30 minutes until cheese is melted.

Nutrition Facts per serving: 396 cal., 1.1 g total fat, 0 mg chol., 2,158 mg sodium, 78 g carbo., 13 g fiber, 21 g pro.
Exchanges: 3 Vegetable, 4 Starch
Carb Choices: 5

Shopping List

Dairy	Packaged
4 oz. nonfat shredded cheddar cheese	8.5-oz. pkg. white corn tortillas

Canned	Condiments
28-oz. can crushed tomatoes in tomato puree	16-oz. jar thick and chunky salsa
6-oz. can roasted garlic tomato paste	
2 15-oz. cans black beans	**Seasonings**
16-oz. can whole kernel corn	chili powder
4-oz. can diced green chiles	garlic powder

Eggplant Parmigiana

Easy | Do Ahead | Serves: 6

½ cup egg substitute

⅓ cup skim milk

3 tbsp. + ⅓ cup seasoned bread crumbs, *divided*

4 large eggplants, *peeled, sliced ½ inch thick, and patted dry*

½ cup nonfat Parmesan cheese

1 28-oz. can nonfat pasta sauce

16 oz. nonfat mozzarella cheese slices

Shopping List

Produce
4 large eggplants

Dairy
egg substitute
skim milk
nonfat Parmesan cheese
16 oz. nonfat mozzarella
cheese slices

Canned
28-oz. can or jar nonfat pasta
sauce

Packaged
seasoned bread crumbs

Combine egg substitute, milk, and 3 tablespoons bread crumbs in shallow baking dish and mix well. Spray large nonstick skillet with cooking spray and heat over medium-high heat. Dip some of the eggplant slices in bread crumb mixture and cook in hot skillet until lightly browned on both sides. Remove from skillet and repeat with remaining eggplant slices. Combine remaining bread crumbs with Parmesan cheese and mix well. Spray inside of slow cooker with cooking spray. Layer a quarter of eggplant slices, a quarter of crumb mixture, a quarter of pasta sauce, and a quarter of mozzarella cheese slices. Repeat layers, ending with cheese. Cover and cook on low heat for 4–5 hours or high heat for 2–2½ hours.

Meatless Meals

Nutrition Facts per serving: 306 cal., 1 g total fat, 1 mg chol., 1,149 mg sodium, 36 g carbo., 1 g fiber, 34 g pro.
Exchanges: 4 Vegetable, 1 Starch, 4 Very Lean Meat
Carb Choices: 2

Vegetarian Slow Cooker Casserole

Easy | Do Ahead | Serves: 8

6 baking potatoes, *sliced*

1 large onion, *sliced*

2 large carrots, *peeled and sliced*

1 zucchini, *sliced*

1 yellow squash, *sliced*

1 11-oz. can Mexicorn, *drained*

1 cup frozen peas, *thawed and drained*

1 cup sliced fresh mushrooms

2½ cups canned tomato sauce with roasted garlic

¼ cup low-sodium soy sauce

1 tsp. dried thyme

1 tsp. dry mustard

1 tsp. dried basil

2 tsp. chili powder

½ tsp. ground cinnamon

⅛ tsp. dried rosemary

2 tbsp. dried parsley

Spray inside of slow cooker with cooking spray. Layer potatoes, onion, carrots, zucchini, squash, Mexicorn, peas, and mushrooms in slow cooker. Combine remaining ingredients and mix well. Pour tomato mixture over vegetables. Cover and cook on low heat for 10–12 hours or high heat for 5–6 hours.

Nutrition Facts per serving: 205 cal., 0.7 g total fat, 0 mg chol., 1,075 mg sodium, 47 g carbo., 6 g fiber, 7 g pro.
Exchanges: 2 Vegetable, 2 Starch
Carb Choices: 3

Shopping List

Produce
6 baking potatoes
large onion
2 large carrots
medium zucchini
medium yellow squash
½ lb. sliced fresh
   mushrooms

Frozen
10-oz. pkg. frozen peas

Canned
11-oz. can Mexicorn
3 8-oz. cans tomato sauce
   with roasted garlic

Condiments
low-sodium soy sauce

Seasonings
dried thyme
dry mustard
dried basil
chili powder
ground cinnamon
dried rosemary
dried parsley

Spicy Vegetarian Special

Easy | **Do Ahead** | **Serves: 8**

3 cups nonfat vegetable broth

1½ cups frozen chopped onions, *thawed and drained*

2 large carrots, *peeled and sliced*

1 tsp. minced garlic

2 11-oz. cans Mexicorn, *drained*

1 15-oz. can red kidney beans, *drained*

1 15-oz. can black beans, *drained*

1 14½-oz. can stewed tomatoes with bell pepper and onion, *drained*

1 4-oz. can diced green chiles, *do not drain*

Spray inside of slow cooker with cooking spray. Combine all ingredients in slow cooker and mix well. Cover and cook on high heat for 1 hour. Reduce heat to low and cook for 7–8 hours.

Nutrition Facts per serving: 192 cal., 1.1 g total fat, 0 mg chol., 1,331 mg sodium, 39 g carbo., 7 g fiber, 10 g pro.
Exchanges: 2 Vegetable, 2 Starch
Carb Choices: 3

Bean Math: A 15-ounce can of drained, rinsed beans equals 1⅔ cups cooked beans.

Meatless Meals

Shopping List

Produce
2 large carrots

Frozen
12-oz. pkg. frozen chopped onions

Canned
2 14-oz. cans nonfat vegetable broth
2 11-oz. cans Mexicorn
15-oz. can red kidney beans
15-oz. can black beans

14½-oz. can stewed tomatoes with bell pepper and onion
4-oz. can diced green chiles

Seasonings
minced garlic

Barbecue Beans

2 15-oz. cans Great Northern beans, *drained*

2 15-oz. cans black beans, *drained*

2 15-oz. cans lima beans, *drained*

1¼ cups barbecue sauce

1 cup thick and chunky salsa

¼ cup + 2 tbsp. brown sugar

¼ tsp. Tabasco sauce

frozen vegetarian burgers (optional)

Spray inside of slow cooker with cooking spray. Combine all ingredients in slow cooker and mix well. Cover and cook on low heat for 2–3 hours until heated through. Serve as a main dish or as a side dish with cooked vegetarian burgers.

Nutrition Facts per serving: 536 cal., 1.9 g total fat, 0 mg chol., 1,948 mg sodium, 107 g carbo., 10 g fiber, 26 g pro.
Exchanges: 5 Starch, 2 Other Carbo.
Carb Choices: 7

Many varieties of mature dry beans are canned. While most beans are sold packed in natural juices, others are available with special sauces such as baked beans with tomato, brown sugar, and molasses sauce or kidney beans in sweet sauce or clear salt brine.

Shopping List

Canned	Condiments
2 15-oz. cans Great Northern beans	12-oz. bottle barbecue sauce
2 15-oz. cans black beans	8-oz. jar thick and chunky salsa
2 15-oz. cans lima beans	Tabasco sauce

Baking Goods	Optional
brown sugar	frozen vegetarian burgers

Garbanzo Beans and Tomatoes

Easy | **Do Ahead** | **Serves: 6**

1 tbsp. nonfat vegetable broth

1½ cups frozen chopped onions, *thawed and drained*

2 tsp. minced garlic

1 tsp. ground ginger

2 tsp. ground coriander

1 tsp. cumin seed

½ tsp. black pepper

½ tsp. cayenne pepper

2 tsp. balsamic vinegar

2 cups petite-cut diced tomatoes with roasted garlic and sweet onion, *drained*

2 19-oz. cans garbanzo beans, *rinsed and drained*

Spray large nonstick skillet with cooking spray. Add broth to skillet and heat over medium-high heat. Add onions and minced garlic to skillet. Cook over medium-high heat, stirring frequently, until vegetables are lightly browned. Add ginger, coriander, cumin, pepper, and cayenne pepper; cook 1 minute. Add vinegar and tomatoes; bring to a boil over high heat. Remove skillet from heat and stir in garbanzo beans. Spray inside of slow cooker with cooking spray. Spoon mixture into slow cooker. Cover and cook on low heat for 6–8 hours or high heat for 3–4 hours.

Meatless Meals

Nutrition Facts per serving: 238 cal., 2 g total fat, 0 mg chol., 653 mg sodium, 45 g carbo., 3 g fiber, 10 g pro.
Exchanges: 3 Vegetable, 2 Starch
Carb Choices: 3

Shopping List

Frozen	Condiments
12-oz. pkg. frozen chopped onions	balsamic vinegar
	Seasonings
Canned	minced garlic
14-oz. can nonfat vegetable broth	ground ginger
	ground coriander
2 14½-oz. cans petite-cut diced tomatoes with roasted garlic and sweet onion	cumin seed
	pepper
	cayenne pepper
2 19-oz. cans garbanzo beans	

Red Beans and Rice

Easy | **Do Ahead** | **Freeze** | **Serves: 6**

1 lb. dry red kidney beans

2 14½-oz. cans stewed tomatoes with bell pepper and onion, *do not drain*

½ cup frozen chopped onions, *thawed and drained*

½ tsp. garlic powder

⅛ tsp. pepper

1 tsp. dried basil

1 tsp. dried thyme

⅛ tsp. cayenne pepper

1½ cups converted brown rice

½ cup dry white wine

Place beans in large soup pot. Cover beans with water and bring to a boil. Boil 10 minutes; reduce heat, cover, and simmer 1½ hours or until beans are tender. Drain. Spray inside of slow cooker with cooking spray. Combine all ingredients except rice and wine in slow cooker and mix well. Cover and cook on high heat for 4 hours. Reduce heat to low and cook 4½ hours. Add rice and wine and cook 1½ hours.

Nutrition Facts per serving: 322 cal., 1.4 g total fat, 0 mg chol., 557 mg sodium, 59 g carbo., 1 g fiber, 18 g pro.
Exchanges: 3 Vegetable, 3 Starch
Carb Choices: 4

Shopping List

Frozen
12-oz. pkg. frozen chopped onions

Canned
2 14½-oz. cans stewed tomatoes with bell pepper and onion

Packaged
1 lb. red kidney beans
converted brown rice

Seasonings
garlic powder
pepper
dried basil
dried thyme
cayenne pepper

Other
dry white wine

Great Grains

Easy | Do Ahead | Serves: 4

1 14½-oz. can petite-cut diced tomatoes, *drained and liquid reserved*

¼ cup quinoa

¼ cup barley

⅓ cup brown rice

1 cup frozen chopped onions, *thawed and drained*

1 cup frozen chopped green bell peppers, *thawed and drained*

½ cup chopped carrot

1 15-oz. can red kidney beans, *drained*

1 8-oz. can tomato sauce with roasted garlic

1½ cups frozen whole kernel corn, *thawed and drained*

1 tsp. dried oregano

1 tsp. dried basil

1 tsp. garlic powder

⅛ tsp. pepper

Spray inside of slow cooker with cooking spray. Drain tomatoes and reserve liquid; add enough water to tomato liquid to equal 2½ cups. Combine all ingredients with tomatoes and liquid in slow cooker and toss to mix. Cover and cook on low heat for 8–10 hours or high heat for 4–5 hours.

Nutrition Facts per serving: 337 cal., 2.1 g total fat, 0 mg chol., 547 mg sodium, 70 g carbo., 11 g fiber, 14 g pro.

Exchanges: 4 Vegetable, 3 Starch

Carb Choices: 5

Meatless Meals

Shopping List

Produce	
large carrot	

Frozen	
12-oz. pkg. frozen chopped onions	
10-oz. pkg. frozen chopped green bell peppers	
10-oz. pkg. frozen whole kernel corn	

Canned	
14½-oz. can petite-cut diced tomatoes	
15-oz. can red kidney beans	
8-oz. can tomato sauce with roasted garlic	

Packaged	
quinoa	
barley	
brown rice	

Seasonings	
dried oregano	
dried basil	
garlic powder	
pepper	

Lentil-Rice Meal

Easy | **Do Ahead** | **Serves: 8**

2 cups dry lentils, *rinsed and drained*

2 cups uncooked brown rice

1 cup chopped carrots

1½ cups frozen seasoning vegetables, *thawed and drained*

6 cups nonfat vegetable broth

3 cups water

1 tsp. garlic powder

½ tsp. pepper

1 cup fresh sliced mushrooms

Shopping List

Produce
2 carrots
½ lb. mushrooms

Frozen
10-oz. pkg. frozen seasoning vegetables

Canned
4 14-oz. cans nonfat vegetable broth

Packaged
8-oz. pkg. dry lentils
8-oz. pkg. brown rice

Seasonings
garlic powder
pepper

Spray inside of slow cooker with cooking spray. Combine lentils, rice, carrots, seasoning vegetables, broth, water, garlic powder, and pepper in slow cooker and mix well. Cover and cook on low heat for 7–8 hours or high heat for 3½–4 hours. Stir in mushrooms and cook 1 hour.

Nutrition Facts per serving: 360 cal., 1.9 g total fat, 0 mg chol., 611 mg sodium, 67 g carbo., 2 g fiber, 20 g pro.
Exchanges: 2 Vegetable, 4 Starch
Carb Choices: 4

Substitution Tip: You can use ½ cup chopped onion, ½ cup chopped green bell pepper, and ½ cup diced celery in place of the frozen seasoning vegetables.

Curried Lentils and Spinach

Easy | **Do Ahead** | **Serves: 4**

- 1 10-oz. pkg. frozen chopped spinach, *thawed and drained*
- ¾ cup frozen chopped onions, *thawed and drained*
- 1 cup dry lentils, *rinsed and drained*
- ¼ cup converted rice
- 1 tsp. crushed garlic
- 1½ tsp. curry powder
- ¼ tsp. chili powder
- 1 tsp. ground ginger
- ¼ tsp. ground turmeric
- ¼ tsp. cayenne pepper
- 2 cups nonfat vegetable broth
- 1 cup petite-cut diced tomatoes with roasted garlic and sweet onion, *drained*

Spray inside of slow cooker with cooking spray. Combine all ingredients except tomatoes in slow cooker and mix well. Cover and cook on low heat for 6–7 hours or high heat for 3–3½ hours. Top with tomatoes and serve.

Nutrition Facts per serving: 231 cal., 1 g total fat, 0 mg chol., 952 mg sodium, 41 g carbo., 2 g fiber, 18 g pro.
Exchanges: 6 Vegetable, 1 Starch
Carb Choices: 3

Meatless Meals

Shopping List

Frozen	Packaged
10-oz. pkg. frozen chopped spinach	dry lentils
12-oz. pkg. frozen chopped onions	converted rice
	Seasonings
Canned	crushed garlic
2 14-oz. cans nonfat vegetable broth	curry powder
14½-oz. can petite-cut diced tomatoes with roasted garlic and sweet onion	chili powder
	ground ginger
	ground turmeric
	cayenne pepper

Curry Vegetable Main Dish

Easy | **Do Ahead** | **Serves: 4**

1¾ lbs. russet potatoes, *peeled and diced*

1 cup frozen chopped onions, *thawed and drained*

1 cup chopped red bell pepper

2 carrots, *peeled and chopped*

1 14½-oz. can petite-cut diced tomatoes, *drained*

1 6-oz. can Italian tomato paste with roasted garlic

¾ cup water

1–2 tbsp. curry powder

2 tsp. chili powder

½ tsp. garlic powder

2 cups 1-inch cauliflower florets

2 cups 1-inch broccoli florets

1 10-oz. pkg. frozen green beans, *thawed and drained*

Spray inside of slow cooker with cooking spray. Combine potatoes, onions, bell pepper, carrots, and tomatoes in bottom of slow cooker. Add tomato paste, water, curry powder, chili powder, and garlic powder and mix well. Top with cauliflower and broccoli florets. Cover and cook on low heat for 8–9 hours or high heat for 4–4½ hours. Stir in green beans. If cooking on low heat, increase to high and cook 15–20 minutes.

Nutrition Facts per serving: 312 cal., 0.9 g total fat, 0 mg chol., 612 mg sodium, 69 g carbo., 7 g fiber, 10 g pro.
Exchanges: 7 Vegetable, 2 Starch
Carb Choices: 5

Shopping List

Produce	Canned
1¾ lbs. russet potatoes	14½-oz. can petite-cut
large red bell pepper	diced tomatoes
2 carrots	6-oz. can Italian tomato
¾ lb. cauliflower	paste with roasted garlic
¾ lb. broccoli	
	Seasonings
Frozen	curry powder
12-oz. pkg. frozen chopped	chili powder
onions	garlic powder
10-oz. pkg. frozen green	
beans	

Curry Couscous with Raisins

Easy | **Do Ahead** | **Serves: 6**

- 1½ lbs. baking potatoes, *peeled and cubed*
- 2 14½-oz. cans diced tomatoes with garlic and onion, *do not drain*
- 2 cups frozen pepper stir-fry, *thawed and drained*
- 1 cup sliced carrots
- 1–2 tbsp. curry powder
- 2 tsp. cumin seed
- ¼ tsp. cayenne pepper
- 2 15-oz. cans garbanzo beans, *rinsed and drained*
- 1½ tsp. minced garlic
- ⅓ cup chopped fresh cilantro
- ¼ cup sliced green onion tops
- 3 cups hot cooked couscous
- 6 tbsp. mango chutney
- 6 tbsp. raisins
- 6 tbsp. nonfat sour cream

Spray inside of slow cooker with cooking spray. Arrange potatoes in bottom of slow cooker. Combine undrained tomatoes, pepper stir-fry, carrots, curry powder, cumin seed, cayenne pepper, garbanzo beans, and minced garlic in medium bowl and mix well. Spoon tomato mixture over potatoes. Cover and cook on low heat for 8–9 hours or high heat for 4–4½ hours. Add cilantro and green onions and heat through. Serve mixture over hot couscous. Top each serving with 1 tablespoon each chutney, raisins, and sour cream.

Nutrition Facts per serving: 475 cal., 3.1 g total fat, 0 mg chol., 823 mg sodium, 96 g carbo., 18 g fiber, 16 g pro.
Exchanges: 4 Vegetable, 1 Fruit, 4 Starch
Carb Choices: 6

Meatless Meals

Shopping List

Produce
1½ lbs. baking potatoes
2 carrots
fresh cilantro
small bunch green onions

Frozen
16-oz. pkg. frozen pepper stir-fry

Dairy
nonfat sour cream

Canned
2 14½-oz. cans diced tomatoes with garlic and onion

2 15-oz. cans garbanzo beans

Packaged
8-oz. pkg. couscous
6-oz. pkg. raisins

Condiments
mango chutney

Seasonings
curry powder
cumin seed
cayenne pepper
minced garlic

Barley, Bean, and Spinach Casserole

Easy | Do Ahead | Serves: 6

2 14-oz. cans nonfat vegetable broth

2 15-oz. cans red kidney beans, *rinsed and drained*

1 8-oz. pkg. sliced fresh mushrooms

1½ cups uncooked pearl barley

1½ cups sliced green onions

1 cup frozen chopped onions, *thawed and drained*

1 tsp. dried Italian seasoning

½ tsp. pepper

1 10-oz. pkg. frozen chopped spinach, *thawed and drained*

¾ cup nonfat Parmesan cheese

Spray inside of slow cooker with cooking spray. Combine broth, beans, mushrooms, barley, green onions, chopped onions, Italian seasoning, and pepper in slow cooker and mix well. Cover and cook on high heat for 3 hours. Add spinach; cover and cook 15 minutes until spinach is heated through. Sprinkle with cheese just before serving.

Nutrition Facts per serving: 375 cal., 1.8 g total fat, 0 mg chol., 1,063 mg sodium, 72 g carbo., 17 g fiber, 21 g pro.
Exchanges: 2 Vegetable, 4 Starch
Carb Choices: 5

Shopping List

Produce
8-oz. pkg. sliced fresh mushrooms
3 bunches green onions

Dairy
3 oz. nonfat Parmesan cheese

Frozen
12-oz. pkg. frozen chopped onions
10-oz. pkg. frozen chopped spinach

Canned
2 14-oz. cans nonfat vegetable broth
2 15-oz. cans red kidney beans

Packaged
8-oz. pkg. pearl barley

Seasonings
dried Italian seasoning
pepper

Spicy Cuban Beans and Rice

Easy | Do Ahead | Serves: 4

2½ cups frozen pepper stir-fry, *thawed and drained*

1 tsp. garlic powder

2 16-oz. cans red kidney beans, *rinsed and drained*

1 14½-oz. can diced tomatoes with green chiles, *do not drain*

2 cups water

1 tsp. ground cumin

½ tsp. dried oregano

¼ tsp. pepper

¼ tsp. cayenne pepper

4 cups hot cooked rice

⅓ cup chopped fresh cilantro

2 tbsp. lime juice

Spray inside of slow cooker with cooking spray. Combine pepper stir-fry, garlic powder, beans, undrained tomatoes, water, cumin, oregano, pepper, and cayenne pepper in slow cooker and mix well. Cover and cook on low heat for 4–5 hours or high heat for 2–2½ hours. Stir in hot cooked rice, cilantro, and lime juice and heat through.

Nutrition Facts per serving: 349 cal., 1.1 g total fat, 0 mg chol., 1,050 mg sodium, 71 g carbo., 3 g fiber, 14 g pro.
Exchanges: 1½ Vegetable, 4 Starch
Carb Choices: 5

Meatless Meals

Shopping List

Produce	Packaged
fresh cilantro	8-oz. pkg. white or brown
lime	rice (regular or instant)
Frozen	**Seasonings**
16-oz. pkg. frozen pepper	garlic powder
stir-fry	ground cumin
	dried oregano
Canned	pepper
2 16-oz. cans red kidney	cayenne pepper
beans	
14½-oz. can diced tomatoes	
with green chiles	

Vegetarian Sauce

1 28-oz. can crushed tomatoes, *do not drain*

1 28-oz. can diced tomatoes, *do not drain*

1 6-oz. can Italian tomato paste with roasted garlic

¾ cup chopped onion

1 tsp. crushed garlic

1 tbsp. dried Italian seasoning

½ lb. sliced fresh mushrooms

½ tsp. sugar

Shopping List

Produce
large onion
½ lb. sliced fresh mushrooms

Canned
28-oz. can crushed tomatoes
28-oz. can diced tomatoes
6-oz. can Italian tomato paste with roasted garlic

Baking Goods
sugar

Seasonings
crushed garlic
dried Italian seasoning

Spray inside of slow cooker with cooking spray. Combine all ingredients except sugar in slow cooker and mix well. Cover and cook on low heat for 7–8 hours or high heat for 3½–4 hours. Stir in sugar and cook 10–15 minutes. Serve over pasta or cooked spaghetti squash, or use as pizza sauce.

Nutrition Facts per serving: 97 cal., 0.5 g total fat, 0 mg chol., 376 mg sodium, 21 g carbo., 4 g fiber, 4 g pro.
Exchanges: 4 Vegetable
Carb Choices: 1

Slow cooking is a true energy-saver! You can save even more energy in the kitchen if you set the refrigerator between 38°F and 40°F, cover all food, check the refrigerator coils twice a year to avoid clogging them, and keep the refrigerator and freezer full.

Pasta with Eggplant and Artichoke Sauce

Easy | Do Ahead | Serves: 4

- 1 26-oz. jar nonfat pasta sauce
- 1 lb. eggplant, *cut into 1/4-inch slices*
- 1 9-oz. pkg. frozen artichoke hearts, *thawed and drained*
- 1 cup nonfat shredded mozzarella cheese
- 1 tsp. dried Italian seasoning
- 4 cups hot cooked angel hair pasta
- 1/2 cup nonfat Parmesan cheese

Spray inside of slow cooker with cooking spray. Pour half the pasta sauce into slow cooker; arrange half of eggplant slices on top. Top with half of the artichoke hearts and sprinkle with half of the mozzarella cheese. Spoon 1/2 cup pasta sauce over mozzarella cheese. Repeat layers with remaining eggplant, artichoke hearts, and mozzarella cheese. Top with remaining pasta sauce and sprinkle with Italian seasoning. Cover and cook on low heat for 5–6 hours. Serve over hot cooked pasta and sprinkle with Parmesan cheese (1–2 tablespoons per serving).

Meatless Meals

Nutrition Facts per serving: 353 cal., 1.4 g total fat, 0 mg chol., 922 mg sodium, 62 g carbo., 2 g fiber, 23 g pro.
Exchanges: 3 Vegetable, 3 Starch
Carb Choices: 4

Shopping List

Produce	**Packaged**
1 lb. eggplant	8-oz. pkg. angel hair pasta
Dairy	**Condiments**
4 oz. nonfat shredded mozzarella cheese	26-oz. jar nonfat pasta sauce
nonfat Parmesan cheese	
	Seasonings
Frozen	dried Italian seasoning
9-oz. pkg. frozen artichoke hearts	

Vegetarian Spaghetti with Super Sauce

Easy | Do Ahead | Serves: 6

- 1 1.25-oz. pkg. spaghetti sauce mix
- 1 8-oz. can tomato sauce with roasted garlic
- 1 cup water
- 1 medium zucchini, *cubed*
- ¾ lb. eggplant, *peeled and cubed*
- 1 medium green or red bell pepper, *cut into 1-inch pieces*
- 1 28-oz. can diced tomatoes, *drained*
- 8 oz. uncooked spaghetti
- ¾ cup nonfat Parmesan cheese

Spray inside of slow cooker with cooking spray. Combine spaghetti sauce mix, tomato sauce, water, zucchini, eggplant, bell pepper, and tomatoes in slow cooker and mix well. Cover and cook on low heat for 4–6 hours or high heat for 2–3 hours. Cook spaghetti according to package directions; drain well. Serve sauce over cooked spaghetti and sprinkle with cheese.

Nutrition Facts per serving: 244 cal., 0.8 g total fat, 0 mg chol., 1,032 mg sodium, 48 g carbo., 2 g fiber, 12 g pro.
Exchanges: 3 Vegetable, 2 Starch
Carb Choices: 3

Shopping List

Produce	Packaged
medium zucchini	1.25-oz. pkg. spaghetti
¾ lb. eggplant	sauce mix
medium bell pepper	8-oz. pkg. spaghetti

Dairy
nonfat Parmesan cheese

Canned
8-oz. can tomato sauce with roasted garlic
28-oz. can diced tomatoes

Five-Vegetable Sauce

Easy | Do Ahead | Serves: 4

1½ cups packed shredded zucchini

1½ cups packed shredded carrots

1 lb. chopped plum tomatoes

1 cup frozen chopped onions, *thawed, drained, and patted dry*

1 cup chopped bell pepper

¼ cup dry red wine

1½ tsp. minced garlic

1 6-oz. can Italian tomato paste with roasted garlic

¼ cup chopped fresh basil

Spray inside of slow cooker with cooking spray. Combine all ingredients except basil in slow cooker and mix well. Cover and cook on low heat for 7–8 hours or high heat for 3½–4 hours. Stir in fresh basil; cook 10–15 minutes. Serve sauce over pasta or spaghetti squash or use as pizza sauce.

Nutrition Facts per serving: 126 cal., 0.6 g total fat, 0 mg chol., 417 mg sodium, 24 g carbo., 6 g fiber, 4 g pro.
Exchanges: 5 Vegetable
Carb Choices: 2

Meatless Meals

Vegetable Pizza: Spread Five-Vegetable Sauce on Boboli or other pizza crust; top with nonfat shredded mozzarella cheese. Bake in 450° oven for 15–18 minutes until lightly browned and crisp.

Shopping List

Produce	Canned
2 medium zucchini	6-oz. can Italian tomato
3 large carrots	paste with roasted garlic
1 lb. plum tomatoes	
large bell pepper	**Seasonings**
fresh basil	minced garlic

Frozen	Other
12-oz. pkg. frozen chopped onions	dry red wine

Eggplant Pasta Sauce

Easy | **Do Ahead** | **Serves: 6**

- 1 lb. eggplant, *cut into 1-inch cubes*
- ¾ cup chopped onion
- ½ cup chopped green bell pepper
- 2 14-oz. cans ready-cut Italian diced tomatoes with garlic, oregano, and basil, *do not drain*
- 1 6-oz. can Italian tomato paste with roasted garlic
- ½ cup sliced fresh mushrooms
- 1 tsp. minced garlic
- 1½ tsp. sugar
- 1 tbsp. red wine vinegar
- ¼ cup water
- 1½ tsp. dried Italian seasoning
- 4 cups hot cooked penne pasta
- 6 tbsp. nonfat Parmesan cheese (optional)

Spray inside of slow cooker with cooking spray. Combine all ingredients except pasta and cheese in slow cooker and mix. Cover and cook on low heat for 7–8 hours or high heat for 3½–4 hours. Serve over hot cooked pasta and top each serving with 1 tablespoon cheese, if desired.

Nutrition Facts per serving: 222 cal., 0.8 g total fat, 0 mg chol., 469 mg sodium, 44 g carbo., 3 g fiber, 7 g pro.
Exchanges: 3 Vegetable, 2 Starch
Carb Choices: 3

Shopping List

Produce	Baking Goods
1 lb. eggplant	sugar
medium onion	
small green bell pepper	**Condiments**
2 oz. fresh mushrooms	red wine vinegar

Canned	Seasonings
2 14-oz. cans ready-cut Italian diced tomatoes with garlic, oregano, and basil	minced garlic
	dried Italian seasoning
6-oz. can Italian tomato paste with roasted garlic	**Optional**
	nonfat Parmesan cheese

Packaged
8-oz. pkg. penne pasta

Okra, Corn, and Bean Soup

Easy | **Do Ahead** | **Serves: 8**

- 3 11-oz. cans Mexicorn, *drained*
- 1 16-oz. pkg. frozen baby lima beans, *thawed and drained*
- 2 14½-oz. cans ready-cut diced tomatoes with garlic, oregano, and basil, *do not drain*
- 2 14-oz. cans nonfat vegetable broth
- 1 10-oz. pkg. frozen sliced okra, *thawed and drained*
- 1¼ cups frozen chopped onions, *thawed and drained*
- 2 tsp. Tabasco sauce
- 2 tsp. Worcestershire sauce
- ¼ tsp. dried basil
- ½ tsp. pepper
- 1½ tsp. minced garlic

Spray inside of slow cooker with cooking spray. Combine all ingredients in slow cooker and mix well. Cover and cook on low heat for 10–12 hours or high heat for 5–6 hours.

Nutrition Facts per serving: 195 cal., 0.5 g total fat, 0 mg chol., 963 mg sodium, 40 g carbo., 7 g fiber, 9 g pro.
Exchanges: 2 Vegetable, 2 Starch
Carb Choices: 3

Meatless Meals

Shopping List

Frozen	Condiments
16-oz. pkg. frozen baby lima beans	Tabasco sauce
10-oz. pkg. frozen sliced okra	Worcestershire sauce
12-oz. pkg. frozen chopped onions	**Seasonings**
	dried basil
	pepper
	minced garlic

Canned
3 11-oz. cans Mexicorn
2 14½-oz. cans ready-cut diced tomatoes with garlic, oregano, and basil
2 14-oz. cans nonfat vegetable broth

Bean and Vegetable Stew

Easy | Do Ahead | Freeze | Serves: 4

8 oz. dry kidney beans

1 cup V-8 juice

⅓ cup + 3 tbsp. vegetable broth

3 tbsp. low-sodium soy sauce

⅓ cup chopped celery

⅓ cup chopped potato

⅓ cup chopped carrot

⅓ cup chopped mushrooms

⅓ cup chopped onion

½ tsp. dried basil

½ tsp. dried parsley

½ tsp. garlic powder

½ tsp. pepper

1 cup cooked rice or pasta

½ cup nonfat Parmesan cheese (optional)

Place beans in large soup pot; cover with water and bring to a boil. Boil 10 minutes; reduce heat, cover, and simmer 1½ hours or until beans are tender. Drain. Spray inside of slow cooker with cooking spray. Combine beans, V-8 juice, broth, and soy sauce in slow cooker. Cover and cook on high heat for 2 hours. Add celery, potato, carrot, mushrooms, onions, basil, parsley, garlic powder, and pepper and mix well. Cook on low heat for 5–6 hours or high heat for 2½–3 hours. Add rice and cook 45–60 minutes. Sprinkle with cheese before serving, if desired.

Nutrition Facts per serving: 263 cal., 1.1 g total fat, 0 mg chol., 813 mg sodium, 50 g carbo., 2 g fiber, 16 g pro.
Exchanges: 4 Vegetable, 2 Starch
Carb Choices: 3

Shopping List

Produce	Condiments
small bunch celery	low-sodium soy sauce
potato	
carrot	**Seasonings**
2 oz. fresh mushrooms	dried basil
small onion	dried parsley
	garlic powder
Canned	pepper
8-oz. can V-8 juice	
14-oz. can nonfat vegetable	**Optional**
broth	nonfat Parmesan cheese
Packaged	
8 oz. dry kidney beans	
rice or pasta	

Vegetable Chili

Easy | **Do Ahead** | **Serves: 4**

1 medium zucchini, *chopped*

1 medium yellow squash, *chopped*

3 carrots, *peeled and chopped*

2 10-oz. pkgs. frozen seasoning vegetables, *thawed and drained*

1 14½-oz. can petite-cut diced tomatoes with roasted garlic and sweet onion, *drained*

1 15¼-oz. can whole kernel corn, *drained*

1 15-oz. can garbanzo beans, *drained*

2½ tsp. chili powder

1 tsp. ground cumin

1 15-oz. jar mild salsa

⅓ cup tomato paste

chopped green onions, nonfat sour cream, and/or nonfat shredded cheese (optional)

Spray inside of slow cooker with cooking spray. Combine all ingredients except tomato paste in slow cooker and mix well. Cover and cook on low heat for 8–9 hours or high heat for 4–4½ hours. Stir in tomato paste and cook 10–15 minutes. Garnish with green onions, sour cream, and/or cheese, if desired.

Nutrition Facts per serving: 364 cal., 2 g total fat, 0 mg chol., 1,583 mg sodium, 76 g carbo., 16 g fiber, 14 g pro.
Exchanges: 5 Vegetable, 3 Starch
Carb Choices: 5

Meatless Meals

Shopping List

Produce
medium zucchini
medium yellow squash
3 carrots

Frozen
2 10-oz. pkgs. frozen seasoning vegetables

Canned
14½-oz. can petite-cut diced tomatoes with roasted garlic and sweet onion
15¼-oz. can whole kernel corn

15-oz. can garbanzo beans
6-oz. can tomato paste

Condiments
15-oz. jar mild salsa

Seasonings
chili powder
ground cumin

Optional
green onions, nonfat sour cream, and/or nonfat shredded cheddar cheese

Vegetarian Minestrone

Easy | Do Ahead | Serves: 6

- ¾ cup frozen chopped onions, *thawed and drained*
- 2 medium carrots, *chopped*
- 1 cup chopped celery
- 1 red bell pepper, *seeded and cut into ½-inch pieces*
- 1 medium zucchini, *cubed*
- 1 tsp. minced garlic
- 2 14-oz. cans nonfat vegetable broth
- 1 28-oz. can crushed tomatoes, *drained*
- 1 15-oz. can red kidney beans, *drained*
- ¾ tsp. dried basil
- ¾ tsp. dried thyme
- ¼ tsp. pepper
- 1½ cups cooked rice

Spray inside of slow cooker with cooking spray. Combine all ingredients except rice in slow cooker and mix well. Cover and cook on low heat for 8–10 hours or high heat for 4–5 hours. Add rice, stir to combine, and heat through.

Nutrition Facts per serving: 268 cal., 1.3 g total fat, 0 mg chol., 1,290 mg sodium, 53 g carbo., 11 g fiber, 14 g pro.
Exchanges: 4 Vegetable, 2 Starch
Carb Choices: 4

For added flavor, shred fresh Parmesan cheese over the soup just before serving.

Shopping List

Produce	
2 medium carrots	28-oz. can crushed tomatoes
small bunch celery	2 15-oz. cans red kidney beans
red bell pepper	
medium zucchini	
	Packaged
Frozen	rice
12-oz. pkg. frozen chopped onions	
	Seasonings
	minced garlic
Canned	dried basil
2 14-oz. cans nonfat vegetable broth	dried thyme
	pepper

Creole Chili

Easy | **Do Ahead** | **Serves: 4**

1 16-oz. can 99% fat-free vegetarian chili with beans

1 14½-oz. can petite-cut diced tomatoes with jalapeños, *do not drain*

2 cups frozen seasoning vegetables, *thawed and drained*

1 tsp. minced garlic

½ cup nonfat shredded cheddar cheese (optional)

chopped green onions (optional)

Spray inside of slow cooker with cooking spray. Combine all ingredients except optional ingredients in slow cooker and mix well. Cover and cook on low heat for 7–9 hours or high heat for 3½–4½ hours. Garnish with cheese and green onions, if desired.

Nutrition Facts per serving: 111 cal., 0 g total fat, 0 mg chol., 408 mg sodium, 19 g carbo., 5 g fiber, 8 g pro.
Exchanges: 1 Vegetable, 1 Starch
Carb Choices: 1

Meatless Meals

Shopping List

Frozen
10-oz. pkg. frozen seasoning vegetables

Canned
16-oz. can 99% fat-free vegetarian chili with beans
14½-oz. can petite-cut diced tomatoes with jalapeños

Seasonings
minced garlic

Optional
nonfat shredded cheddar cheese
green onions

Vegetarian's Dream Chili

Easy | **Do Ahead** | **Serves: 6**

- 2 14½-oz. cans petite-cut diced tomatoes with jalapeños, *do not drain*
- 1 15-oz. can garbanzo beans, drained
- 1 zucchini, *cubed*
- 1 yellow squash, *cubed*
- 2 carrots, *sliced*
- 3 cups frozen seasoning vegetables, *thawed and drained*
- 1–2 tbsp chili powder
- 1 4-oz. can diced green chiles, *do not drain*
- 1 tsp. minced garlic
- 1 tbsp. dried oregano
- 2 tsp. ground cumin

Spray inside of slow cooker with cooking spray. Combine all ingredients in slow cooker and mix well. Cover and cook on low heat for 6–8 hours or high heat for 3–4 hours.

Nutrition Facts per serving: 135 cal., 1.4 g total fat, 0 mg chol., 745 mg sodium, 25 g carbo., 8 g fiber, 6 g pro.
Exchanges: 2 Vegetable, 1 Starch
Carb Choices: 2

For a full-meal deal, add ½ cup cooked brown rice, couscous, or lentils to Vegetarian's Dream Chili.

Shopping List

Produce	Seasonings
medium zucchini	chili powder
medium yellow squash	minced garlic
2 carrots	dried oregano
	ground cumin

Frozen
2 10-oz. pkgs. frozen seasoning vegetables

Canned
2 14½-oz. cans petite-cut diced tomatoes with jalapeños
15-oz. can garbanzo beans
4-oz. can diced green chiles

Meatless Stew

2 lbs. potatoes, *sliced*

1 large onion, *sliced*

2 carrots, *sliced*

1 green bell pepper, *cored, seeded, and sliced*

1 zucchini, *sliced*

1 cup frozen whole kernel corn, *thawed and drained*

1 cup frozen peas, *thawed and drained*

1 cup frozen cut green beans, *thawed and drained*

2½ cups tomato sauce

¼ cup low-sodium soy sauce

2 tsp. dried Italian seasoning

1 tsp. dry mustard

2 tsp. chili powder

½ tsp. ground cinnamon

2 tbsp. dried parsley

⅛ tsp. dried rosemary

Spray inside of slow cooker with cooking spray. Layer potatoes, onion, carrots, bell pepper, zucchini, corn, peas, and green beans in slow cooker. Combine remaining ingredients in a medium bowl and mix well. Pour tomato sauce mixture over vegetables. Cover and cook on low heat for 10–12 hours or high heat for 5–6 hours.

Nutrition Facts per serving: 245 cal., 0.7 g total fat, 0 mg chol., 1,048 mg sodium, 56 g carbo., 7 g fiber, 8 g pro.
Exchanges: 1 Vegetable, 3 Starch
Carb Choices: 4

Meatless Meals

Shopping List

Produce	Canned
2 lbs. potatoes (about 6)	2 14½-oz. cans tomato
large onion	sauce
2 carrots	
medium green bell pepper	**Condiments**
medium zucchini	low-sodium soy sauce
Frozen	**Seasonings**
10-oz. pkg. frozen whole	dried Italian seasoning
kernel corn	dry mustard
10-oz. pkg. frozen peas	chili powder
10-oz. pkg. frozen cut	ground cinnamon
green beans	dried parsley
	dried rosemary

Hearty Vegetarian Chili

Easy | **Do Ahead** | **Serves: 6**

1 12-oz. pkg. frozen vegetarian beef crumbles, *thawed and drained*

2 15-oz. cans red kidney beans, *drained*

3 cups frozen seasoning vegetables, *thawed and drained*

1 tbsp. + 1½ tsp. chili powder

2 tbsp. + ¾ tsp. molasses

¾ cup nonfat vegetable broth

1 tbsp. chopped fresh cilantro

¾ tsp. Tabasco sauce

¼ tsp. pepper

2 tbsp. + ¾ tsp. flour

¾ cup water

Spray inside of slow cooker with cooking spray. Combine beef crumbles, beans, seasoning vegetables, chili powder, molasses, broth, cilantro, Tabasco, and pepper in slow cooker and mix well. Cover and cook on high heat for 3 hours. Mix flour and water until blended smooth; add to cooker and stir to mix. Cover and cook 1 hour.

Nutrition Facts per serving: 233 cal., 0.6 g total fat, 0 mg chol., 852 mg sodium, 37 g carbo., 10 g fiber, 20 g pro.
Exchanges: 2 Vegetable, 2 Starch, 1 Very Lean Meat
Carb Choices: 2

Shopping List

Produce	Baking Goods
fresh cilantro	flour

Frozen	Condiments
12-oz. pkg. frozen vegetarian beef crumbles	molasses
2 10-oz. pkgs. frozen seasoning vegetables	Tabasco sauce
	Seasonings
	chili powder
Canned	pepper
2 15-oz. cans red kidney beans	
14-oz. can nonfat vegetable broth	

Mediterranean-Style Stew

Easy | **Do Ahead** | **Serves: 4**

- 1 butternut squash, *seeded and cubed*
- ½ lb. eggplant, *unpeeled, cubed*
- 1 medium zucchini, *cubed*
- 1 yellow squash, *cubed*
- 1 10-oz. pkg. frozen okra, *thawed and drained*
- 1 8-oz. can tomato sauce with roasted garlic
- 1 cup frozen chopped onions, *thawed and drained*
- 1 14½-oz. can petite-cut diced tomatoes, *drained*
- 6 baby carrots, *cut into thirds*
- ½ cup nonfat vegetable broth
- ⅓ cup raisins
- ½ tsp. minced garlic
- ¼ tsp. chili powder
- ½ tsp. ground turmeric
- ¼ tsp. crushed red pepper
- ¼ tsp. ground cinnamon
- ¼ tsp. paprika

Spray inside of slow cooker with cooking spray. Combine all ingredients in slow cooker and mix well. Cover and cook on low heat for 8–10 hours or high heat for 4–5 hours.

Nutrition Facts per serving: 207 cal., 1.1 g total fat, 0 mg chol., 307 mg sodium, 48 g carbo., 8 g fiber, 7 g pro.
Exchanges: 3 Vegetable, 1 Fruit, 1 Starch
Carb Choices: 3

Turmeric is a spice used extensively in Indian and Southeast Asian cooking. It is known for its brilliant yellow color, mildly aromatic scent, and pungent, bitter flavor.

Meatless Meals

Shopping List

Produce
medium butternut squash
½ lb. eggplant
medium zucchini
medium yellow squash
8-oz. pkg. baby carrots

Frozen
10-oz. pkg. frozen okra
12-oz. pkg. frozen chopped onions

Canned
8-oz. can tomato sauce with roasted garlic

14½-oz. can petite-cut diced tomatoes
14-oz. can vegetable broth

Packaged
raisins

Seasonings
minced garlic
chili powder
ground turmeric
crushed red pepper
ground cinnamon
paprika

Black Bean and Lentil Soup

Easy | **Do Ahead** | **Serves: 4**

8 oz. dry black beans

3 cups water

1 carrot, *chopped*

½ cup chopped celery

½ cup chopped red onion

1½ tsp. minced garlic

¾ cup chopped green bell pepper

¼ cup dry lentils, *rinsed and drained*

1 14½-oz. can petite-cut diced tomatoes with jalapeños, *do not drain*

1 tbsp. + 1 tsp. chili powder

¼ tsp. dried oregano

¼ tsp. pepper

1½ tbsp. red wine vinegar

¼ cup uncooked converted rice

Place beans in large soup pot; cover with water and bring to a boil. Boil 10 minutes. Cover pot, remove from heat, and let stand 1 hour. Drain beans and rinse. Spray inside of slow cooker with cooking spray. Combine beans and 3 cups water in slow cooker. Cover and cook on high heat for 3 hours. Add remaining ingredients except rice and mix well. Cover and cook on low heat for 2–3 hours. Add rice and cook 20–30 minutes. Puree half of soup in food processor or blender until smooth; return to slow cooker and mix well.

Nutrition Facts per serving: 155 cal., 0.5 g total fat, 0 mg chol., 1,079 mg sodium, 32 g carbo., 4 g fiber, 9 g pro.
Exchanges: 3 Vegetable, 1 Starch
Carb Choices: 2

Shopping List

Produce
1 carrot
small bunch celery
small red onion
medium green bell pepper

Canned
14½-oz. can petite-cut diced tomatoes with jalapeños

Packaged
8 oz. dry black beans
dry lentils
converted rice

Condiments
red wine vinegar

Seasonings
minced garlic
chili powder
dried oregano
pepper

Not Just Another Vegetarian Chili

Easy | **Do Ahead** | **Serves: 8**

- 1 15-oz. can 99% fat-free black bean soup
- 1 15-oz. can red kidney beans, *drained*
- 1 15-oz. can garbanzo beans, *drained*
- 1 16-oz. can 99% fat-free vegetarian baked beans
- 1 14½-oz. can petite-cut diced tomatoes with roasted garlic and sweet onion, *do not drain*
- 1 11-oz. can Mexicorn, *drained*
- 2 cups frozen seasoning vegetables, *thawed and drained*
- 1½ tsp. minced garlic
- 2 tbsp. chili powder
- 2 tsp. dried oregano
- 2 tsp. dried basil
- nonfat shredded cheddar cheese (optional)

Spray inside of slow cooker with cooking spray. Combine all ingredients in slow cooker and mix well. Cover and cook on low heat for 4–6 hours or high heat for 2–3 hours. Garnish with cheese before serving, if desired.

Nutrition Facts per serving: 247 cal., 1.9 g total fat, 0 mg chol., 1,042 mg sodium, 49 g carbo., 13 g fiber, 13 g pro.
Exchanges: 4 Vegetable, 2 Starch
Carb Choices: 3

Meatless Meals

Shopping List

Frozen	Seasonings
10-oz. pkg. frozen seasoning vegetables	minced garlic
	chili powder
	dried oregano
Canned	dried basil
15-oz. can 99% fat-free black bean soup	
15-oz. can red kidney beans	**Optional**
15-oz. can garbanzo beans	nonfat shredded cheddar cheese
16-oz. can 99% fat-free vegetarian baked beans	
14½-oz. can petite-cut diced tomatoes with roasted garlic and sweet onion	
11-oz. can Mexicorn	

Black Bean-Corn Chili

Easy | **Do Ahead** | **Freeze** | **Serves: 6**

2 tbsp. nonfat vegetable broth

1½ cups frozen chopped onions, *thawed and drained*

1 tsp. minced garlic

1½ cups frozen chopped green bell peppers, *thawed and drained*

1½ tsp. chili powder

1 tsp. cayenne pepper

2 28-oz. cans crushed tomatoes, *do not drain*

2 11-oz. cans Mexicorn, *drained*

2 15-oz. cans black beans, *drained*

1 cup thick and chunky salsa

nonfat shredded cheddar cheese, chopped green onions, and/or nonfat sour cream (optional)

Spray large nonstick skillet with cooking spray. Add broth to skillet and heat over medium-high heat. Add onions, minced garlic, and bell peppers to skillet; cook over medium-high heat, stirring frequently, until vegetables are softened. Add chili powder and cayenne pepper and heat 1 minute. Remove skillet from heat. Spray inside of slow cooker with cooking spray. Spoon onion mixture into slow cooker. Add undrained tomatoes, Mexicorn, beans, and salsa and mix well. Cover and cook on low heat for 8–10 hours or high heat for 4–5 hours. Garnish with cheese, green onions, and/or sour cream, if desired.

Nutrition Facts per serving: 308 cal., 1.4 g total fat, 0 mg chol., 1,811 mg sodium, 66 g carbo., 9 g fiber, 15 g pro.
Exchanges: 3 Vegetable, 3 Starch
Carb Choices: 5

Shopping List

Frozen
12-oz. pkg. frozen chopped onions
10-oz. pkg. frozen chopped green bell peppers

Canned
14-oz. can nonfat vegetable broth
2 28-oz. cans crushed tomatoes
2 11-oz. cans Mexicorn
2 15-oz. cans black beans

Condiments
8-oz. jar thick and chunky salsa

Seasonings
minced garlic
chili powder
cayenne pepper

Optional
nonfat shredded cheddar cheese, green onions, and/or nonfat sour cream

Side Dishes

Ratatouille Italian-Style

Baked Beans

Easy | Do Ahead | Serves: 12

- 4 15-oz. cans 99% fat-free vegetarian beans, *lightly drained*
- ¼ cup chopped onion
- ⅓ cup lite maple syrup
- 2 tbsp. prepared mustard
- ⅓ cup Bacon Crumbles (optional)

Shopping List

Produce
small onion

Canned
4 15-oz. cans 99% fat-free vegetarian beans

Condiments
lite maple syrup
prepared mustard

Optional
1.3-oz. bottle Bacon Crumbles

Spray inside of slow cooker with cooking spray. Combine all ingredients except Bacon Crumbles in slow cooker and mix well. Cover and cook on low heat for 6–8 hours or high heat for 3–4 hours. Serve with Bacon Crumbles, if desired.

Nutrition Facts per serving: 160 cal., 1.3 g total fat, 0 mg chol., 727 mg sodium, 33 g carbo., 11 g fiber, 8 g pro.
Exchanges: 1½ Starch, ½ Other Carbo.
Carb Choices: 2

Substitution Tip: You can use 2 teaspoons dry mustard and a dash of vinegar in place of prepared mustard.

Rice and Beans

Easy | Do Ahead | Serves: 24

- 1 16-oz. can black beans, *drained*
- 1 16-oz. can cannellini beans, *drained*
- 1 14-oz. can nonfat vegetable broth
- 1 cup uncooked long grain rice (not instant)
- 4 cups salsa
- 1 cup water
- 1 tsp. garlic powder

Spray inside of slow cooker with cooking spray. Combine all ingredients in slow cooker and mix well. Cover and cook on low heat for 10 hours or high heat for 5 hours.

Nutrition Facts per serving: 79 cal., 0.2 g total fat, 0 mg chol., 337 mg sodium, 16 g carbo., 1 g fiber, 4 g pro.
Exchanges: 1 Starch
Carb Choices: 1

Side Dishes

Shopping List

Canned
16-oz. can black beans
16-oz. can cannellini beans
14-oz. can vegetable broth

Packaged
rice (not instant)

Condiments
2 16-oz. jars salsa

Seasonings
garlic powder

Portobello Rice Pilaf

¾ cup wild rice

½ cup long grain brown rice

½ lb. portobello mushrooms, *cut into 1-inch pieces*

1 10¾-oz. can low-fat cream of mushroom soup

½ cup nonfat chicken broth

1 cup water

¼ tsp. pepper

Spray inside of slow cooker with cooking spray. Combine all ingredients in slow cooker and mix well. Cover and cook on low heat for 6–7 hours or high heat for 3–3½ hours.

Nutrition Facts per serving: 169 cal., 1.5 g total fat, 1 mg chol., 275 mg sodium, 34 g carbo., 2 g fiber, 7 g pro.
Exchanges: 1 Vegetable, 2 Starch
Carb Choices: 2

Shopping List

Produce
½ lb. portobello mushrooms

Canned
10¾-oz. can low-fat cream of mushroom soup
14-oz. can nonfat chicken broth

Packaged
wild rice
long grain brown rice

Seasonings
pepper

Portobello mushrooms are mature cremini mushrooms and are noted for their rich flavor and meaty texture. Select firm, plump mushrooms that are not slimy or bruised. Refrigerate portobellos, unwashed, lightly wrapped in paper towels or in a paper bag, never in plastic.

German Potato Salad

Easy | **Do Ahead** | **Serves: 6**

3 lbs. potatoes, *sliced*

1 cup frozen chopped onions, *thawed and drained*

1 cup chopped celery

½ cup water

¼ cup cider vinegar

1½ tbsp. sugar

2 tbsp. quick-cooking tapioca

2 tbsp. chopped fresh parsley

2 tbsp. Bacon Crumbles

Spray inside of slow cooker with cooking spray. Combine potatoes, onions, and celery in slow cooker. Combine remaining ingredients except Bacon Crumbles in medium bowl and mix well. Pour vinegar mixture over potatoes and toss to coat. Cover and cook on low heat for 8–10 hours or high heat for 4–5 hours. Stir in Bacon Crumbles and heat through.

Nutrition Facts per serving: 256 cal., 0.7 g total fat, 0 mg chol., 114 mg sodium, 58 g carbo., 6 g fiber, 6 g pro.
Exchanges: 3 Starch, ½ Other Carbo.
Carb Choices: 4

Side Dishes

Shopping List

Produce
3 lbs. potatoes
small bunch celery
fresh parsley

Frozen
12-oz. pkg. frozen chopped onions

Packaged
1.3-oz. bottle Bacon Crumbles

Baking Goods
sugar
quick-cooking tapioca

Condiments
cider vinegar

Storage Tip: Potatoes store for 2–3 weeks in a cool, dark, well-ventilated place—not in the refrigerator. Avoid warm, light places, which encourage sprouting and shriveling. Store potatoes in paper or burlap bags. Never store potatoes near onions; onions emit gases that cause potatoes to spoil faster.

Onion-Cheese Potatoes

¼ cup instant minced onion

¾ tsp. garlic powder

1 32-oz. pkg. frozen hash brown potatoes, *thawed and drained*

8 oz. nonfat cream cheese, *cubed*

Spray inside of slow cooker with cooking spray. Combine onion and garlic powder in small bowl and mix well. Layer a quarter of potatoes in bottom of slow cooker; sprinkle with a quarter of seasonings and top with a third of cream cheese cubes. Repeat layers, ending with potatoes and seasonings. Cover and cook on low heat for 6–8 hours or high heat for 3–4 hours. Remove lid and stir during last hour of cooking to mix cheese evenly.

Nutrition Facts per serving: 116 cal., 0 g total fat, 0 mg chol., 237 mg sodium, 23 g carbo., 2 g fiber, 7 g pro.
Exchanges: 1½ Starch
Carb Choices: 2

Shopping List

Dairy
8 oz. nonfat cream cheese

Frozen
32-oz. pkg. frozen hash brown potatoes

Seasonings
instant minced onion
garlic powder

Mashed Potatoes

Easy | Do Ahead | Serves: 8

- 2 16-oz. pkgs. roasted onion potato cubes
- 1 3-oz. pkg. nonfat cream cheese, softened
- ½ cup nonfat sour cream
- 1 tsp. onion powder
- ½ tsp. garlic powder
- ¼ tsp. pepper
- 2 tbsp. egg substitute
- 1 tbsp. nonfat margarine

Spray inside of slow cooker with cooking spray. Cook potatoes according to package directions; drain well and mash. Add cream cheese, sour cream, onion powder, garlic powder, pepper, egg substitute, and margarine and mix well. Spoon potato mixture into slow cooker. Cover and cook on low heat for 3 hours, stirring once or twice while cooking.

Nutrition Facts per serving: 126 cal., 0 g total fat, 0 mg chol., 320 mg sodium, 25 g carbo., 3 g fiber, 5 g pro.
Exchanges: 1 Starch, ½ Other Carbo.
Carb Choices: 2

Side Dishes

Shopping List

Produce
2 16-oz. pkgs. roasted onion potato cubes

Dairy
3-oz. pkg. nonfat cream cheese
4 oz. nonfat sour cream
egg substitute
nonfat margarine

Seasonings
onion powder
garlic powder
pepper

Substitution Tip: For a sour cream substitute, puree 1 cup nonfat cottage cheese with ¼ cup nonfat yogurt or simply substitute 1 cup nonfat yogurt or buttermilk.

Baked Potatoes

6 baking potatoes

Scrub potatoes and prick with fork in several places. Arrange potatoes in a pyramid in slow cooker but do not allow potatoes to touch sides of cooker. Cover and cook on low heat for 8–9 hours or high heat for 4–4½ hours. Garnish and serve as desired.

Nutrition Facts per serving: 145 cal., 0.1 g total fat, 0 mg chol., 8 mg sodium, 34 g carbo., 4 g fiber, 3 g pro.
Exchanges: 2 Starch
Carb Choices: 2

Shopping List

Produce
6 baking potatoes

When selecting potatoes, always consider whether you will bake, broil, mash, roast, or fry them. Favorite potato varieties include russets (also referred to as baking or Idaho potatoes), which are best for baking, french fries, or mashing; boiling potatoes (red or white), which are best for potato salads, oven roasting, or frying; new potatoes, which can be roasted, grilled, or boiled; and Yukon golds, which are excellent for boiling and mashing.

Baked Sweet Potatoes

6 sweet potatoes, washed and dried

Butter Buds, nonfat margarine, crushed pineapple, brown sugar and ground cinnamon, or lite maple syrup (optional)

Scrub sweet potatoes and prick in several places with a fork. Wrap each potato in foil and place in slow cooker. Cover and cook on low heat for 7–9 hours or high heat for 3½–4½ hours. Serve with Butter Buds, margarine, pineapple, brown sugar and ground cinnamon, or maple syrup, if desired.

Nutrition Facts per serving: 117 cal., 0 g total fat, 0 mg chol., 11 mg sodium, 28 g carbo., 3 g fiber, 2 g pro.
Exchanges: 1½ Starch
Carb Choices: 2

Side Dishes

Shopping List

Produce
6 sweet potatoes

Optional
Butter Buds, nonfat margarine, crushed pineapple, brown sugar and ground cinnamon, or lite maple syrup

Did you know that sweet potatoes and regular potatoes are not even related? When buying, select uniform, heavy, firm sweet potatoes without cracks, bruises, soft spots, or mold. You can store sweet potatoes in a cool, dry place for up to 1 month, but it is best to use them within a week of purchase. Avoid storing sweet potatoes in the refrigerator because it will affect the flavor.

Cinnamon Sweet Potatoes

Easy | **Do Ahead** | **Serves: 6**

6 medium sweet potatoes, *peeled and cut into 1-inch cubes*

1½ cups + 2 tbsp. chunky-style applesauce

½ cup brown sugar

2 tsp. ground cinnamon

¼ tsp. ground nutmeg

Spray inside of slow cooker with cooking spray. Place sweet potatoes in slow cooker. Combine remaining ingredients and mix well. Pour over top of potatoes. Cover and cook on low heat for 6–8 hours or high heat for 3–4 hours.

Nutrition Facts per serving: 238 cal., 0.2 g total fat, 0 mg chol., 19 mg sodium, 59 g carbo., 4 g fiber, 2 g pro.
Exchanges: 1 Fruit, 2 Starch, ½ Other Carbo.
Carb Choices: 4

Shopping List

Produce
6 medium sweet potatoes

Canned
16-oz. jar chunky-style applesauce

Baking Goods
brown sugar

Seasonings
ground cinnamon
ground nutmeg

Skins on or off? Keeping the skins on when baking or boiling sweet potatoes retains flavor and color and makes peeling easier.

Pineapple Sweet Potatoes

Easy | Do Ahead | Serves: 8

1 40-oz. can cut sweet
   potatoes in light syrup,
   drained
1½ tbsp. brown sugar
½ tsp. ground cinnamon
⅓ cup pineapple preserves

Spray inside of slow cooker with cooking spray. Combine sweet potatoes, brown sugar, cinnamon, and preserves in slow cooker and mash lightly (potatoes should be slightly chunky). Cover and cook on low heat for 6–7 hours.

Nutrition Facts per serving: 176 cal., 0.2 g total fat, 0 mg chol., 77 mg sodium, 42 g carbo., 4 g fiber, 2 g pro.
Exchanges: 2 Starch, ½ Other Carbo.
Carb Choices: 3

Side
Dishes

Shopping List

Canned
40-oz. can cut sweet potatoes
   in light syrup

Baking Goods
brown sugar

Condiments
12 oz. pineapple preserves

Seasonings
ground cinnamon

Holiday Sweet Potatoes

Easy | Do Ahead | Serves: 8

1 40-oz. can cut sweet
potatoes in light syrup,
drained

1 16-oz. can crushed
pineapple in juice, *drained*

2 tbsp. brown sugar

¾ tsp. ground cinnamon

¼ tsp. ground nutmeg

Spray inside of slow cooker with cooking spray. Combine all ingredients in medium mixing bowl and beat with mixer until creamy and smooth. Spoon into slow cooker. Cover and cook on low heat for 2–4 hours.

Nutrition Facts per serving: 176 cal., 0.3 g total fat, 0 mg chol., 77 mg sodium, 42 g carbo., 4 g fiber, 3 g pro.
Exchanges: 1 Fruit, 1 Starch, ½ Other Carbo.
Carb Choices: 3

Shopping List

Canned
40-oz. can cut sweet potatoes
in light syrup
16-oz. can crushed pineapple
in juice

Baking Goods
brown sugar

Seasonings
ground cinnamon
ground nutmeg

To soften hard brown sugar, add a few drops of water to the box and microwave on high for 15–30 seconds.

Savory Stuffing

Easy | **Do Ahead** | **Serves: 8**

7 cups croutons or bread cubes

2 cups frozen seasoning vegetables, *thawed and drained*

3 Golden Delicious apples, *peeled, cored, and chopped*

1 tbsp. dried parsley

¼ tsp. paprika

1 tsp. poultry seasoning

1¼ cups nonfat chicken broth

Shopping List

Produce
3 Golden Delicious apples

Frozen
10-oz. pkg. frozen seasoning vegetables

Canned
14-oz. can nonfat chicken broth

Packaged
2 6-oz. pkgs. croutons or bread cubes

Seasonings
dried parsley
paprika
poultry seasoning

Spray inside of slow cooker with cooking spray. Combine all ingredients in slow cooker and mix well. Cover and cook on high heat for 1 hour, then stir. Reduce heat to low and cook for 3–4 hours.

Nutrition Facts per serving: 96 cal., 0.1 g total fat, 0 mg chol., 252 mg sodium, 24 g carbo., 2 g fiber, 3 g pro.
Exchanges: 1 Vegetable, 1 Starch
Carb Choices: 2

Side Dishes

Superb Stuffing

Easy | Do Ahead | Serves: 12

4½ cups nonfat chicken broth,
  divided

2 10-oz. pkgs. frozen
  seasoning vegetables,
  thawed and drained

2 8-oz. cans mushrooms,
  drained

12 cups day-old bread cubes

½ cup egg substitute

1 tsp. poultry seasoning

1½ tsp. dried sage

1 tsp. dried thyme

½ tsp. pepper

½ tsp. garlic powder

Spray large nonstick skillet or Dutch oven with cooking spray. Add 1 cup chicken broth to skillet and heat over medium-high heat. Add seasoning vegetables and mushrooms and cook, stirring frequently, until vegetables are softened. Remove skillet from heat. Place bread cubes in large bowl. Pour vegetable mixture over cubes, add egg substitute and remaining ingredients, and mix until moistened. Spray inside of slow cooker with cooking spray. Pack stuffing into slow cooker. Cover and cook on low heat for 6–8 hours or high heat for 3–4 hours.

Nutrition Facts per serving: 111 cal., 1.4 g total fat, 0 mg chol., 652 mg sodium, 19 g carbo., 3 g fiber, 6 g pro.
Exchanges: 1 Vegetable, 1 Starch
Carb Choices: 1

Shopping List

Dairy
egg substitute

Frozen
2 10-oz. pkgs. frozen
  seasoning vegetables

Canned
3 14-oz. cans nonfat chicken
  broth
2 8-oz. cans mushrooms

Packaged
bread purchased from
  bakery or four 12-oz.
  pkgs. Kellogg's Croutettes
  Stuffing Mix

Seasonings
poultry seasoning
dried sage
dried thyme
pepper
garlic powder

Substitution Tip:
For variety, use corn bread cubes in place of regular bread cubes and prepare as directed.

Corn on the Cob

6 whole ears of corn,
*unshucked, trimmed to fit
into your slow cooker*

Butter Buds, nonfat
Parmesan cheese, or other
seasonings (optional)

Place corn in slow cooker. Fill cooker three-quarters full with hot water. Cover and cook on low heat for 3–4 hours. Using tongs, remove corn from cooker. Wearing oven mitts, remove husks and silk from corn. Serve with Butter Buds, cheese, or other seasonings.

Nutrition Facts per serving: 83 cal., 0.9 g total fat, 0 mg chol., 13 mg sodium, 19 g carbo., 3 g fiber, 3 g pro.
Exchanges: 1 Starch
Carb Choices: 1

Side
Dishes

Shopping List

Produce

6 whole ears of corn

Optional

Butter Buds, nonfat Parmesan
cheese, or other seasonings

Corn Pudding

Easy | **Do Ahead** | **Serves: 4**

- 1 tsp. nonfat vegetable broth
- ¼ cup frozen chopped onions, *thawed and drained*
- ¼ cup frozen chopped green bell peppers, *thawed and drained*
- ¼ cup canned petite-cut diced tomatoes, *drained*
- 1 16-oz. can cream-style corn
- 1 cup egg substitute
- ½ cup evaporated skim milk
- ¼ tsp. pepper
- ½ cup nonfat shredded cheddar cheese

Spray large nonstick skillet with cooking spray. Add broth to skillet and heat over medium-high heat. Add onions and bell peppers. Cook over medium-high heat, stirring frequently, until vegetables are softened. Stir in tomatoes and cook 1 minute. Spray inside of slow cooker with cooking spray. Combine all ingredients except cheese in slow cooker and mix well. Cover and cook on low heat for 5–6 hours or high heat for 2½–3 hours. Sprinkle cheese evenly over top and cook until melted.

Nutrition Facts per serving: 153 cal., 0.5 g total fat, 1 mg chol., 689 mg sodium, 26 g carbo., 2 g fiber, 13 g pro.
Exchanges: 2 Vegetable, 1 Starch, 1 Very Lean Meat
Carb Choices: 2

Shopping List

Dairy
8 oz. egg substitute
nonfat shredded cheddar cheese

Frozen
12-oz. pkg. frozen chopped onions
10-oz. pkg. frozen chopped green bell peppers

Canned
14-oz. can nonfat vegetable broth
14½-oz. can petite-cut diced tomatoes
16-oz. can cream-style corn
8-oz. can evaporated skim milk

Seasonings
pepper

When buying canned vegetables or fruits, avoid bulging, swelled, or dented cans. They may indicate spoilage.

Hot Bean and Corn Salad

Easy | Do Ahead | Serves: 10

2 16-oz. cans nonfat vegetarian baked beans, *drained*

2 11-oz. cans Mexicorn, *drained*

½ cup chopped red bell pepper

1 cup chopped onion

¾ cup barbecue sauce

1½ tbsp. brown sugar

Spray inside of slow cooker with cooking spray. Combine all ingredients in slow cooker. Cover and cook on low heat for 8–9 hours or high heat for 4–4½ hours.

Nutrition Facts per serving: 161 cal., 1.1 g total fat, 0 mg chol., 730 mg sodium, 36 g carbo., 9 g fiber, 6 g pro.
Exchanges: 1 Vegetable, 1 Starch, 1 Other Carbo.
Carb Choices: 2

Side Dishes

Shopping List

Produce
small red bell pepper
large onion

Canned
2 16-oz. cans nonfat vegetarian baked beans
2 11-oz. cans Mexicorn

Baking Goods
brown sugar

Condiments
barbecue sauce

Substitution Tip: You can substitute two 8-oz. cans whole kernel corn or one 16-oz. package frozen whole kernel corn, thawed and drained, for the Mexicorn.

Mexicorn with Salsa

1 16-oz. can cream-style corn

2 cups Mexicorn, *well drained*

1 cup chunky salsa

Spray inside of slow cooker with cooking spray. Combine all ingredients in slow cooker and mix well. Cover and cook on low heat for 2–3 hours or high heat for 1–1½ hours.

Nutrition Facts per serving: 91 cal., 0.5 g total fat, 0 mg chol., 516 mg sodium, 22 g carbo., 2 g fiber, 3 g pro.
Exchanges: 1 Vegetable, 1 Starch
Carb Choices: 2

Shopping List

Canned
16-oz. can cream-style corn
2 11-oz. cans Mexicorn

Condiments
8 oz. chunky salsa

Southwest Corn Bread

Easy | **Do Ahead** | **Serves: 16**

⅔ cup + 2 tbsp. chunky salsa

½ cup whole kernel corn,
  drained and patted dry

¼ cup applesauce

½ cup egg substitute

1 17.5-oz. pkg. nonfat corn
  bread mix

Spray inside of slow cooker with cooking spray. Combine salsa, corn, applesauce, and egg substitute in medium bowl and mix well. Stir in corn bread mix until batter is mixed but still slightly lumpy. Pour batter into slow cooker. Cover and cook on low heat for 3 hours or high heat for 1½ hours.

Nutrition Facts per serving: 123 cal., 0 g total fat, 0 mg chol., 475 mg sodium, 27 g carbo., 1 g fiber, 3 g pro.
Exchanges: 1½ Starch
Carb Choices: 2

Side
Dishes

Shopping List

Dairy
egg substitute

Canned
8-oz. can whole kernel corn
4 oz. applesauce

Packaged
17.5-oz. pkg. nonfat corn
  bread mix

Condiments
8 oz. chunky salsa

Candied Carrots

Easy | Do Ahead | Serves: 8

2 16-oz. pkgs. frozen sliced carrots, *thawed and drained*
¼ cup brown sugar
¾ cup lite pancake syrup
½ cup chopped walnuts

Spray inside of slow cooker with cooking spray. Combine all ingredients in slow cooker and mix well. Cover and cook on high heat for 5 hours.

Nutrition Facts per serving: 160 cal., 4.5 g total fat, 0 mg chol., 156 mg sodium, 29 g carbo., 5 g fiber, 3 g pro.
Exchanges: 3 Vegetable, 1 Other Carbo., 1 Fat
Carb Choices: 2

Shopping List

Frozen
2 16-oz. pkgs. frozen sliced carrots

Packaged
chopped walnuts

Baking Goods
brown sugar

Condiments
lite pancake syrup

Carrot Pudding

2 8-oz. pkgs. shredded carrots

1 cup grated onion

½ tsp. ground cinnamon

1 tbsp. sugar

½ cup nonfat half and half

½ cup skim milk

¾ cup egg substitute

Spray inside of slow cooker with cooking spray. Combine all ingredients in slow cooker and mix well. Cover and cook on high heat for 3–4 hours.

Nutrition Facts per serving: 86 cal., 0.2 g total fat, 1 mg chol., 128 mg sodium, 16 g carbo., 3 g fiber, 5 g pro.
Exchanges: 2 Vegetable, ½ Other Carbo.
Carb Choices: 1

Side Dishes

Shopping List

Produce
2 8-oz. pkgs. shredded carrots
large onion

Dairy
4 oz. nonfat half and half
4 oz. skim milk
egg substitute

Baking Goods
sugar

Seasonings
ground cinnamon

Each 8-oz. package of shredded carrots contains approximately 2–2½ cups. One pound of whole carrots shredded or sliced provides about 3 cups; 1 large carrot provides about ¾–1 cup.

Sweet and Sour Red Cabbage

2½ lbs. shredded red cabbage

1 cup chopped dried apricot bits

¼ cup honey

2 tbsp. lemon juice

½ cup dry red wine

Spray inside of slow cooker with cooking spray. Combine cabbage and dried apricots in slow cooker. Combine remaining ingredients in small bowl and pour over cabbage. Toss mixture until coated. Cover and cook on low heat for 5–6 hours or high heat for 2½–3 hours.

Nutrition Facts per serving: 161 cal., 0.5 g total fat, 0 mg chol., 25 mg sodium, 37 g carbo., 6 g fiber, 3 g pro.
Exchanges: 3 Vegetable, 1 Fruit, ½ Other Carbo.
Carb Choices: 2

Shopping List

Produce
2½ lbs. shredded red cabbage

Packaged
6-oz. pkg. dried apricot bits

Condiments
honey
lemon juice

Other
dry red wine

Apples and Red Cabbage

Easy | **Do Ahead** | **Serves: 4**

8 cups shredded red cabbage

3 medium apples, *peeled, cored, and grated*

½ cup red wine vinegar

¾ cup sugar

1 tsp. ground allspice

⅛ tsp. crushed red pepper

2 tbsp. Bacon Crumbles

Spray inside of slow cooker with cooking spray. Combine all ingredients except Bacon Crumbles in slow cooker and mix well. Cover and cook on high heat for 5–6 hours. Stir halfway through cooking. Sprinkle with Bacon Crumbles just before serving.

Nutrition Facts per serving: 249 cal., 1.4 g total fat, 0 mg chol., 137 mg sodium, 63 g carbo., 5 g fiber, 3 g pro.
Exchanges: 3 Vegetable, 1 Fruit, 2 Other Carbo.
Carb Choices: 4

Side Dishes

Shopping List

Produce
1 head red cabbage or 16-oz. pkg. shredded red cabbage
3 medium apples

Packaged
1.3-oz. bottle Bacon Crumbles

Baking Goods
sugar

Condiments
red wine vinegar

Seasonings
ground allspice
crushed red pepper

Pair this side dish with barbecue pork, meat loaf, or turkey roast for the perfect slow-cooked meal.

Fresh Artichokes

Easy | Do Ahead | Serves: 4

2 large fresh artichokes

6 cups hot water

4 lemons, sliced thin

nonfat salad dressing, creamy dip, or melted nonfat margarine seasoned with garlic powder (optional)

Cut about 1 inch off the top of each artichoke and cut off the stem near the base. Using sharp kitchen scissors, trim about ½ inch off the top of each leaf. Using a sharp knife, cut each artichoke in half vertically; scoop out and discard fuzzy center of artichoke. Place artichoke halves in slow cooker; add hot water and lemon slices. Cover and cook on high heat for 4–5 hours. Drain artichokes and serve with salad dressing, dip, or nonfat margarine seasoned with garlic powder.

Nutrition Facts per serving: 49 cal., 0.1 g total fat, 0 mg chol., 82 mg sodium, 11 g carbo., 3 g fiber, 3 g pro.
Exchanges: 2 Vegetable
Carb Choices: 1

Shopping List

Produce
2 large artichokes
4 lemons

Optional
nonfat salad dressing, creamy dip, or nonfat margarine and garlic powder

Ratatouille Italian-Style

Easy | **Do Ahead** | **Serves: 8**

1 lb. eggplant, *peeled, cut into 1-inch chunks, drained, and patted dry*

5½ cups frozen pepper stir-fry, *thawed and drained*

3 medium zucchini, *sliced*

2 lbs. plum tomatoes, *cut into ½-inch wedges*

3 tbsp. Italian tomato paste with roasted garlic

2 tbsp. nonfat vegetable or chicken broth

¼ tsp. pepper

2 tbsp. minced garlic

2 tbsp. dried Italian seasoning

Spray inside of slow cooker with cooking spray. Layer half of the eggplant, pepper stir-fry, zucchini, and tomatoes in slow cooker. Combine tomato paste, broth, pepper, minced garlic, and Italian seasoning in small bowl and mix well. Spoon half of tomato paste mixture over vegetables. Repeat layers. Cover and cook on low heat for 5–6 hours or high heat for 2½–3 hours.

Nutrition Facts per serving: 75 cal., 0.6 g total fat, 0 mg chol., 89 mg sodium, 16 g carbo., 3 g fiber, 3 g pro.
Exchanges: 3 Vegetable
Carb Choices: 1

Side Dishes

Shopping List

Produce
1 lb. eggplant
3 medium zucchini
2 lbs. plum tomatoes

Frozen
2 16-oz. pkgs. frozen pepper stir-fry

Canned
6-oz. can Italian tomato paste with roasted garlic
14-oz. can nonfat vegetable or chicken broth

Seasonings
pepper
minced garlic
dried Italian seasoning

Serving Tip: Serve ratatouille as a side dish or as a topping for baked potatoes, rice, or pasta.

Simple Spaghetti Squash

Easy | Do Ahead | Serves: 4

- 1 large spaghetti squash
- 2 cups nonfat pasta sauce, *heated*
- ¼ cup nonfat Parmesan cheese

Spray inside of slow cooker with cooking spray. Pierce several holes in squash. Pour 2 cups water in slow cooker; set whole spaghetti squash in water. Cover and cook on low heat for 8–9 hours. Split squash open and transfer "spaghetti" strands to a bowl. Serve with heated pasta sauce and cheese.

Nutrition Facts per serving: 124 cal., 0.6 g total fat, 0 mg chol., 435 mg sodium, 25 g carbo., 3 g fiber, 5 g pro.
Exchanges: 5 Vegetable
Carb Choices: 2

Shopping List

Produce
large spaghetti squash

Dairy
nonfat Parmesan cheese

Condiments
16-oz. jar nonfat pasta sauce

Averaging 4–8 pounds, spaghetti squash is generally available year-round. Select hard, heavy, pale squash without soft spots or green color. The average 4-pound spaghetti squash yields about 5 cups of "spaghetti" strands. Spaghetti squash stores at room temperature for about 1 month. After cutting, wrap in plastic wrap and refrigerate for up to 2 days. You can freeze spaghetti squash in freezer bags; partially thaw before using and steam about 5 minutes until tender but still firm.

Creamy Vegetable Bake

Easy | **Do Ahead** | **Serves: 6**

- 1 17-oz. can cream-style corn
- 1 16-oz. pkg. frozen cut green beans, *thawed and drained*
- 1 16-oz. pkg. frozen peas, *thawed and drained*
- 1 cup petite-cut diced tomatoes with roasted garlic and sweet onion, *drained*
- ¼ cup nonfat mayonnaise
- ½ tsp. dried tarragon
- ½ tsp. dried basil
- ⅛ tsp. pepper

Spray inside of slow cooker with cooking spray. Combine all ingredients in slow cooker and mix well. Cover and cook on low heat for 4–6 hours or high heat for 2–3 hours.

Nutrition Facts per serving: 153 cal., 0.7 g total fat, 0 mg chol., 376 mg sodium, 33 g carbo., 3 g fiber, 7 g pro.
Exchanges: 3 Vegetable, 1 Starch
Carb Choices: 2

Side Dishes

Shopping List

Frozen
16-oz. pkg. frozen cut green beans
16-oz. pkg. frozen peas

Canned
17-oz. can cream-style corn
14½-oz. can petite-cut diced tomatoes with roasted garlic and sweet onion

Condiments
nonfat mayonnaise

Seasonings
dried tarragon
dried basil
pepper

Select frozen vegetable packages that are firm and do not have signs of defrosting. Avoid packages that are limp, wet, or sweating and those that have ice on the outside. These may be signs that the package has been defrosted and refrozen, and the contents may not be safe to eat.

Maple-Granola-Stuffed Baked Apples

Easy | **Do Ahead** | **Serves: 4**

¾ cup Grape Nuts cereal

¼ cup raisins

½ cup lite maple syrup

ground cinnamon (optional)

4 large McIntosh apples, *cored*

Mix cereal, raisins, maple syrup, and, if desired, cinnamon in a small bowl. Fill cavity of each apple with cereal mixture. Arrange apples in slow cooker and add 1 inch water to bottom of cooker. Cover and cook on low heat for 3–4 hours. Remove apples from cooker and sprinkle with cinnamon just before serving, if desired.

Nutrition Facts per serving: 275 cal., 0.8 g total fat, 0 mg chol., 266 mg sodium, 69 g carbo., 6 g fiber, 3 g pro.
Exchanges: 2 Fruit, 2 Starch
Carb Choices: 5

Shopping List

Produce
4 large McIntosh apples

Packaged
Grape Nuts cereal
6-oz. pkg. raisins

Condiments
lite maple syrup

Optional
ground cinnamon

Store small quantities of apples in plastic bags in the refrigerator to prevent shriveling; store larger quantities in a cool, dark, airy place. Apples can be refrigerated for 1–2 weeks, depending on the type and maturity of the apples, or sliced and frozen for up to 1 year.

Apple-Cranberry Dessert

Easy | Do Ahead | Serves: 8

1 21-oz. can More Fruit Cinnamon 'n' Spice Apple pie filling

1 16-oz. can whole-berry cranberry sauce

½ cup raisins

1½ tsp. ground cinnamon

¼ tsp. ground nutmeg

angel food cake, nonfat ice cream, or frozen yogurt

Spray inside of slow cooker with cooking spray. Spoon apple pie filling into bowl and chop apples into small pieces. Add cranberry sauce, raisins, cinnamon, and nutmeg and mix. Spoon mixture into slow cooker. Cover and cook on low heat for 4 hours. Serve warm or cold as a topping for angel food cake, ice cream, or frozen yogurt.

Nutrition Facts per serving: 187 cal., 0.2 g total fat, 0 mg chol., 50 mg sodium, 49 g carbo., 1 g fiber, 1 g pro.
Exchanges: 3 Fruit
Carb Choices: 3

Side Dishes

Shopping List

Canned
21-oz. can More Fruit Cinnamon 'n' Spice Apple pie filling
16-oz. can whole-berry cranberry sauce

Packaged
6-oz. pkg. raisins
angel food cake, nonfat ice cream, or frozen yogurt

Seasonings
ground cinnamon
ground nutmeg

Baked Apple Slices with Frozen Yogurt

Easy | Do Ahead | Serves: 6

2 lbs. Granny Smith apples, *cored and cut into ½-inch slices*
¼ cup sugar
¾ tsp. ground cinnamon
⅛ tsp. ground nutmeg
2 tbsp. lemon juice
3 cups nonfat frozen yogurt

Spray inside of slow cooker with cooking spray. Arrange apple slices in bottom of slow cooker. Combine sugar, cinnamon, and nutmeg in small bowl and mix well. Sprinkle sugar mixture over apples. Drizzle with lemon juice. Cover and cook on low heat for 7–8 hours or high heat for 3½–4 hours. Spoon hot apples into dessert dishes; top each dish with ½ cup frozen yogurt and serve immediately.

Nutrition Facts per serving: 165 cal., 0.5 g total fat, 3 mg chol., 71 mg sodium, 39 g carbo., 3 g fiber, 4 g pro.
Exchanges: 1 Fruit, 1½ Other Carbo.
Carb Choices: 3

Shopping List

Produce
2 lbs. Granny Smith apples

Frozen
24 oz. nonfat frozen yogurt

Baking Goods
sugar

Condiments
lemon juice

Seasonings
ground cinnamon
ground nutmeg

Applesauce

Easy | Do Ahead | Serves: 8

3 lbs. Granny Smith apples,
peeled, cored, and sliced

½ cup brown sugar

1½ tbsp. lemon juice

1½ tsp. ground cinnamon

Spray inside of slow cooker with cooking spray. Combine apples, brown sugar, and lemon juice in slow cooker and toss to mix. Cover and cook on high heat for 3–4 hours. Mash apple mixture until smooth. Sprinkle with cinnamon and mix well. Serve warm or refrigerate and serve cold.

Nutrition Facts per serving: 152 cal., 0.6 g total fat, 0 mg chol., 5 mg sodium, 40 g carbo., 4 g fiber, 0.3 g pro.
Exchanges: 2½ Fruit
Carb Choices: 3

Side Dishes

Shopping List

Produce
3 lbs. Granny Smith apples

Baking Goods
brown sugar

Condiments
lemon juice

Seasonings
ground cinnamon

Baked Apples

- 6 large baking apples, *peeled, cored, and cut in half*
- 2 tbsp. lemon juice
- 2 tbsp. low-fat margarine, *melted*
- 3 tbsp. brown sugar
- 1½ tsp. ground cinnamon
- nonfat ice cream, frozen yogurt, or whipped topping (optional)

Shopping List

Produce
6 large baking apples (Rome or York)

Dairy
low-fat margarine

Baking Goods
brown sugar

Condiments
lemon juice

Seasonings
ground cinnamon

Optional
nonfat ice cream, frozen yogurt, or whipped topping

Spray inside of slow cooker with cooking spray. Arrange prepared apples in slow cooker; drizzle with lemon juice and melted margarine. Sprinkle with brown sugar and cinnamon. Cover and cook on low heat for 4 hours or high heat for 2 hours. Serve with ice cream, frozen yogurt, or whipped topping, if desired.

Nutrition Facts per serving: 166 cal., 2.7 g total fat, 0 mg chol., 20 mg sodium, 39 g carbo., 5 g fiber, 1 g pro.
Exchanges: 2 Fruit, ½ Other Carbo.
Carb Choices: 3

Cherry Bread Pudding

Easy | Do Ahead | Serves: 6

2 egg whites

¼ cup egg substitute

¼ cup sugar

½ tsp. ground cinnamon

1 cup nonfat half and half

1 tsp. vanilla extract

4 cups French bread, *cut into ½-inch cubes*

¼ cup dried cherries

nonfat whipped topping or frozen yogurt (optional)

Shopping List

Dairy
eggs
egg substitute
8 oz. nonfat half and half

Packaged
1-lb. loaf French bread
6-oz. pkg. dried cherries

Baking Goods
sugar
vanilla extract

Seasonings
ground cinnamon

Optional
nonfat whipped topping or frozen yogurt

Spray inside of slow cooker with cooking spray. Preheat slow cooker on high heat. Combine egg whites, egg substitute, sugar, cinnamon, half and half, and vanilla in medium bowl and mix well. Stir in bread and cherries and toss until bread is saturated with egg mixture. Spread mixture in bottom of slow cooker. Cook on high heat for 1¾–2 hours. Uncover and serve pudding hot or cold directly from cooker. Top with whipped topping or frozen yogurt, if desired.

Nutrition Facts per serving: 144 cal., 0.8 g total fat, 0 mg chol., 151 mg sodium, 28 g carbo., 1 g fiber, 4 g pro.
Exchanges: 2 Other Carbo.
Carb Choices: 2

Side Dishes

Cherry Rice Pudding

3 cups cooked white rice

½ cup dried cherries

2 tsp. almond extract

1 14-oz. can nonfat sweetened condensed milk

1 12-oz. can evaporated skim milk

1 tbsp. sugar

1 tsp. ground cinnamon

Spray inside of slow cooker with cooking spray. Combine all ingredients except sugar and cinnamon in slow cooker. Cover and cook on low heat for 3–4 hours until liquid is absorbed. Stir pudding. Mix sugar and cinnamon in small bowl; sprinkle over pudding. Serve warm.

Nutrition Facts per serving: 292 cal., 0.3 g total fat, 1 mg chol., 74 mg sodium, 63 g carbo., 1 g fiber, 8 g pro.
Exchanges: 1 Fruit, 2 Starch, 1 Other Carbo.
Carb Choices: 4

Shopping List

Canned
14-oz. can nonfat sweetened condensed milk
12-oz. can evaporated skim milk

Packaged
8-oz. pkg. white rice (instant or regular)
6-oz. pkg. dried cherries

Baking Goods
sugar

Seasonings
almond extract
ground cinnamon

You can refrigerate leftover rice in a tightly sealed container for up to 1 week or freeze it for up to 6 months.

Raisin Rice Pudding

Easy | Do Ahead | Serves: 8

3 cups cooked white rice

½ cup golden raisins

2 tsp. vanilla extract

1 14-oz. can nonfat sweetened condensed milk

1 12-oz. can evaporated skim milk

1 tbsp. sugar

1 tsp. ground cinnamon

Spray inside of slow cooker with cooking spray. Combine all ingredients except sugar and cinnamon in slow cooker and mix well. Cover and cook on low heat for 3–4 hours until liquid is absorbed. Stir pudding. Mix sugar and cinnamon in small bowl. Sprinkle over pudding just before serving. Serve warm.

Nutrition Facts per serving: 313 cal., 0.3 g total fat, 2 mg chol., 103 mg sodium, 67 g carbo., 1 g fiber, 9 g pro.
Exchanges: 2 Fruit, 2 Starch, ½ Other Carbo.
Carb Choices: 4

Side Dishes

Shopping List

Canned
14-oz. can nonfat sweetened condensed milk
12-oz. can evaporated skim milk

Packaged
8-oz. pkg. white rice (regular or instant)
6-oz. pkg. golden raisins

Baking Goods
sugar
vanilla extract

Seasonings
ground cinnamon

Devil's Food Cake

Easy | Do Ahead | Freeze | Serves: 12

- 1 18.25-oz. pkg. Super Moist devil's food cake mix
- 1⅓ cups water
- ¼ cup egg substitute
- 2 egg whites
- 1 tbsp. instant coffee
- 1 tsp. ground cinnamon
- ½ cup cinnamon applesauce

Spray inside of cooker with cooking spray. Preheat slow cooker for 10 minutes on high heat. Combine all ingredients in large mixing bowl and beat with electric mixer on low speed for 1 minute, scraping bowl constantly. Pour batter into slow cooker; place paper towel over top of cooker and cover with lid. Cook on high heat for 2 hours or until knife inserted in center comes out clean. Remove crock and let cake cool for 10 minutes. Run knife around edge of cake to loosen. Place plate on top of slow cooker and turn it upside down to remove cake.

Nutrition Facts per serving: 204 cal., 5 g total fat, 0 mg chol., 435 mg sodium, 37 g carbo., 1 g fiber, 3 g pro.
Exchanges: 2½ Other Carbo.
Carb Choices: 2

Shopping List

Dairy
egg substitute
eggs

Canned
cinnamon applesauce

Baking Goods
18.25-oz. pkg. Super Moist devil's food cake mix

Seasonings
ground cinnamon

Other
instant coffee

Chocolate Chocolate Chip Cake

Easy | Do Ahead | Serves: 12

1 18.25-oz. pkg. Super Moist
   devil's food cake mix

4 egg whites

¼ cup egg substitute

½ cup nonfat vanilla yogurt

¾ cup cold water

½ cup mini chocolate chips

Spray inside of slow cooker with cooking spray. Preheat slow cooker on high heat for 10 minutes. Combine all ingredients in a medium bowl and mix well. Pour into slow cooker. Place paper towel over top of cooker and cover with lid. Cook on high heat for 1½ hours. Remove crock and let cake cool for 10–15 minutes. Run knife around edge of cake to loosen. Place plate on top of slow cooker and turn it upside down to remove cake, or serve directly from slow cooker.

Nutrition Facts per serving: 204 cal., 5.1 g total fat, 1 mg chol., 449 mg sodium, 36 g carbo., 0 g fiber, 4 g pro.
Exchanges: 2½ Other Carbo., 1 Fat
Carb Choices: 2

Side Dishes

Shopping List

Dairy
eggs
egg substitute
6 oz. nonfat vanilla yogurt

Baking Goods
18.25-oz. pkg. Super Moist
   devil's food cake mix
mini chocolate chips

Accurate measuring of ingredients is important for successful baking. Measure liquid ingredients such as milk, water, and egg substitute in a glass or plastic measuring cup with a pour spout. Measure dry or solid ingredients such as flour, sugar, and chopped nuts in plastic or metal graduated measuring cups.

Pumpkin Spice Cake

Easy | Do Ahead | Serves: 12

- 1 18.25-oz. pkg. Super Moist white or yellow cake mix
- 1 16-oz. can pumpkin
- 2 egg whites
- ¼ cup egg substitute
- ¾ cup brown sugar
- ¼ cup sugar
- 1½ tsp. ground cinnamon
- ½ tsp. pumpkin pie spice

Spray inside of slow cooker with cooking spray. Preheat slow cooker on high heat for 10 minutes. Combine all ingredients in medium bowl and mix well. Pour mixture into slow cooker; place paper towel on top of cooker and cover with lid, leaving a slight gap. Cook on high heat for 1½ hours until toothpick inserted in center comes out clean. Remove crock from slow cooker and let cool for 10 minutes. Run knife around edge of cake to loosen. Place plate on top of slow cooker and turn it upside down to remove cake, or serve directly from slow cooker.

Nutrition Facts per serving: 255 cal., 2.1 g total fat, 0 mg chol., 280 mg sodium, 58 g carbo., 1 g fiber, 3 g pro.
Exchanges: 4 Other Carbo., ½ Fat
Carb Choices: 4

Shopping List

Dairy
eggs
egg substitute

Canned
16-oz. can pumpkin (not pumpkin pie mix)

Baking Goods
18.25-oz. Super Moist white or yellow cake mix
brown sugar
sugar

Seasonings
ground cinnamon
pumpkin pie spice

Coffee Cake

Easy | Do Ahead | Freeze | Serves: 12

1 17.5- to 19-oz. pkg. fat-free muffin mix

½ cup nonfat half and half

¼ cup egg substitute

¼ tsp. ground cinnamon

2 tbsp. powdered sugar

fresh fruit (optional)

Shopping List

Dairy
4 oz. nonfat half and half
egg substitute

Baking Goods
17.5- to 19-oz. box fat-free muffin mix (any flavor)
powdered sugar

Seasonings
ground cinnamon

Optional
fresh fruit

Spray inside of cooker with cooking spray. Preheat slow cooker on high heat for 10 minutes. Remove ½ cup muffin mix from package and set aside. Combine remaining muffin mix with half and half and egg substitute in medium bowl and mix well. Spread mixture in slow cooker. Combine reserved muffin mix with cinnamon and mix well; sprinkle mixture over batter in slow cooker. Place paper towel over top of cooker and cover with lid. Cook on high heat for 1 hour. Remove crock from slow cooker and let cool 10 minutes. Run knife around edge of cake to loosen. Place plate on top of slow cooker and turn it upside down to remove cake. When cake is completely cooled, sprinkle with powdered sugar. Cut into wedges and serve with fresh fruit, if desired.

Side Dishes

Nutrition Facts per serving: 176 cal., 0 g total fat, 0 mg chol., 416 mg sodium, 41 g carbo., 3 g fiber, 3 g pro.
Exchanges: 2½ Other Carbo.
Carb Choices: 3

For best results when baking or cooking, measure liquid ingredients on a flat surface, lining up the markings at eye level. For dry ingredients, use a straight-edge spatula to level.

Hot Fruit Compote

4 fresh oranges, *peeled and sectioned*

3 cups fresh pineapple chunks

3 fresh pears, *peeled and sliced ¼ inch thick*

3 fresh peaches, *peeled and sliced ¼ inch thick*

1½ cups fresh cherries

1½ cups seedless grapes

¼ cup sugar

¼ cup water

1 tbsp. lemon juice

low-fat ice cream, nonfat frozen yogurt, or angel food cake

Shopping List

Produce

4 oranges

3-lb. pineapple

3 pears

3 peaches

pint cherries

pint seedless grapes

lemon

Packaged

low-fat ice cream, nonfat frozen yogurt, or angel food cake

Baking Goods

sugar

Spray inside of slow cooker with cooking spray. Combine all ingredients in slow cooker and mix well. Cover and cook on low heat for 3–4 hours. Serve over ice cream, frozen yogurt, or angel food cake.

Nutrition Facts per serving: 158 cal., 0.7 g total fat, 0 mg chol., 2 mg sodium, 41 g carbo., 5 g fiber, 1.7 g pro.
Exchanges: 3 Fruit
Carb Choices: 3

Bonus Recipes 7

Berry Meringue Dessert

Ginger Spice Slaw

½ lb. Red or Golden Delicious apples, *grated*

¾ cup shredded red or green cabbage

1 tbsp. chopped green onion

½ cup chopped celery

¼ cup nonfat mayonnaise

¼ cup nonfat plain yogurt

¼ tsp. ground ginger

2 tbsp. toasted slivered almonds

Combine apples, cabbage, onion, and celery in medium bowl. Combine mayonnaise, yogurt, and ginger in small bowl and mix until blended. Spoon mayonnaise mixture over apple mixture and toss to mix. Cover and refrigerate several hours so flavors can blend. Sprinkle with slivered almonds just before serving; toss lightly.

Nutrition Facts per serving: 40 cal., 1 g total fat, 0 mg chol., 66 mg sodium, 7 g carbo., 1 g fiber, 1 g pro.
Exchanges: ½ Vegetable, ½ Fruit
Carb Choices: 0

Shopping List

Produce
½ lb. Red or Golden Delicious apples
8-oz. pkg. shredded cabbage (red, green, or blended)
small bunch green onions
small bunch celery

Dairy
4 oz. nonfat plain yogurt

Packaged
slivered almonds

Condiments
nonfat mayonnaise

Seasonings
ground ginger

Citrus Salad with Jicama and Butterleaf Lettuce

Easy | **Serves: 6**

- 4 cups torn butterleaf lettuce
- 2 kiwifruits, *peeled and chopped*
- 2 11-oz. cans mandarin oranges, *chopped and drained*
- 1 cup jicama, *peeled and chopped*
- 1 cup nonfat raspberry and balsamic salad dressing

Combine lettuce, kiwifruits, oranges, and jicama in large bowl. Pour salad dressing over top and toss to mix. Serve immediately.

Nutrition Facts per serving: 125 cal., 0.2 g total fat, 0 mg chol., 176 mg sodium, 30 g carbo., 1 g fiber, 1 g pro.
Exchanges: 1 Vegetable, 1½ Fruit
Carb Choices: 2

Bonus Recipes

Shopping List

Produce
2 10-oz. pkgs. torn butterleaf lettuce
2 kiwifruits
small jicama

Canned
2 11-oz. cans mandarin oranges

Condiments
8 oz. nonfat raspberry and balsamic salad dressing

Store all cut fruits and vegetables on a refrigerator shelf above raw meat, poultry, or fish and use within 1 day. To prevent cut fruits and vegetables from darkening, brush the cut surface with citrus juice such as lemon, orange, grapefruit, or lime juice.

Couscous with Dried Fruit and Almonds

Easy | Do Ahead | Serves: 6

1 14-oz. can nonfat vegetable broth

½ tsp. ground ginger

1⅓ cups couscous

3 tbsp. chopped green onions

¼ cup dried fruit bits

¼ tsp. pepper

2 tbsp. toasted slivered almonds

Shopping List

Produce
green onions

Canned
14-oz. can nonfat vegetable broth

Packaged
couscous
7-oz. pkg. dried fruit bits
slivered almonds

Seasonings
ground ginger
pepper

Combine broth and ginger in medium saucepan; bring to a boil over high heat. Stir in couscous, onions, dried fruit bits, and pepper. Remove saucepan from heat, cover, and let stand 7–8 minutes until liquid is absorbed; fluff with a fork. Sprinkle with almonds just before serving.

Nutrition Facts per serving: 197 cal., 1.7 g total fat, 0 mg chol., 235 mg sodium, 38 g carbo., 7 g fiber, 7 g pro.
Exchanges: ½ Fruit, 2 Starch
Carb Choices: 3

4 Easy Ways to Toast Almonds

1. Spray a skillet with cooking spray, add almonds, and cook over medium heat until golden brown.
2. Bake on a shallow baking pan in a 350° oven for 10–15 minutes until golden brown.
3. Place in a glass pie plate, spray with I Can't Believe It's Not Butter Spray, and microwave on high for 4–5 minutes, stirring every minute until golden brown.
4. Place raw almonds on a toaster oven tray and bake at 350° until golden brown.

Apple-Zucchini Slaw

Easy | Do Ahead | Serves: 8

1 tbsp. chopped green onion

½ cup chopped celery

½ lb. Granny Smith apples, *grated*

¾ cup grated zucchini

1 tbsp. chopped walnuts

¼ cup nonfat mayonnaise

¼ cup nonfat plain yogurt

½ tsp. dried Italian seasoning

Combine onion, celery, apples, zucchini, and walnuts in medium bowl. Combine remaining ingredients in small bowl and mix well. Spoon mayonnaise mixture over vegetables and toss to mix. Cover and refrigerate several hours to blend flavors.

Nutrition Facts per serving: 35 cal., 0.6 g total fat, 1 mg chol., 65 mg sodium, 7 g carbo., 1 g fiber, 1 g pro.
Exchanges: 1 Vegetable
Carb Choices: 0

Shopping List

Produce
small bunch green onions
small bunch celery
½ lb. Granny Smith apples
medium zucchini

Dairy
4 oz. nonfat plain yogurt

Packaged
chopped walnuts

Condiments
nonfat mayonnaise

Seasonings
dried Italian seasoning

Bonus Recipes

Berry Delicious Salad

1 20-oz. can crushed
   pineapple in juice,
   undrained

2 tbsp. unflavored gelatin

2 cups fresh cranberries,
   chopped

1 cup frozen unsweetened
   raspberries

1 cup frozen orange juice
   concentrate, *thawed*

1 cup water

1 tbsp. grated orange peel

Drain pineapple, pouring juice into microwave-safe glass container. Microwave on High about 3 minutes until liquid comes to a boil. Add gelatin to hot juice and mix until gelatin is dissolved. Combine chopped cranberries, pineapple, raspberries, hot juice (with dissolved gelatin), orange juice concentrate, water, and orange peel in medium bowl and mix well. Place in refrigerator several hours or overnight until mixture completely sets.

Nutrition Facts per serving: 248 cal., .5 g total fat, 0 mg chol., 7 mg sodium, 61 g carbo., 3 g fiber, 4 g pro.
Exchanges: 4 Fruit
Carb Choices: 4

Shopping List

Produce
12-oz. pkg. fresh cranberries
orange

Frozen
10-oz. pkg. frozen raspberries
6-oz. can orange juice
   concentrate

Canned
20-oz. can crushed pineapple
   in juice

Packaged
unflavored gelatin

Apple-Cranberry Relish

Easy | **Do Ahead** | **Serves: 8**

2 Golden Delicious apples, *cored, peeled, and chopped*

1 orange, *peeled, seeded, and chopped fine*

1½ cups fresh cranberries, *coarsely chopped*

½ cup sugar

¼ lb. seedless grapes, *sliced in half*

1 8-oz. can unsweetened pineapple chunks, *finely chopped*

Shopping List

Produce
2 Golden Delicious apples
orange
12-oz. bag fresh cranberries
¼ lb. seedless grapes

Canned
8-oz. can unsweetened pineapple chunks

Baking Goods
sugar

Combine all ingredients in large bowl and toss to mix. Cover and refrigerate several hours or overnight.

Nutrition Facts per serving: 101 cal., 0.2 g total fat, 0 mg chol., 1 mg sodium, 27 g carbo., 2 g fiber, 1 g pro.
Exchanges: 1½ Fruit
Carb Choices: 2

Bonus Recipes

Storing Cranberries: Store fresh cranberries in their original packaging. They'll keep for up to a year in the freezer. You can cook frozen cranberries without defrosting. Simply pat them dry before using.

Fresh Pineapple Salsa

1½ cups chopped fresh pineapple

1 cup chopped cucumber

¾ cup minced sweet onion

4 tsp. chopped fresh cilantro

2 tbsp. chopped green chiles

1 tsp. minced garlic

1 tsp. ground ginger

¼ cup lemon juice

Combine all ingredients in medium bowl and mix well. Cover and refrigerate at least 2–3 hours or overnight. Serve over chicken or fish, or with baked pita chips or crackers.

Nutrition Facts per serving: 32 cal., 0.2 g total fat, 0 mg chol., 35 mg sodium, 8 g carbo., 1 g fiber, 1 g pro.
Exchanges: ½ Fruit
Carb Choices: 1

Shopping List

Produce
fresh pineapple
large cucumber
large sweet onion
fresh cilantro

Canned
4-oz. can chopped green chiles

Condiments
lemon juice

Seasonings
minced garlic
ground ginger

Vidalia and Walla Walla onions, named for the areas they come from, are two of the most popular sweet onions available. Other varieties include the Texas 1015, Imperial, Oso Sweet, Maui, Bermuda, and Italian red.

Peachy Keen Salsa

2 cups fresh peeled and chopped peaches

½ cup chopped red onion

¾ cup chopped yellow bell pepper

2 tbsp. lemon juice

1 tsp. chopped fresh cilantro

2 tsp. sugar

⅛ tsp. cayenne pepper

Combine all ingredients in medium bowl and mix well. Cover and refrigerate at least 2–3 hours. Serve over cooked chicken or fish.

Nutrition Facts per serving: 39 cal., 0 g total fat, 0 mg chol., 1 mg sodium, 10 g carbo., 1 g fiber, 1 g pro.
Exchanges: ½ Fruit
Carb Choices: 1

Bonus
Recipes

Shopping List

Produce
4 medium peaches
small red onion
medium yellow bell pepper
fresh cilantro

Baking Goods
sugar

Condiments
lemon juice

Seasonings
cayenne pepper

Cut your sugar intake. You can substitute Splenda or Splenda baking product for sugar without affecting flavor, texture, or overall quality of most foods.

Fiberful Salad

Easy | **Do Ahead** | **Serves: 6**

4½ cups torn romaine lettuce

1½ cups cauliflower florets

1½ cups broccoli florets

¼ cup chopped red onion

¼ cup chopped bell pepper

½ cup nonfat ranch salad dressing

½ cup nonfat mayonnaise

2 tbsp. nonfat Parmesan cheese

3 tbsp. sugar

Combine lettuce, cauliflower, broccoli, onion, and bell pepper in large bowl and toss to mix. Combine remaining ingredients in small bowl and mix until smooth. Pour mayonnaise mixture over salad; toss and serve.

Nutrition Facts per serving: 87 cal., 0.2 g total fat, 0 mg chol., 356 mg sodium, 18 g carbo., 2 g fiber, 3 g pro.
Exchanges: 2 Vegetable, ½ Other Carbo.
Carb Choices: 1

Shopping List

Produce

16-oz. pkg. torn romaine lettuce
¾ lb. cauliflower
½ lb. broccoli
small red onion
small bell pepper

Dairy

nonfat Parmesan cheese

Baking Goods

sugar

Condiments

nonfat ranch salad dressing
nonfat mayonnaise

Avocado Ranch Salad

Easy | **Serves: 6**

3 cups bean sprouts

1 cup shredded carrots

½ cup shredded cucumber

½ cup chopped bell pepper

1 tbsp. dried parsley

1 medium avocado, *peeled, seeded, and sliced*

⅔ cup nonfat ranch salad dressing

Combine bean sprouts, carrots, cucumber, bell pepper, parsley, and avocado in large bowl. Pour salad dressing over top and toss to mix.

Nutrition Facts per serving: 103 cal., 5.2 g total fat, 0 mg chol., 277 mg sodium, 13 g carbo., 2 g fiber, 2 g pro.
Exchanges: 3 Vegetable, 1 Fat
Carb Choices: 1

Bonus Recipes

Shopping List

Produce
bean sprouts
8-oz. pkg. shredded carrots
small cucumber
bell pepper
medium avocado

Condiments
nonfat ranch salad dressing

Seasonings
dried parsley

While bean sprouts are often stir-fried or sauteed, they are best eaten raw. Select crisp-looking sprouts with buds attached. Refrigerate bean sprouts in a plastic bag for no more than 3 days.

Italian Salad Bowl

- 1 10-oz. pkg. broccoli florets
- 1 10-oz. pkg. romaine lettuce, *torn into bite-size pieces*
- ¾ cup shredded carrots
- 1 red onion, *thinly sliced*
- 8 oz. sliced fresh mushrooms
- 8 oz. cherry tomatoes, *cut in half*
- ¾ cup chopped red bell pepper
- ½ cup finely chopped canned hearts of palm, *drained*
- ½ cup finely chopped canned artichoke hearts, *drained*
- ½ cup nonfat seasoned croutons
- 2 tbsp. nonfat Parmesan cheese
- ½ cup nonfat Italian salad dressing

If broccoli packaging is microwave-safe, cut a slit in the top of package. If packaging is not microwave-safe, transfer broccoli to microwave-safe dish. Microwave broccoli on High 3–5 minutes until crisp-tender. Remove broccoli from bag and drain well. Combine lettuce, cooked broccoli, carrots, onion, mushrooms, tomatoes, bell pepper, hearts of palm, and artichokes in large bowl and toss to mix. (Salad can be prepared to this point, covered, and refrigerated until ready to serve.) Add croutons and sprinkle with cheese; pour salad dressing over salad and toss to coat. Serve immediately.

Nutrition Facts per serving: 143 cal., 1 g total fat, 0 mg chol., 241 mg sodium, 29 g carbo., 6 g fiber, 9 g pro.
Exchanges: 4 Vegetable, ½ Other Carbo.
Carb Choices: 2

Shopping List

Produce	Canned
10-oz. pkg. broccoli florets	16-oz. can hearts of palm
10-oz. pkg. romaine lettuce	16-oz. can artichoke hearts
8-oz. pkg. shredded carrots	
red onion	**Packaged**
8 oz. sliced fresh mushrooms	6-oz. pkg. nonfat seasoned croutons
8 oz. cherry tomatoes	
medium red bell pepper	**Condiments**
	nonfat Italian salad dressing
Dairy	
nonfat Parmesan cheese	

Sweet and Sour Coleslaw

Easy | Do Ahead | Serves: 8

4 cups shredded cabbage

2 cups shredded carrots

1 cup golden raisins

1 cup nonfat mayonnaise

1 tbsp. honey

1½ tsp. Splenda

1½ tsp. prepared mustard

¼ tsp. celery salt

Combine cabbage, carrots, and raisins in large bowl and mix well. Combine remaining ingredients in small bowl and mix well. Pour mayonnaise mixture over cabbage mixture and toss to mix. Cover and refrigerate several hours before serving.

Nutrition Facts per serving: 106 cal., 0.2 g total fat, 0 mg chol., 276 mg sodium, 26 g carbo., 3 g fiber, 1 g pro.
Exchanges: 2 Vegetable, 1 Fruit
Carb Choices: 2

Bonus Recipes

Shopping List

Produce
1–1½ lbs. cabbage or 16-oz. pkg. shredded cabbage
12-oz. pkg. shredded carrots

Packaged
6-oz. pkg. golden raisins

Baking Goods
Splenda

Condiments
8 oz. nonfat mayonnaise
honey
prepared mustard

Seasonings
celery salt

Wild Rice and Cherry Salad

Easy | Do Ahead | Serves: 4

- 1 cup uncooked instant brown rice
- ½ cup uncooked wild rice
- ½ cup dried cherries or Craisins
- 2 tbsp. minced red onion
- 2 tbsp. toasted slivered almonds
- ¼ cup nonfat honey-Dijon salad dressing

Cook brown and wild rice according to package directions, omitting any butter or salt. Cool 10–15 minutes. Combine rice and remaining ingredients and mix well. Cover and refrigerate several hours.

Nutrition Facts per serving: 325 cal., 3.4 g total fat, 0 mg chol., 69 mg sodium, 67 g carbo., 3 g fiber, 7 g pro.
Exchanges: 2 Fruit, 2½ Starch, ½ Fat
Carb Choices: 4

Shopping List

Produce
red onion

Packaged
brown rice (instant)
wild rice
6-oz. pkg. dried cherries or Craisins
6-oz. pkg. slivered almonds

Condiments
nonfat honey-Dijon salad dressing

Vegetable-Rice Salad with Creamy Dijon Dressing

Easy | **Do Ahead** | **Serves: 8**

4 cups cooked rice

1 14½-oz. can petite-cut diced tomatoes with roasted garlic and sweet onion, *drained*

1 10-oz. pkg. broccoli cuts, *cooked and drained*

¾ cup nonfat mayonnaise

1 tbsp. Dijon mustard

2 tbsp. lemon juice

Combine rice, tomatoes, and broccoli in large bowl. Combine remaining ingredients in small bowl and mix well. Spoon mayonnaise mixture over rice mixture and toss to mix. Serve immediately or cover and refrigerate until ready to serve.

Nutrition Facts per serving: 174 cal., 0.5 g total fat, 0 mg chol., 277 mg sodium, 37 g carbo., 3 g fiber, 4 g pro.
Exchanges: 1 Vegetable, 2 Starch
Carb Choices: 2

Bonus Recipes

Shopping List

Frozen
10-oz. pkg. broccoli cuts

Canned
14½-oz. can petite-cut diced tomatoes with roasted garlic and sweet onion

Packaged
rice (instant or regular)

Condiments
nonfat mayonnaise
Dijon mustard
lemon juice

Timesaver Tip: When preparing recipes that call for cooked rice, use instant rice or Minute Rice, which drastically cuts cooking time.

Good Grains Salad

1 cup pearl barley

1 16-oz. pkg. frozen asparagus cuts

1 10-oz. pkg. frozen peas

⅓ cup nonfat Italian salad dressing

1½ tbsp. lemon juice

1½ tsp. grated lemon peel

Bring 6 cups water to a boil in large saucepan over high heat. Add barley to saucepan and return water to a boil. Reduce heat to medium-low and simmer 40–45 minutes until barley is tender. Drain barley and cool. Spray 9×13-inch microwave-safe baking dish with cooking spray; combine asparagus and peas in baking dish. Microwave on High 3–5 minutes until vegetables are crisp-tender. Combine salad dressing, lemon juice, and lemon peel in medium bowl and mix well. Add barley and vegetables; toss lightly to mix.

Nutrition Facts per serving: 178 cal., 1.2 g total fat, 0 mg chol., 62 mg sodium, 35 g carbo., 5 g fiber, 9 g pro.
Exchanges: 1 Vegetable, 2 Starch
Carb Choices: 2

Shopping List

Produce
lemon

Frozen
16-oz. pkg. frozen asparagus cuts
10-oz. pkg. frozen peas

Packaged
pearl barley

Condiments
nonfat Italian salad dressing

FYI: One cup of uncooked barley yields 3 cups of cooked barley.

Couscous with Feta and Mint

Easy | **Serves: 4**

1½ cups nonfat vegetable broth

1 cup couscous

3 green onions, *trimmed and chopped*

1 tbsp. fresh mint, *chopped fine*

¼ cup reduced-fat feta cheese crumbles

Pour broth in medium saucepan and bring to a boil over high heat. Stir in couscous, cover pan, and remove from heat. Let stand 10–12 minutes. Add remaining ingredients and toss to mix.

Nutrition Facts per serving: 193 cal., 1.2 g total fat, 3 mg chol., 394 mg sodium, 36 g carbo., 7 g fiber, 8 g pro.
Exchanges: 2 Starch, ½ Very Lean Meat
Carb Choices: 2

Bonus Recipes

Shopping List

Produce
small bunch green onions
fresh mint

Dairy
reduced-fat feta cheese
    crumbles

Canned
14-oz. can nonfat vegetable
    broth

Packaged
couscous

Spinach Risotto

Easy | **Serves: 6**

4 cups + 1 tbsp. nonfat chicken broth, *divided*

½ cup frozen chopped onions, *thawed and drained*

1½ cups Arborio rice

½ cup nonfat Parmesan cheese

⅛ tsp. pepper

1 10-oz. pkg. frozen chopped spinach, *thawed and drained*

Shopping List

Frozen
12-oz. pkg. frozen chopped onions
10-oz. pkg. frozen chopped spinach

Dairy
nonfat Parmesan cheese

Canned
3 14-oz. cans nonfat chicken broth

Packaged
8-oz. pkg. Arborio rice

Seasonings
pepper

Bring 4 cups broth to a boil in saucepan over high heat. Reduce heat to low and keep warm. Spray medium saucepan with cooking spray; add 1 tablespoon broth and heat over medium-high heat. Add onions and cook, stirring frequently, until onions are softened and translucent. Add rice and mix with onions; reduce heat to low. Gradually add 1 cup hot broth and stir until absorbed. Continue adding broth 1 cup at a time, stirring constantly, and allowing rice to absorb broth before adding more. Once all broth has been added and absorbed, add cheese, pepper, and spinach; heat through and serve.

Nutrition Facts per serving: 233 cal., 1 g total fat, 0 mg chol., 909 mg sodium, 46 g carbo., 3 g fiber, 11 g pro.
Exchanges: 1 Vegetable, 2 Starch, ½ Other Carbo.
Carb Choices: 3

Pumpkin Spice Pilaf

Easy | **Serves: 6**

1¾ cups nonfat chicken or
vegetable broth

1 cup long grain brown rice

1 cup canned pumpkin

½ tsp. ground cinnamon

⅛ tsp. ground nutmeg

2 tbsp. chopped green onion

Spray large saucepan with cooking spray. Add 1 tablespoon of the broth to saucepan and heat over medium-high heat. Add rice and cook, stirring constantly, until rice is coated. Add remaining broth, pumpkin, cinnamon, and nutmeg; bring to a boil over high heat. Reduce heat to low, cover, and simmer 25–30 minutes until liquid is absorbed. Stir in green onion and serve.

Nutrition Facts per serving: 134 cal., 1.1 g total fat, 0 mg chol., 241 mg sodium, 27 g carbo., 3 g fiber, 4 g pro.
Exchanges: 1½ Starch
Carb Choices: 2

Bonus Recipes

Shopping List

Produce
small bunch green onions

Canned
14-oz. can nonfat chicken or
vegetable broth
15-oz. can pumpkin

Packaged
long grain brown rice

Seasonings
ground cinnamon
ground nutmeg

Vegetable-Rice Pilaf

Do Ahead | Serves: 6

2 tbsp. + 1½ cups nonfat vegetable broth, *divided*

1 medium onion, *sliced*

1 tsp. minced garlic

1 tsp. chili powder

2 tsp. paprika

¼ tsp. ground cinnamon

⅛ tsp. ground nutmeg

⅛ tsp. ground cloves

1½ cups long grain rice

⅔ cup + 2 tbsp. dry white wine

1 14½-oz. can petite-cut diced tomatoes with roasted garlic and sweet onion, *drained*

¼ lb. sliced fresh mushrooms

1 medium zucchini, *cubed*

1 yellow squash, *cubed*

Spray large nonstick skillet with cooking spray. Add 2 tablespoons broth to skillet and heat over medium-high heat. Add onion and cook over medium-high heat, stirring frequently, until onions are lightly browned. Add minced garlic, chili powder, paprika, cinnamon, nutmeg, and cloves. Cook, stirring constantly, 1 minute. Add rice and mix well. Add remaining broth, wine, tomatoes, mushrooms, zucchini, and squash. Bring to a boil over high heat. Reduce heat to low, cover pan, and simmer 15–18 minutes until rice and vegetables are tender.

Nutrition Facts per serving: 234 cal., 0.6 g total fat, 0 mg chol., 326 mg sodium, 45 g carbo., 3 g fiber, 6 g pro.
Exchanges: 3 Vegetable, 2 Starch
Carb Choices: 3

Shopping List

Produce	Packaged
medium onion	8-oz. pkg. long grain rice
¼ lb. sliced fresh mushrooms	
medium zucchini	**Seasonings**
medium yellow squash	minced garlic
	chili powder
	paprika
Canned	ground cinnamon
14-oz. can nonfat vegetable broth	ground nutmeg
	ground cloves
14½-oz. can petite-cut diced tomatoes with roasted garlic and sweet onion	
	Other
	dry white wine

Vegetable Barley

Easy | **Serves: 4**

1 tbsp. + ¾ cup nonfat
   vegetable broth, *divided*

½ cup chopped onion

½ cup chopped mushrooms

¼ cup chopped green bell
   pepper

¼ lb. eggplant, *peeled and
   cubed*

1 tbsp. minced garlic

1 14½-oz. can diced
   tomatoes with garlic and
   onion, *do not drain*

¾ cup water

¾ cup quick-cooking barley

½ cup ketchup

1 tbsp. horseradish

2 tbsp. lemon juice

1 tbsp. dried parsley

1 tsp. honey

1 tsp. Worcestershire sauce

¼ tsp. dried thyme

   pepper to taste

Spray large nonstick skillet with cooking spray. Add 1 tablespoon broth to skillet and heat over medium-high heat. Add onion, mushrooms, bell pepper, eggplant, and minced garlic to skillet. Cook, stirring frequently, 5–6 minutes until softened. Add undrained tomatoes, water, barley, ketchup, horseradish, lemon juice, parsley, honey, Worcestershire sauce, thyme, and pepper; bring to a boil over high heat. Reduce heat to low and simmer 20–25 minutes until barley is cooked through.

Nutrition Facts per serving: 208 cal., 1 g total fat, 0 mg chol., 44 g carbo., 7 g fiber, 7 g pro.
Exchanges: 2 Vegetable, 1½ Starch, ½ Other Carbo.
Carb Choices: 3

Bonus
Recipes

Shopping List

Produce	Condiments
small onion	ketchup
mushrooms	horseradish
small green bell pepper	lemon juice
small eggplant	honey
	Worcestershire sauce

Canned	
14-oz. can nonfat vegetable	**Seasonings**
broth	minced garlic
14½-oz. can diced tomatoes	dried parsley
with garlic and onion	dried thyme
	pepper

Packaged
quick-cooking barley

Couscous Salad with Feta Cheese

Easy | **Do Ahead** | **Serves: 6**

1 cup uncooked couscous

1 cup chopped cucumber

1 14½-oz. can petite-cut diced tomatoes with roasted garlic and sweet onion, *drained*

1 4-oz. pkg. reduced-fat feta cheese crumbles

1 tbsp. chopped fresh dillweed

½ cup nonfat Italian salad dressing

Shopping List

Produce
medium cucumber
fresh dillweed

Dairy
4-oz. pkg. reduced-fat feta cheese crumbles

Canned
14½-oz. can petite-cut diced tomatoes with roasted garlic and sweet onion

Packaged
couscous

Condiments
nonfat Italian salad dressing

Cook couscous according to package directions (without adding butter or salt); fluff with a fork. Place couscous in large bowl and let cool 10–15 minutes. Add remaining ingredients and toss lightly to mix. Cover and refrigerate several hours.

Nutrition Facts per serving: 165 cal., 0.2 g total fat, 0 mg chol., 495 mg sodium, 30 g carbo., 5 g fiber, 9 g pro.
Exchanges: 2 Vegetable, 1½ Starch
Carb Choices: 2

Sweet and Sour Bean Salad

Easy | **Serves: 6**

- 1 16-oz. can red kidney beans, *drained*
- 1 cup garbanzo beans, *drained*
- 1 cup chopped onion
- 1 cup chopped bell pepper
- ½ cup canned whole kernel corn, *drained*
- ¾ cup chopped celery
- ½ cup balsamic vinegar
- 2 tbsp. minced garlic
- 2 tbsp. lemon juice
- 3 tbsp. sugar
- 2 tbsp. dried parsley
- pepper to taste

Combine kidney beans, garbanzo beans, and onion in medium saucepan; bring to a boil over high heat. Reduce heat to medium-high and cook 4–5 minutes. Drain. Combine bean mixture, bell pepper, corn, and celery in large bowl and toss to mix. Combine balsamic vinegar, minced garlic, lemon juice, sugar, parsley, and pepper in small bowl and mix well. Pour vinegar mixture over bean mixture; toss lightly to coat. Serve while still warm.

Nutrition Facts per serving: 189 cal., 0.8 g total fat, 0 mg chol., 387 mg sodium, 39 g carbo., 5 g fiber, 8 g pro.
Exchanges: 2 Vegetable, 1 Starch, 1 Other Carbo.
Carb Choices: 3

Bonus Recipes

Shopping List

Produce	**Condiments**
large onion	balsamic vinegar
large bell pepper	lemon juice
small bunch celery	
	Seasonings
Canned	minced garlic
16-oz. can red kidney beans	dried parsley
15-oz. can garbanzo beans	pepper
8-oz. can whole kernel corn	
Baking Goods	
sugar	

Summer Squash with Lemon-Parmesan Sauce

Easy | **Serves: 4**

- 2 tbsp. nonfat chicken or vegetable broth
- 1 lb. zucchini, *cut into 3-inch sticks*
- 1 lb. yellow squash, *cut into 3-inch sticks*
- 1 tsp. grated lemon peel
- 2–3 tbsp. nonfat Parmesan cheese
- ¼ tsp. pepper

Spray large nonstick skillet with cooking spray. Add broth to skillet and heat over medium-high heat. Add zucchini, squash, and lemon peel and cook, stirring frequently, over medium-high heat 4–5 minutes until vegetables are lightly browned. Stir in cheese and pepper and cook 1–2 minutes. Serve immediately.

Nutrition Facts per serving: 51 cal., 0.5 g total fat, 0 mg chol., 63 mg sodium, 10 g carbo., 3 g fiber, 4 g pro.
Exchanges: 2 Vegetable
Carb Choices: 1

Shopping List

Produce
1 lb. zucchini
1 lb. yellow squash
lemon

Dairy
nonfat Parmesan cheese

Canned
14-oz. can nonfat chicken or vegetable broth

Seasonings
pepper

Stir-Fry Spinach with Feta Cheese

Easy | **Serves: 4**

1 16-oz. pkg. frozen chopped spinach, *thawed and drained*

1½ tbsp. dried minced onion

¾ tsp. dried oregano

½ tsp. dried basil

1½ tsp. minced garlic

1½ tsp. balsamic vinegar

3 tbsp. reduced-fat feta cheese crumbles

Spray large nonstick skillet with cooking spray and heat over medium-high heat. Add spinach, minced onion, oregano, basil, minced garlic, and vinegar to skillet and cook, stirring frequently, until spinach is cooked through and liquid is absorbed. Spoon spinach into serving dish and sprinkle with cheese; toss lightly to mix.

Nutrition Facts per serving: 53 cal., 0.2 g total fat, 0 mg chol., 213 mg sodium, 10 g carbo., 2 g fiber, 5 g pro.
Exchanges: 2 Vegetable
Carb Choices: 1

Bonus Recipes

Shopping List

Dairy
reduced-fat feta cheese crumbles

Frozen
16-oz. pkg. frozen chopped spinach

Condiments
balsamic vinegar

Seasonings
dried minced onion
dried oregano
dried basil
minced garlic

Substitution Tip: For a change of pace, you can substitute frozen chopped broccoli for the spinach.

Roasted Vegetables

Easy | **Serves: 8**

½ lb. baby red potatoes, *cut in half*

1 10-oz. bag baby carrots

1 onion, *peeled and sliced*

1 small zucchini, *cubed*

4 cloves garlic, *peeled*

6 tbsp. nonfat vegetable broth

1 tbsp. grated lemon peel

½ tsp. chili powder

½ tsp. mustard seed

¼ tsp. pepper

¼ cup chopped fresh parsley

Shopping List

Produce
½ lb. baby red potatoes
10-oz. bag baby carrots
onion
small zucchini
whole garlic
lemon
fresh parsley

Canned
14-oz. can nonfat vegetable broth

Seasonings
chili powder
mustard seed
pepper

Preheat oven to 425°. Line baking sheet with foil and spray with cooking spray. Combine potatoes, carrots, onion, zucchini, and garlic on baking sheet. Combine broth, lemon peel, chili powder, mustard seed, and pepper in small bowl and mix well. Pour broth mixture over vegetables and toss to coat. Bake 25–30 minutes, stirring occasionally, until vegetables are tender and lightly browned. Garnish with parsley before serving.

Nutrition Facts per serving: 150 cal., 0.3 g total fat, 0 mg chol., 66 mg sodium, 35 g carbo., 6 g fiber, 3 g pro.
Exchanges: 3 Vegetable, 1 Starch
Carb Choices: 2

Roasted Brussels Sprouts

Easy | **Do Ahead** | **Serves: 6**

1 lb. fresh Brussels sprouts

2–3 tbsp. nonfat vegetable broth

Mrs. Dash seasoning to taste

pepper to taste

Preheat oven to 400°. Line baking sheet with foil and spray with cooking spray. Arrange Brussels sprouts on baking sheet; sprinkle with broth, Mrs. Dash seasoning, and pepper. Bake 30–35 minutes until tender.

Nutrition Facts per serving: 30 cal., 0.3 g total fat, 0 mg chol., 32 mg sodium, 7 g carbo., 3 g fiber, 2 g pro.
Exchanges: 1 Vegetable
Carb Choices: 0

Bonus Recipes

Shopping List

Produce
1 lb. fresh Brussels sprouts

Canned
14-oz. can nonfat vegetable broth

Seasonings
Mrs. Dash seasoning
pepper

Select bright green, firm, and compact Brussels sprouts. Pass on those with wilted leaves or soft spots. Do not wash or trim sprouts before storing them. Store sprouts in a perforated plastic bag; for freshness, use in 3–5 days.

Eggplant Parmesan Sticks

Easy | Do Ahead | Serves: 4

⅓ cup seasoned bread crumbs

½ tsp. dried Italian seasoning

½ tsp. garlic powder

⅓ cup nonfat Parmesan cheese

½ cup nonfat ranch salad dressing

2 tbsp. skim milk

1 lb. eggplant, *cut into 3-inch-long sticks*

1 cup nonfat pasta or marinara sauce

Preheat oven to 425°. Line baking sheet with foil and spray with cooking spray. Combine bread crumbs, Italian seasoning, garlic powder, and cheese in shallow dish and mix well. Combine salad dressing and milk in small bowl and mix well. Dip eggplant in salad dressing mixture; roll in bread crumb mixture to coat and place on baking sheet. Repeat with remaining eggplant. Bake 8–10 minutes; turn eggplant over and bake 8–10 minutes until browned and crisp on both sides. Serve with hot or cold pasta sauce.

Nutrition Facts per serving: 133 cal., .6 g total fat, 1 mg chol., 572 mg sodium, 26 g carbo., 1 g fiber, 5 g pro.
Exchanges: 2 Vegetable, 1 Other Carbo.
Carb Choices: 2

Shopping List

Produce
1 lb. eggplant

Dairy
skim milk
nonfat Parmesan cheese

Packaged
seasoned bread crumbs

Condiments
nonfat ranch salad dressing
8-oz. jar pasta or marinara sauce

Seasonings
dried Italian seasoning
garlic powder

FYI: One pound eggplant equals 3–4 cups chopped eggplant. One average-size eggplant serves about 3 people. One medium eggplant usually weighs in at about 1 pound.

Cauliflower with Red Pepper

Easy | Serves: 4

- 2 8-oz. pkgs. cauliflower florets
- 1 tbsp. nonfat vegetable broth
- 1 tsp. crushed garlic
- ¼ cup thinly sliced red bell pepper strips
- ⅛ tsp. pepper

If cauliflower packaging is microwave-safe, cut a slit in the top of cauliflower packages. If packaging is not microwave-safe, transfer cauliflower to microwave-safe dish. Microwave cauliflower on High 2–3 minutes until slightly softened. Spray large nonstick skillet with cooking spray. Add broth to skillet and heat over medium-high heat. Add garlic and cook 1 minute; add bell pepper and cook 1–2 minutes until softened. Add cauliflower and pepper; toss with garlic and bell peppers and cook 3–4 minutes until tender. Serve immediately.

Bonus Recipes

Nutrition Facts per serving: 30 cal., 0.2 g total fat, 0 mg chol., 30 mg sodium, 6 g carbo., 3 g fiber, 2 g pro.
Exchanges: 1 Vegetable
Carb Choices: 0

Shopping List

Produce
2 8-oz. pkgs. cauliflower florets
small red bell pepper

Canned
14-oz. can nonfat vegetable broth

Seasonings
crushed garlic
pepper

Select firm cauliflower with compact florets. Store wrapped tightly in plastic wrap in the refrigerator for up to 5 days.

Very Veggie Stuffed Potato

Serves: 4

4 large baking potatoes,
  8–10 oz. each

1 16-oz. pkg. frozen chopped
  spinach, *thawed and
  drained*

1 cup shredded carrots

½ cup nonfat cream cheese

1 tbsp. nonfat Parmesan
  cheese

pepper to taste

Preheat oven to 425°. Wash potatoes and prick with fork in several places. Bake for 50–60 minutes. While potatoes are baking, combine spinach and carrots in microwave-safe bowl; microwave on High 3–4 minutes until carrots are softened. Stir cream cheese, Parmesan cheese, and pepper into spinach mixture; mix until creamy and smooth. Cut potatoes in half; scoop out pulp and place in medium bowl. Mash potato pulp until smooth; add spinach-cheese mixture to pulp and mix well. Spoon mixture into potato shells. Heat oven to 450°. Line baking sheet with foil and spray with cooking spray. Arrange potato halves on baking sheet; bake 5–10 minutes until heated through and lightly browned.

Nutrition Facts per serving: 216 cal., 0.4 g total fat, 0 mg chol., 326 mg sodium, 45 g carbo., 7 g fiber, 11 g pro.
Exchanges: 2 Vegetable, 1½ Starch, ½ Other Carbo.
Carb Choices: 3

Shopping List

Produce
4 large baking potatoes
8-oz. pkg. shredded carrots

Dairy
4-oz. pkg. nonfat cream cheese
nonfat Parmesan cheese

Frozen
16-oz. pkg. frozen chopped
  spinach

Seasonings
pepper

Scalloped Potatoes and Carrots

Easy | **Serves: 4**

- 1 lb. potatoes, *peeled and sliced*
- ¾ lb. carrots, *peeled and sliced*
- 1 tsp. garlic powder
- 1 tsp. onion powder
- ½ cup + 2 tbsp. nonfat Parmesan cheese, *divided*
- ¼ cup nonfat mayonnaise

Shopping List

Produce
1 lb. potatoes
¾ lb. carrots

Dairy
nonfat Parmesan cheese

Condiments
nonfat mayonnaise

Seasonings
garlic powder
onion powder

Preheat oven to 350°. Line baking sheet with foil and spray with cooking spray. Arrange potatoes and carrots on baking sheet; sprinkle with garlic powder and onion powder. Combine ½ cup cheese and mayonnaise in small bowl and mix well. Spread cheese mixture over vegetables. Spray another piece of foil with cooking spray and place on top; seal lightly around edges without pressing down on top. Bake 45 minutes. Remove top foil and continue baking until potatoes and carrots are tender and lightly browned on top. Sprinkle with remaining cheese and serve.

Bonus Recipes

Nutrition Facts per serving: 194 cal., 0.2 g total fat, 0 mg chol., 253 mg sodium, 41 g carbo., 5 g fiber, 8 g pro.
Exchanges: 2 Vegetable, 2 Starch
Carb Choices: 3

Select firm, smooth, well-shaped potatoes that are free of cracks and blemishes. Avoid potatoes with green-tinged skins or buds.

Pecan Sweet Potato Casserole

Easy | Serves: 8

6 medium sweet potatoes,
   6–8 oz. each

½ cup brown sugar, *divided*

¼ cup egg substitute

¼ cup nonfat half and half

1 tsp. cinnamon, *divided*

¼ cup cornflake crumbs

2 tbsp. chopped pecans

1–1½ tbsp. Butter Buds

water

Shopping List

Produce
6 medium sweet potatoes

Dairy
egg substitute
nonfat half and half

Packaged
cornflake crumbs
chopped pecans

Baking Goods
brown sugar

Seasonings
cinnamon
Butter Buds

Preheat oven to 425°. Wash sweet potatoes and prick with a fork in several places. Bake for 40–50 minutes. Spray 9×13-inch baking dish with cooking spray. Peel skin from potatoes and place potato pulp in medium bowl. Mash potato pulp until smooth; add ¼ cup brown sugar, egg substitute, half and half, and ½ teaspoon cinnamon and mix well. Spread potato mixture in baking dish. Combine cornflake crumbs, ¼ cup brown sugar, ½ teaspoon cinnamon, and pecans in small bowl. Sprinkle dry Butter Buds over crumb mixture; drizzle with water and mix with fingertips just until moistened and crumbly. Sprinkle crumb mixture over potatoes and spread evenly. Bake 40–45 minutes until lightly browned and cooked through.

Nutrition Facts per serving: 169 cal., 1.2 g total fat, 0 mg chol., 65 mg sodium, 37 g carbo., 3 g fiber, 3 g pro.
Exchanges: 1 Starch, 1 Other Carbo.
Carb Choices: 2

Substitution Tip: You can use canned evaporated skim milk in place of nonfat half and half.

Parmesan Corn Bread

Easy | **Do Ahead** | **Serves: 12**

1 14.5-oz. pkg. fat-free corn muffin mix

¼ cup nonfat Parmesan cheese

½ tsp. dried rosemary

1¼ cups water

1 8-oz. can whole kernel corn, *drained*

Preheat oven to 400°. Spray 8×8-inch baking dish with cooking spray. Combine all ingredients in medium bowl and mix well. Spread mixture evenly in baking dish and bake 18–22 minutes until lightly browned. Cool 5 minutes before slicing. Serve warm.

Nutrition Facts per serving: 141 cal., 0.1 g total fat, 0 mg chol., 480 mg sodium, 32 g carbo., 2 g fiber, 3 g pro.
Exchanges: 2 Starch
Carb Choices: 2

Bonus Recipes

Shopping List

Dairy
nonfat Parmesan cheese

Canned
8-oz. can whole kernel corn

Baking Goods
14.5-oz. pkg. fat-free corn muffin mix

Seasonings
dried rosemary

Garlic Cheese Bread

Easy | Serves: 8

8 slices French or sourdough bread

I Can't Believe It's Not Butter Spray

2 tsp. garlic powder

½ cup nonfat Parmesan cheese

Preheat broiler on high heat. Line baking sheet with foil and spray with cooking spray. Arrange bread slices in a single layer on baking sheet. Spray each bread slice lightly with I Can't Believe It's Not Butter Spray; sprinkle each slice with ¼ teaspoon garlic powder and 1 tablespoon cheese. Broil 45–60 seconds until lightly browned and bubbly on top. Serve immediately.

Nutrition Facts per serving: 115 cal., 1.3 g total fat, 0 mg chol., 238 mg sodium, 20 g carbo., 1 g fiber, 5 g pro.
Exchanges: 1½ Starch, 1 Lean Meat
Carb Choices: 1

Shopping List

Dairy
I Can't Believe It's Not Butter Spray
nonfat Parmesan cheese

Packaged
½-lb. loaf French or sourdough bread

Seasonings
garlic powder

Substitution Tip: You can use any low-calorie "butter-spray," or sprinkle with "butter" granules, garlic powder, and Parmesan cheese, then spray lightly with cooking spray before baking.

Peach-Apricot Tortilla Roll-Ups

Easy | **Do Ahead** | **Serves: 6**

1 20-oz. can peach pie filling

2 tsp. ground cinnamon, *divided*

¼ cup chopped dried apricots

6 98% fat-free flour tortillas

1 tbsp. sugar

Preheat oven to 375°. Line baking sheet with foil and spray with cooking spray. Combine pie filling, 1 teaspoon cinnamon, and apricots and mix well. Spread peach mixture over half of each tortilla. Fold tortillas in half. Place tortillas in a single layer on baking sheet. Combine remaining cinnamon and sugar in small bowl and mix well. Sprinkle cinnamon-sugar over tortillas; spray lightly with cooking spray. Bake 8–10 minutes until lightly browned.

Nutrition Facts per serving: 237 cal., 0.6 g total fat, 0 mg chol., 382 mg sodium, 55 g carbo., 2 g fiber, 4 g pro.
Exchanges: 4 Other Carbo.
Carb Choices: 4

Bonus
Recipes

Shopping List

Packaged
6-oz. pkg. dried apricots
17.5-oz. pkg. 98% fat-free
flour tortillas

Baking Goods
20-oz. can peach pie filling
sugar

Seasonings
ground cinnamon

Berry Meringue Dessert

2 cups whole strawberries, *hulled and cut in half*

2 cups raspberries, *rinsed, drained, and patted dry*

1½ cups blueberries, *rinsed, drained, and patted dry*

1½ cups blackberries, *rinsed, drained, and patted dry*

1 tbsp. grated orange peel

½ cup orange juice

2 egg whites

¼ tsp. cream of tartar

¼ cup sugar

2 tsp. powdered sugar

Shopping List

Produce
pint strawberries
pint raspberries
pint blueberries
pint blackberries
large orange

Dairy
whole eggs

Baking Goods
cream of tartar
sugar
powdered sugar

Preheat oven to 475°. Lightly spray 1½-quart baking dish with cooking spray. Combine berries, orange peel, and orange juice in baking dish and toss lightly. Place egg whites in medium mixing bowl; beat with electric mixer until frothy. Add cream of tartar and sugar; beat until egg whites are stiff and shiny peaks form. Spoon meringue over center of fruit; leave about a 1-inch edge around fruit. Bake 4–5 minutes until meringue is lightly browned. Sprinkle with powdered sugar and serve.

Nutrition Facts per serving: 91 cal., 0.5 g total fat, 0 mg chol., 16 mg sodium, 22 g carbo., 5 g fiber, 2 g pro.
Exchanges: 1½ Fruit
Carb Choices: 2

Freezing Berries: Savor the fresh flavor of berries even after the season passes. Lay them on a plastic tray in a single layer, not touching, and place tray in freezer. When frozen, put fruit into plastic bags and return to freezer.

Angel Food Cake with Creamy Banana Sauce

Easy | **Do Ahead** | **Serves: 8**

1½ cups nonfat plain yogurt

1 banana, *cut into small pieces*

1½ tsp. honey

¾ tsp. vanilla extract

8 slices prepared angel food cake

2 cups sliced strawberries

Combine yogurt, banana, honey, and vanilla in food processor or blender and process until smooth. Spoon mixture into bowl; cover tightly and refrigerate until ready to serve. Arrange cake slices in individual dessert dishes; top each with ¼ cup sliced strawberries and drizzle with banana mixture.

Nutrition Facts per serving: 195 cal., 0.4 g total fat, 1 mg chol., 175 mg sodium, 42 g carbo., 1 g fiber, 7 g pro.
Exchanges: 3 Other Carbo.
Carb Choices: 3

Bonus Recipes

Shopping List

Produce
banana
pint strawberries

Dairy
12 oz. nonfat plain yogurt

Packaged
angel food cake mix or
    prepared angel food cake

Baking Goods
vanilla extract

Condiments
honey

Substitution Tip: You can use any flavored yogurt instead of plain, but if you do, eliminate the vanilla from the recipe.

Crème Brûlée

2 cups skim milk
1 cup egg substitute
8 egg whites
¾ cup sugar
2 tsp. potato starch
1 tbsp. vanilla extract
½ cup brown sugar

Shopping List

Dairy
pint skim milk
8 oz. egg substitute
dozen eggs

Baking Goods
sugar
vanilla extract
potato starch
brown sugar

Preheat oven to 300°. Pour milk into heavy saucepan; heat milk over medium heat until hot but do not boil. While milk is heating, combine egg substitute, egg whites, sugar, potato starch, and vanilla in large bowl and mix until sugar is dissolved and mixture is blended. Slowly whisk egg mixture into hot milk. Cook over medium heat, stirring constantly with a wooden spoon, until the mixture coats the back of the spoon. Remove saucepan from heat and divide the mixture among 8 small oven- and broiler-proof glass dishes. Place dessert dishes in a 9×13-inch baking dish; pour hot water in the bottom of the baking dish until the water comes halfway up the sides of the dessert dishes. Place baking dish in oven and bake 35–40 minutes until knife inserted in center comes out clean. Remove dessert dishes from baking dish and set aside to cool completely. Refrigerate 2–3 hours. Preheat broiler on high heat. Sprinkle each dish of custard with brown sugar and spread evenly to edges. Place dessert dishes on a baking sheet and broil for about 1 minute until the sugar is bubbly and melted. Remove from broiler and serve immediately or chill until ready to serve.

Nutrition Facts per serving: 355 cal., 0.2 g total fat, 2 mg chol., 362 mg sodium, 71 g carbo., 0 g fiber, 17 g pro.
Exchanges: 5 Other Carbo.
Carb Choices: 5

Cinnamon-Spice Baked Bananas

Easy | Serves: 4

- 1½ cups + 1 tbsp. orange-pineapple juice, *divided*
- ¼ cup shredded orange peel
- 1 tsp. ground cinnamon
- 4 bananas, *cut in half lengthwise*
- 1½ tbsp. sugar
- ground cinnamon (optional)

Preheat oven to 350°. Spray 2-quart square glass baking dish with cooking spray. Combine 1½ cups orange-pineapple juice, orange peel, and cinnamon in dish; toss to mix. Place bananas cut side down in dish; drizzle juice mixture over top. Bake bananas 10–12 minutes until softened. Remove bananas from baking dish and arrange on 4 dessert plates. Combine liquid from baking dish with sugar and remaining orange-pineapple juice; pour over bananas and serve immediately. Sprinkle with additional cinnamon, if desired.

Nutrition Facts per serving: 176 cal., 0.5 g total fat, 0 mg chol., 4 mg sodium, 46 g carbo., 2 g fiber, 1 g pro.
Exchanges: 3 Other Carbo.
Carb Choices: 3

Bonus Recipes

Shopping List

Produce
4 bananas
4 oranges

Refrigerated
16 oz. orange-pineapple juice

Baking Goods
sugar

Seasonings
ground cinnamon

Optional
ground cinnamon

Glazed Oranges

4 large navel oranges, *peeled and cut into ¼-inch slices*

¼ cup brown sugar

¼ cup balsamic vinegar

⅛ tsp. pepper

Arrange orange slices on 4 dessert plates. Combine brown sugar and vinegar in small saucepan and bring to a boil over high heat. Reduce heat to medium-low and cook, stirring constantly, until liquid is reduced by half. Remove saucepan from heat and stir in pepper. Drizzle glaze over orange slices and serve.

Nutrition Facts per serving: 159 cal., 0.2 g total fat, 0 mg chol., 7 mg sodium, 40 g carbo., 5 g fiber, 2 g pro.
Exchanges: 2 Fruit, ½ Other Carbo.
Carb Choices: 3

Shopping List

Produce
4 large navel oranges

Baking Goods
brown sugar

Condiments
balsamic vinegar

Seasonings
pepper

Strawberry-Banana Treat

Easy | Do Ahead | Serves: 4

- 2 bananas, *peeled and cut in half*
- 2 cups fresh strawberries
- 2 cups nonfat strawberry-banana yogurt
- 2 tbsp. toasted chopped almonds

Place 1 banana half in each of 4 dessert dishes. Top each banana half with ½ cup strawberries, ½ cup yogurt, and 1½ teaspoons chopped almonds.

Nutrition Facts per serving: 144 cal., 2.6 g total fat, 3 mg chol., 72 mg sodium, 26 g carbo., 3 g fiber, 6 g pro.
Exchanges: ½ Milk, 1½ Fruit, ½ Fat
Carb Choices: 2

Bonus Recipes

Shopping List

Produce
2 bananas
pint fresh strawberries

Dairy
16 oz. nonfat strawberry-banana yogurt

Packaged
6-oz. pkg. chopped almonds

When selecting strawberries, look for bright, firm, dry, clean berries that still have the cap and stem attached. Avoid strawberries that have large seedy areas, a shrunken appearance, soft spots, or mold.

Index

Index

Index

Index

Metric Information

The charts on this page provide a guide for converting measurements from the U.S. customary system, used throughout this book, to the metric system.

Product Differences

Most of the ingredients called for in the recipes in this book are available in most countries. However, some are known by different names. Here are some common American ingredients and their possible counterparts:

- Sugar (white) is granulated, fine granulated, or castor sugar.
- Powdered sugar is icing sugar.
- All-purpose flour is enriched, bleached or unbleached white household flour. When self-rising flour is used in place of all-purpose flour in a recipe that calls for leavening, omit the leavening agent (baking soda or baking powder) and salt.
- Light-colored corn syrup is golden syrup.
- Cornstarch is cornflour.
- Baking soda is bicarbonate of soda.
- Vanilla or vanilla extract is vanilla essence.
- Bell peppers are capsicums.
- Golden raisins are sultanas.

Volume and Weight

The United States traditionally uses cup measures for liquid and solid ingredients. The chart below shows the approximate imperial and metric equivalents. If you are accustomed to weighing solid ingredients, the following approximate equivalents will be helpful.

- 1 cup butter, castor sugar, or rice = 8 ounces = ½ pound = 250 grams
- 1 cup flour = 4 ounces = ¼ pound = 125 grams
- 1 cup icing sugar = 5 ounces = 150 grams

Canadian and U.S. volume for a cup measure is 8 fluid ounces (237 ml), but the standard metric equivalent is 250 ml.

1 British imperial cup is 10 fluid ounces.

In Australia, 1 tablespoon equals 20 ml, and there are 4 teaspoons in the Australian tablespoon.

Spoon measures are used for smaller amounts of ingredients. Although the size of the tablespoon varies slightly in different countries, for practical purposes and for recipes in this book, a straight substitution is all that's necessary. Measurements made using cups or spoons should be level unless stated otherwise.

Common Weight Range Replacements

Imperial / U.S.	Metric
½ ounce	15 g
1 ounce	25 g or 30 g
4 ounces (¼ pound)	115 g or 125 g
8 ounces (½ pound)	225 g or 250 g
16 ounces (1 pound)	450 g or 500 g
1¼ pounds	625 g
1½ pounds	750 g
2 pounds or 2¼ pounds	1,000 g or 1 Kg

Oven Temperature Equivalents

Fahrenheit Setting	Celsius Setting*	Gas Setting
300°F	150°C	Gas Mark 2 (very low)
325°F	160°C	Gas Mark 3 (low)
350°F	180°C	Gas Mark 4 (moderate)
375°F	190°C	Gas Mark 5 (moderate)
400°F	200°C	Gas Mark 6 (hot)
425°F	220°C	Gas Mark 7 (hot)
450°F	230°C	Gas Mark 8 (very hot)
475°F	240°C	Gas Mark 9 (very hot)
500°F	260°C	Gas Mark 10 (extremely hot)
Broil	Broil	Grill

*Electric and gas ovens may be calibrated using celsius. However, for an electric oven, increase celsius setting 10 to 20 degrees when cooking above 160°C. For convection or forced air ovens (gas or electric) lower the temperature setting 25°F/10°C when cooking at all heat levels.

Baking Pan Sizes

Imperial / U.S.	Metric
9×1½-inch round cake pan	22- or 23×4-cm (1.5 L)
9×1½-inch pie plate	22- or 23×4-cm (1 L)
8×8×2-inch square cake pan	20×5-cm (2 L)
9×9×2-inch square cake pan	22- or 23×4.5-cm (2.5 L)
11×7×1½-inch baking pan	28×17×4-cm (2 L)
2-quart rectangular baking pan	30×19×4.5-cm (3 L)
13×9×2-inch baking pan	34×22×4.5-cm (3.5 L)
15×10×1-inch jelly roll pan	40×25×2-cm
9×5×3-inch loaf pan	23×13×8-cm (2 L)
2-quart casserole	2 L

U.S. / Standard Metric Equivalents

⅛ teaspoon = 0.5 ml	
¼ teaspoon = 1 ml	
½ teaspoon = 2 ml	
1 teaspoon = 5 ml	
1 tablespoon = 15 ml	
2 tablespoons = 25 ml	
¼ cup = 2 fluid ounces = 50 ml	
⅓ cup = 3 fluid ounces = 75 ml	
½ cup = 4 fluid ounces = 125 ml	
⅔ cup = 5 fluid ounces = 150 ml	
¾ cup = 6 fluid ounces = 175 ml	
1 cup = 8 fluid ounces = 250 ml	
2 cups = 1 pint = 500 ml	
1 quart = 1 litre	

Metric

ways to
take control of mealtime

Meredith® **BOOKS**

Five more great cookbooks for busy moms

Make it easy. Make it quick. Make it healthy.